FISHING ON THE ASPHALT

Fishing on the Asphalt

EFFECTIVE EVANGELISM IN MAINLINE DENOMINATIONS

Herb Miller

CBP Press

St. Louis   Missouri

Second printing, 1987

© 1983 by CBP Press

Library of Congress Catalog Card Number 83-10006
1. Evangelistic work. I. Title
BY3790. M623 1983, 253.7
ISBN: 0-8272-1011-6

Manufactured in the United States of America

To Nancy Miller and Brax Wright,
daughter-in-law and son-in-law,
highly valued additions to our
growing family.

CONTENTS

ACKNOWLEDGMENTS

A cast of thousands gave various forms of assistance to collecting this stack of words. It all began with Margo Woodworth, administrative director for the National Evangelism Workshop, whose months of research located the fastest growing Christian Churches (Disciples of Christ) in North America. Countless members of congregations and church boards worked to answer complex questions. More than fifty ministers and staff members gave time, energy, and brain power to various kinds of questionnaires and psychological instruments. Dr. Bill Erwin, a clinical psychologist, provided research designs, graduate student assistance, and computer time for the personality studies of growing church pastors. Lynda Maunder, resource director for the National Evangelistic Association of the Christian Church (Disciples of Christ), donated time from a crowded schedule to move several fragments from cassette tapes to typing paper. Jeanette Camp's nimble fingers and quick eye for grammatical mistakes fed in and out of a word processor's silicone brain the semifinal and final piles of sentences.

Barbara, the ever patient and tolerant mate, avoided negative comments as the gestation period stretched into two years of time larceny from an already overbooked schedule. She also suggested the discussion questions at the end of each chapter that help the book to meet a broader range of needs.

But especially, thanks be to God, from whom all ideas and insights flow.

Introduction

Four major skyscrapers dominate the current landscape of mainline denominations.

First, the drought. A severe rain shortage crippled Russian agriculture a few years ago. Visiting a fair in Kiev, a Soviet official strolled through the displays of farm produce. Stopping to run his fingers through a bushel of golden grain, he said knowingly, "This must be a sample of wheat from the Ukraine!"

"No, Comrade," the attendant said. "That's the entire crop."

Mainline churches know that feeling. Down, down, down go the totals in their last two decades of evanglism statistics. Episcopalians, Disciples, United Methodists, Presbyterians, members of the United Church of Christ, and other ecclesiastical giants are united in more than ecumenicity. "Bringing in the sheaves" has been slow business lately.

Second, confusion. An older lady who lived in the canyons of New York inherited a giant block of oil company stock. Knowing little about stock, she knew even less about oil. At year's end, a stockholder notice announced the company's annual meeting. Having nothing scheduled, she decided to attend. Perhaps she could learn something about her investments. The day dragged dully on. Lengthy fiscal summaries. A synopsis of the overseas division. Reports on new technology from the engineering department, et cetera ad nauseum. Finally, the board chairman put a period to the boredom by calling for questions from the stockholders. Timidly, the novice raised her hand from the back of the room. "Yes, ma'am?" said the chairman politely.

"I'm new in our company," she said. "I don't know much about the oil business. But I've just been dying to ask a question. Tell me, when our company decides to build a filling station on the corner of a street in a particular town—how do we know we'll strike oil there?"

The confusion about what makes some churches grow while other nearby congregations decline may not be quite that severe. But it's somewhere in that neighborhood.

Third, a new grass roots surge of interest in evangelism. After twenty years of preoccupation with other issues, mainline pastors are digging into the subject. Many of their parishioners have waited for this a long time. They feel like the parakeet owned by a recently married young couple. The bird had a most limited vocabulary. He could only say two words: "Let's neck." It's a bit embarrassing to have a parakeet who sits around the house all day saying, "Let's neck." So the newlyweds were delighted to hear that their pastor had a parakeet, also. *Surely,* they thought, *his bird will know some other words, perhaps some religious words. If we get the two birds together, maybe ours can get an education.* They put the two birds together in the same cage. Immediately, the young couple's bird said, "Let's neck." The minister's parakeet instantly replied, "My prayers have been answered."

Many persons in major denominations are beginning to feel this is a great time to be alive. Their prayers have been answered. They have always been interested in evangelism. Now, others are, too.

Fourth, mounting evidence that mainline churches can grow if they use appropriate methods. The drought is ending. Some mainline congregations, bucking the general trend in their denomination, are growing. This book adds to that optimistic evidence. The rain of evangelism principles and methods cased between these covers did not fall from clouds of theoretical speculation. Using a five-year measuring stick, an exhaustive statistical study of all 4,389 Christian Churches (Disciples of Christ) congregations in the United States and Canada uncovered forty fast-growing churches which ranked at the top of four different size categories—small, medium-sized, large, and extra-large. The axioms outlined in these chapters emerged from the lifestyles of those forty rapidly growing congregations.

Other evangelism sleuths have mined methodological diamonds from the ore of a few growing *conservative* churches. But the present research analyzed all the significantly growing congregations in an entire mainline denomination. Others have painted a picture of what worked in a few superchurches flourishing in metrosprawl population centers. This study turned churches of every size in many different sociological settings upside down and shook them. Several items fell out of their carpenter aprons onto the pavement. These tools were collected, compared, and catalogued. The following pages describe that assortment.

The massive research undertaken to isolate these principles and methods was postulated on three simple premises: (1) If you wish to learn how to play tennis, why not take lessons from instructors who, when they play tennis, win a lot? Interviews were not, therefore, conducted among seminary professors. They do not play tennis; they teach tennis. In evanglism, as with other skills, theorizing has its place. But the bottom line validity measurement of all evangelism conjecture is: Does this idea actually help to win new persons to an active and continuing allegiance to Jesus Christ? Sophisticated theories that haven't proven themselves in the parish are as handy as shirt buttons with no thread holes. (2) Growing churches must surely do things differently from their declining sister congregations in the same judicatory. (3) Can we uncover observable, measurable qualities that help these churches succeed at evangelism? If so, why not bottle them? Other church leaders may wish to try the prescriptions.

This book is that bottle. From stacks of research data, taped interviews, personality profiles of pastors, tests to uncover the theological stance of pastors, and factor analysis from the computers of a major university, nineteen key growth principles emerged. Like fishing corks on a pond, they came bobbing to the surface of every numerically growing church in every size category. These nineteen principles resemble those consistent similarities found by walking into fast-food restaurants of the same chain throughout the country. Some features are alike everywhere. Various growing churches use many different methods. But close examination reveals that these infinite subspecies of ideas cluster around a few key fundamentals. These principles apply universally, in churches of every size and socioeconomic makeup. Most of the nineteen evangelism principles displayed herein are *essentials*. Mainline churches cannot grow numerically without them. A few of the principles (such as location of the building and a growing community population) are helpful but not absolutely essential—some churches grow without them. All of the principles are important. Any mainline church will be strengthened by their application.

This is not a book of advice for your church. This volume lifts up key principles and illustrates methods which have helped bring these principles alive in churches of different sizes and environments.

Using the book in adult classes and discussion groups will help the ideas penetrate the cerebral systems of members. Each chapter, therefore, concludes with study/discussion questions. In evangelism, as in many other disciplines, changed minds can come from changed behavior. Get a congregation started on new roads of action, and the people start thinking differently, but the reverse is also true; get people thinking differently about what they need to do in evangelism, and they begin acting differently. Whichever road you take, minds and behavior must change before a congregation can move out of the dark shadows of numerical decline toward a resurrected future of new life and growth.

Do these principles and methods apply in *every* denomination in North America? Not necessarily. Systems that work in one com-munion may not be acceptable to leaders in another. Cultural tra-ditions, psychological barriers, or theological hangups may block their efficaciousness. But these methods certainly do apply in that large cluster of American denominations who call themselves "main-line"—most of whom started declining in membership about 1960. These pages furnish those shrinking churches good news about the Good News: *congregations of shriveling mainline churches can grow!* We know they can, because these churches *did!* And they grew using these ideas.

What is honored in a country will be cultivated there.
—*Plato, circa 427-347 B.C.*

Since they had no root, they withered away.
— *Jesus of Nazareth*

1

Sold on the Product

A recent study shows that 100 percent of Americans believe in regular physical exercise. The same study reports that only 45 percent of Americans actively engage in any form of regular physical exercise. Nor do all churches who say they believe in evangelism practice it.

Axiom #1: Growing churches have a theological belief system that motivates pastor and people toward evangelism efforts. Their faith is ambidextrous. They both preach and do evangelism. They don't just *believe* in jogging. They actually run. As the student associate minister from a growing congregation said, "For us it is quite simple. Always be steady in faith, in hope and in love. Do the work of an evangelist. Fulfill your ministry. That is our motto. The congregation is empowered by believing that God has called us to this. The pastors participate in that call by seeing that theologically it is reinforced, biblically it is reinforced, and with a sense of religiosity it is carried out."

Growing churches don't believe that evangelism is the *only* work of the church. But they do understand that evangelism is the only work upon which all other works of the church depend. The continuous recruitment of new Sunday school teachers, for example, is directly dependent on evangelistic work. High levels of mission giving require consistent numbers of people in the church. Annual

13

stewardship campaigns are contingent on a pool of givers. Even in community action causes, success is directly linked to evangelism. Programs require people. If you're shooting a rocket off to the moon, the size of the launching pad determines the size of the vehicle you can fire. Everything churches do is *directly* dependent on success in evangelism.

Growing churches are not duped by the "let your light so shine" misapplication of Matthew 5:16. This myth, heralded in hymn and cliché, says that you accomplish evangelism by living a Christian life. According to this theory, people are attracted to you like moths to a light bulb. By spiritual osmosis, they then come to Christian commitment. Except for a few exceptional saints (like Mother Teresa or St. Francis of Assisi), this theory does not produce numerical results. It only makes Christians feel better about doing nothing.

Leaders in growing churches do not lift up one tiny shred of Jesus' teaching and say, "Let us look no farther! This is the sum total of Jesus' instruction about evangelism." They understand that these New Testament scriptures must be taken with equal seriousness and balanced against all other New Testament scriptures.

People in growing churches notice that when Jesus talks with the disciples for the last time, he says, "Go therefore and make disciples of all nations..." (Matthew 28:19). In fact, his *only* command to his followers in *all* his last recorded conversations was the instruction to evangelize: "Go into all the world and preach the gospel to the whole creation" (Mark 16:15). "Repentance and forgiveness of sins should be preached in his name to all nations..." (Luke 24:47). "You shall be my witnesses in Jerusalem and in all Judea and Samaria and to the end of the earth" (Acts 1:8).

Critics of declining congregations often say, "The ministers and members just don't have enough enthusiasm!" But what causes this lack of enthusiasm? Failure to stay in touch with the biblical roots that bring evangelistic fruits. Leaders in growing congregations remember that the Old Testament prophets called unceasingly for conversion—that John the Baptist called for conversion—that Peter called for conversion when he spoke to the Pentecost crowd (Acts 2)—that Paul called for conversion in his synagogue preaching. They remember Jesus saying in his triple parables of the lost coin, the lost sheep, and the lost son, "...there will be more joy in heaven over one sinner who repents than over ninety-nine righteous persons who need no repentance" (Luke 15:7). They know that few lost anythings find themselves. Some faithful someone must go looking.

This doesn't mean that a church cannot grow unless all its members become charismatics or wild-eyed religious fanatics. Studies of growing churches across the country reveal virtually every color of theological belief on the spectrum. Many are middle-of-the-streeters, theologically. But the unchurched cannot come in unless Christians get out of their steepled banquet hall and onto the street. Do we believe that people need Christ? Then we will find some way to get off our pew pads and invite them. Firm belief leads to concrete action. When that happens, a church will grow...just about anywhere.

Paul really means it when he says, "Now you are the body of Christ and individually members of it" (1 Corinthians 12:27). The church exists for the purpose of *being* the continuing body of Christ on this earth. A church which intends to live up to its name must therefore do and say on this earth exactly what Jesus did and said when he was here.

And just what did Jesus say and do? Walk back through the pages of the New Testament and take a look. You'll find three golden threads. Woven together, these three threads sum up his teachings and work.

A young lawyer asked Jesus a tricky question one day. "Teacher, what shall I do to inherit eternal life?" (Luke 10:25). But if you study the context of the question, you see that he was saying something deeper. "What is the point of your teachings?" he was asking. "What are you trying to say to us? You slam our sacred rituals and criticize our precious religious laws. Precisely what do you think religious faith should be like? Sum it up."

Jesus, unlike most preachers, summed it up in much less than twenty minutes. "You shall love the Lord your God with all your heart, and with all your soul, and with all your strength, and with all your mind; and your neighbor as yourself" (Luke 10:27). There you have two of Jesus' golden threads: Love God. That is the *main* thing. The second thing is very near to the main thing: love people.

The third golden thread becomes visible when you examine how Jesus went about accomplishing these two tasks. When compared to modern methods, Jesus had a clumsy way of doing his work. Why didn't he rent some good office space right across the street from the temple? The high traffic flow would have ensured his success. Why didn't he put a lighted sign out in front of his building which said, "Spiritual Healing" or "Catechisms Taught Here"? Why didn't he hire a good staff of nurses and a pleasant receptionist? Jesus had the greatest power available for healing and helping people that the world has ever known. Yet, he didn't get properly organized to treat the maximum number of people in the minimum amount of time.

What was Jesus' approach? He wandered around the countryside talking to people, many of them one at a time. Occasionally, he gathered great groups on the hillsides. Sometimes they crowded along a seashore as he stood in a fishing boat. But so much of the time Jesus intersected lives one at a time. He stopped to talk with a woman drawing well water. Touching her life at the core, he sent her away marveling and different. He stopped in a city street where a woman was being stoned to death for a sexual sin. In Capernaum, he stopped where a man was working in his office. We may not know all of what he said to that man. Surely, Jesus must have said more that the two words, "Follow me." That man arose from his desk and walked away. Many years later, he wrote the first Gospel of the New

Testament. His name was Matthew.

Jesus stopped by the boat where a commercial fisherman was repairing his nets. Did he say more than those two words: "Follow me"? We aren't sure. But we do know the fisherman's response. He did follow. He walked out of the seashore sand into the sands of history. Later, Jesus would say of this big fisherman, "On this rock—Petros—I will build my church, and the gates of hell will not prevail against it."

In one of history's most unprejudiced acts, Jesus stopped one day as a great mass of people pressed on every side. Looking up in a tree, he saw a short little Internal Revenue agent. Calling the IRS man down, he went to lunch with him. Again and again we see Jesus contacting people one at a time. He did not erect a building on the corner of some Fourth and Caesar Street in Jerusalem. He did not expect the world to beat a path to his better ideas. He didn't even take out an ad in the yellow pages. He did most of the walking himself.

There you have the three golden threads—the grand summation of Christ's message and method. Love God. Love people. Get the Word out. Do you want to dazzle your Sunday school class next week? Tell them you can summarize the entire New Testament in eight words. You won't be far off. Few lines in the New Testament fail to categorize under one of these three headings: Love God. Love people. Get the Word out! That was Jesus' message and his method.

We sometimes feel that a church fails to grow because the people in the community don't understand their church and what it tries to do for them. But the real problem is somewhere else altogether. *Church people don't understand themselves and their role.*

A business is designed to produce a *profit*. Money is the bottom line of its success. A business may have many vital things going for it—like service and quality products. But when it stops making money, it loses the ability to provide those items. It goes out of business.

What is the bottom line in church life? Certainly not money! Churches are not created in order to make a profit. No, a church is designed to *be* a *prophet*. Its objective is to achieve these three purposes of Christ: Love God. Love people. Get the Word out. If it accomplishes these three objectives, it becomes a successful or *prophetable* church.

Golden Thread #1

The first thread is *vertical*. It reaches up to the Father. Some people accuse fast-growing churches of being little more than "Religious Lion's Clubs" with good membership sign-up systems. Ministers in status quo congregations sometimes slam growing church pastors by saying, "They don't have much theological depth. They're just after numbers."

But studies of growing churches do not confirm that widely held opinion. Nor do they tell us that churches must become conservative or charismatic in order to grow. Rapid membership escalation comes in all kinds of theological packaging. A few growing churches are charismatic. Some are conservative. Others are pastored by ministers who classify themselves as "liberals" in the faith. Many are middle-of-the-road: their pastors hold the same theological persuasion as 90 percent of the other ministers in their denomination.

But regardless of how you describe their theology, growing churches hold one thing in common: their preaching and teaching is transcendent. They aren't just social clubs, psychological groups, or social service agencies. Their proclamation to the world answers the bottom line question of the faith in the affirmative. And what is the bottom line question of the faith? Different Christians phrase it differently, but it comes down to this: "Are we or are we not alone in the universe?" Is there just us? Or, is there more than us? Are we or are we not alone in this room? Is there just what we can see and touch? Or, is there *something more?* Is there an invisible other—a mysterious, inscrutable, eternal, yet knowable force—which the generations of the earth ahead of us have called *God?*

Growing churches answer this question with a resounding, "No, we are not alone!" These churches believe that God is *here.* They preach and teach Christ as a real and present power, not just a great teacher or historical figure. Without that vertical thread, a church starts becoming something less than a church. It also starts to die.

Golden Thread #2

The second thread is *horizontal.* The first thread reaches *up* to God. The second thread reaches *over* to other people in the church. We could describe this quality in numerous ways.

Fast-growing churches have a warm, positive spirit of fellowship among their people. This quality is immediately obvious. Strangers feel it before anyone says a word to them. This quality goes *beyond* friendliness. People can act friendly without caring about each other.

One way to explain this quality is to think about its opposite. Did you ever enter a room where people were angry with each other? Did someone have to tell you what was happening? No, you could feel the hackles standing out from their necks. The air was blue with hostility.

The warmth that pervades the atmosphere of growing churches is the ultra-opposite of feelings found in that board. This warmth is fostered in relationships between pastor and people. It is expressed in caring concern of members for other members in times of illness and other stress. It reaches outside the church in social helping efforts toward less fortunate members of society. But one of the most obvious places where this horizontal dimension expresses itself is in "multifaceted programming" within congregational life.

Have you noticed that people are different from each other? Have you noticed that they don't all like the same things? Have you noticed that even Christian people are different from each other? Fast-growing churches have picked that up. They understand that church programming must meet the needs of many different kinds of people at many different ages and stages of emotional, spiritual, physical, and mental development.

Some women, for example, love to participate in a women's organization. Others wouldn't be caught dead "wasting their time" in a women's circle. But they *would* like to teach a fourth-grade Sunday school class. Some people who need a bowling league this year may need a prayer group next year. Vice versa can be equally true. Leaders in growing churches know that. They don't try to pour every person into the same mold. They try to open as many different doors from the church into the world as they possibly can. They know that different kinds of people will come through different doors on their way to God and Christian maturity.

Golden Thread #3

The third thread reaches out *beyond* the church to people outside the church for the purpose of attracting them *toward* the church. The first thread reaches *up*. The second thread reaches *over*. The third one reaches *out*. Every growing church uses some method for contacting people outside their group and attracting them toward the group. This usually involves some kind of weekly, systematic visiting by members in the homes of non-members. Among the forty fastest growing Christian Churches (Disciples of Christ) in North America, only one lacked a systematic lay calling program. The stated "contact system" in that church is frequent impromptu personal witnessing and church invitations to business associates, fellow workers, and friends. Even there, the congregation had employed a part-time layperson to do a large volume of calling.

Contrast these three golden threads to those found in the average church. Most status quo congregations have medium strength in the first thread. You find very few atheists in mainline churches. They do reach up. The second thread is usually much weaker. Many mainline churches have relatively strong programming in a few aspects of their life. But they are often weak in youth work, weak in music programs for youth, and weak in singles ministries. You rarely find a mainline church with programmatic strength across the board. The third thread is virtually invisible. Most mainline churches depend on the first and second threads to take care of the third thread's work. Results: Decline.

He who has ears to hear, let him hear.

Group Discussion Questions

1. What is the actual record of growth or decline in your congregation over the past ten years? (See the annual yearbooks of your denomination for these statistics.)
2. What is the population growth pattern of your surrounding community during the past ten years? (See the Chamber of Commerce or the United States county and city population figures for 1970 and 1980.)
3. How would you describe the *growth potential* and the *will to grow* of this congregation?
4. Illustrate some things God has done in your own life that cause you to believe in the importance of evangelism.
5. To what extent do you agree or disagree with this definition of evangelism: "Winning new persons to an active and continuing allegiance to Jesus Christ"?
6. Which of the three golden threads do you feel are strongest in your church? Weakest?

> For some patients, though conscious that their condition is perilous, recover their health simply through their contentment with the goodness of the physician.
>
> *—Hippocrates, 460-377 B.C.*

2

God's Quarterback

In the movie *Airport*, a giant jet is stuck at the edge of a snowbound runway. The swirling snow drifting around the plane blocks all air traffic. But an injured plane loaded with passengers needs to land. Precious fuel drains away as time runs out. All forces focus on moving the snowlocked 747 off the runway.

Petrone, the mechanical genius engineer, directs a brilliant maneuver. He will force the plane out of the snowbank under its own engine power. The multimillion-dollar aircraft's owners raise objections. What about the damage this enormous stress might cause to the plane's superstructure? Petrone dismisses their concern with a wave of his hand. "The 747 is built so well it will stand just about anything," he says, "except a bad pilot."

Churches are much the same. They do well in almost any circumstances, except with a bad pilot. The pastor cannot guarantee a congregation's success in evangelism, but he/she can definitely block it. Without the pastor's commitment, lay efforts will prove futile. A recent bumper sticker says, "Warning: This car under the influence of driver." Like an automobile, churches are a complex organization of interrelated parts. If any one of them goes awry, the whole system stops getting anywhere. But the driver is by far the most significant piece.

Twenty-year membership charts repeatedly reveal change for the better after a new pastor arrives. Other factors remain constant—same parishioners, same building, same budget, same key leaders. One new person comes and the chart "upclines" dramatically. Not because he or she does all the work. Not because people flock to church to hear the new pastor. Not because of any personal charisma. But because the new pastor sets a new *style*. Pastors either create a mood for growth or a mood for something else. A church cannot grow if the pastor does not create a growth atmosphere. Leadership is the pearl without price.

Axiom #2: Growing churches have an effective pastor-leader who gives time and energy to evangelism. Lay leaders in rapidly growing churches were polled for a list of factors that they believe caused their growth. They inevitably put the pastor high on that list. He or she doesn't do all the evangelism work, but provides many of the ideas and does much of the motivating. She or he works at it, believes in it, and organizes others to work at it.

Many have described effective pastors with the "coaching" metaphore. But "coach" doesn't adequately illustrate the pastor's role in a growing church. A coach sits on the bench and watches. He gives directions but doesn't actually get on the field and play the game. The denominational executive or the seminary professor most nearly matches the coaching metaphor. Neither of these persons actually play ball. They talk about playing ball. They meet frequently with the team. They drink lots of coffee with the quarterbacks. They analyze and discuss training films. But they never actually block or carry the ball.

Quarterbacks play the game as well as talk about the game. Along with encouraging the team, they actually run down the field. They don't just write about the game or watch replays on closed circuit TV. Pastors of growing churches don't just preach to the team. They help move the ball toward the goal line. Some days they feel like guards, with lots of bruises from getting clobbered. Some days they feel like an end, way out for a long pass, with the whole team running the other direction. But more than anything else, pastors are quarterbacks. They are the nerve centers, the ball carriers, the signal callers, the pivots on which the teams turn.

The Association of Theological Schools in the United States and Canada has attempted to identify the qualities by which ministers in forty-eight denominations are judged effective. From a massive study, involving more than 5,000 respondents, they identified six characteristics as the most universally desirable ministerial qualities: (1) serves without regard for acclaim or public recognition; (2) honors commitments without fail, has personal integrity; (3) sets a Christian example; (4) functions responsibly, without avoiding tasks which he or she does not enjoy; (5) helps develop a sense of community within the congregation; and (6) manifests warmth in personal and counseling relationships. The three least desirable ministerial qualities were: (1) emotionally insecure behavior; (2) undisciplined living, often involving poor money management and extramarital sex; (3) self-serving, behaving abruptly, impatiently, judgmentally.

Psychological studies of pastors in growing churches do not directly compare with this earlier A.T.S. study. The twenty-three pastors in the present study have already proven their "readiness for ministry." They currently serve the fastest-growing churches in their denomination. The following report from Dr. Bill Erwin, a clinical psychologist, points toward the personality traits of quarterbacks who made the growing church all-star list.

Characteristics of the Growing Church Pastor

Trying to define the principles of church growth is a very inexact science. As indicated in other parts of this book, many of the factors are of an intangible nature that make them very difficult to define. However, it would likely be an almost universally accepted hypothesis to assume that the role of the pastor in church growth is quite significant. Becker and Schuller have outlined the historical development of the relationship between the Christian Church (Disciples of Christ) minister and the local congregation.

> ...The Christian Church (Disciples of Christ), born on the American frontier, still possesses a concept of ministry in which the twin principles of voluntarism and congregational policy are evident. These result in the demand that its ministers be both skillful in meeting the personal needs of church and possess the capacity to keep a congregation intact and vital.[1]

After this initial introduction, Becker and Schuller spend some time analyzing the various characteristics of the ministry deemed to be important by both ministers and the laity as gleaned from the responses given by persons within the Christian Church (Disciples of Christ) and compared with other denominations.

The present study evaluated only the responses of ministers of the forty fastest growing churches in the denomination. Of the forty pastors who were sent personality inventories, twenty-three were able to return their inventories for scoring and evaluation. The pastors involved in the study had been kind enough to volunteer their time for several types of questionnaires prior to the administration of the personality inventories which represent only a portion of the total study.

The inventories chosen for this section were *The Adjective Check*

---

[1]Edwin L. Becker and David S. Schuller, "Christian Church (Disciples of Christ)," *Ministry in America,* ed. David S. Schuller, Merton P. Strommen, and Milo L. Brekke. Harper & Row, 1980, pp. 307-330.

List[2] and the *Temperament and Values Inventory*[3]. These instruments were chosen for their ease of administration and scoring in the hope that they would, at the same time, tap some of the motivational components of the personalities of the various ministers. With the utilization of time being of great importance to most ministers, it was felt that it was essential to use instruments requiring minimum administration time.

The Adjective Check List (ACL) and the *Temperament and Values Inventory* (TVI) are standardized instruments that are scored by computer as a means of reducing subjective interpretation of the data. After the answer sheets were scored, the profiles were condensed into one composite profile and interpretations were made on the basis of this composite profile. The group profile for the ministers was then compared to the scores for the general population and not a population specifically made up only of ministers. Any time a group is reduced to a composite profile, some measure of individuality is lost, but something equally important is gained in terms of ease of interpretation. See pages 33 and 34.

"*The Adjective Check List* consists of 300 adjectives commonly used to describe attributes of a person." The respondent is simply required to check each of the adjectives which he believes to describe himself most of the time. The computerized results reflect each individual's standard score on each of fifteen scales which were designed to measure a need or disposition according to Murray's[4] need-press system.

Maybe the outstanding feature of the scores of the ministers on the ACL is the diversity of the individual personality profiles. In comparing the various patterns, there doesn't appear to be a "typical" profile that would characterize the group as a whole. The successful minister is a unique blend with his particular congregation.

In common usage of *The Adjective Check List* by one of the authors of this chapter, standard scores between 40 and 60 represent a mid-range with more extreme scores in either direction representing characteristics of the person taking the test that may be noteworthy in his or her personality dynamics. For the ministers in the present study only three scales—Intraception, Autonomy and Aggression—fall outside this arbitrary range (Fig. 1). These three scores would suggest that the ministers in the fastest growing churches in the denomination consider themselves to be curious individuals who are

[2]H.G. Gough, and A.B. Heilbrun, *The Adjective Check List Manual*. Consulting Psychologists Press, 1965.

[3]C.B. Johansson, *Manual for the Temperament and Values Inventory*. National Computer Systems, Inc., 1977.

[4]H.A. Murray, *Exploration in Personality*. Science Editions, 1962.

constantly seeking to expand their range of knowledge. They also value their independence in making decisions and may not always seek the immediate approval of others in making these decisions. However, they are such self-assured individuals they may simply feel they have the confidence of their "flock" in the decisions they are called upon to make. As a group they are competitive and assertive with a strong desire to win. Negative implications of these three characteristics would suggest that these ministers may be insensitive to the needs of their congregations and tend to go their own way. However, the success they have had in building their churches would indicate that more than likely they are in tune with their congregations, and they have been given more or less free rein to do those things which are productive for the congregations and the growth of the church as a whole.

The remaining scales may be considered less meaningful in describing the composite group since the scores fall so close to the mean. However, a brief examination of some of these traits may help us to better understand the ministers and their personalities. Scales six and one, Nurturance and Achievement are the next highest scales and fall closely within the same range. The similar elevation of these two scales would suggest that the ministers have achieved some degree of balance between their need to achieve for their own recognition for themselves and, at the same time, their desire to provide emotional and material support for others.

The next three scales, also similar in range, can be grouped together for examination. The score on the Dominance scale likely is a reflection of the leadership capacity of the minister in the local church and his relative contentment with this position. A person manifesting a high score in this area usually displays confidence in his own leadership skills and is able to persuade others to endorse his position in many significant areas of church growth and development. Gough and Heilbrun, the authors of the ACL, define the *Affiliation* on page 10 as the need "to seek and sustain numerous personal friendships." Such a quality would be invaluable in providing a coalescence of the many divergent views found in almost every congregation. The Endurance score reflects the individual's ability to persevere in any task and see it through to its eventual completion.

The next four scales are closely grouped around the mean and thus offer limited insight into the personality dynamics of the minister. The Order score suggests a nice balance between a need for neatness and planning and the spontaneity that is necessary in handling the various tasks imposed upon a minister. The Heterosexuality scale measures the individual's zest for life. An average score is probably a healthy sign that is found in many professional groups. The Exhibition score reflects a balance between narcissism and diffidence. The Change score is in keeping with the similar score on the Order scale.

Still close to the mean, but giving us some insight into the personality characteristics of these ministers is their composite score on the need for Abasement. They are not handicapped particularly by feelings of inferiority and tend to be responsive to others without a display of a self-effacing attitude. The low Succorance score reflects an attitude of independence and self-sufficiency that allows ministers to relate to others without needing to evoke unnecessary feelings of sympathy. The low Deference score reaffirms the desire of the ministers to lead and/or supervise others while maintaining an ambitious attitude in an energetic manner.

"The Temperament and Values Inventory (TVI)[5] is designed to measure individual differences in temperament and work values." This instrument allows still another look at the qualities that motivate the minister of a rapidly growing church. The final profile (Fig. 2) of the individual taking the test yields scores on seven temperament scales and seven measures of reward values. Again, as with the ACL, because of the use of the composite profile, many of the scores averaged out to be quite near the mean.

The temperament scales are bi-polar dimensions avoiding the connotation of a "good-bad" continuum for each scale. Three of the dimensions yielded a score almost exactly on the mean, suggesting a balance in the temperaments measured by these dimensions—Routine-Flexible, Quiet-Active and Attentive-Distractible. Of the remaining scales, we find scores that present a picture of what might be expected of a minister—one who is cheerful, consistent, sociable and persuasive.

The reward values scales also lend support to the traditional description we might write for our minister. These scales measure what is important to a minister, within the limitations of the evaluation instrument, and provide some insight as to what a minister finds rewarding in his chosen vocation. What is of least importance to the ministers in these churches is shown by their score on Managerial/Sales Benefits. Fringe benefits traditionally found in managerial or sales-oriented professions have little reinforcement value for these individuals. Apparently, they find intrinsic satisfaction in their work in terms of their duties or as a by-product of watching their churches grow. More research will be needed to shed further light on this aspect of their motivation.

Next highest of these scales is the score on Task Specificity. Apparently, the ministers enjoy the variety of tasks offered them in their role as minister and would prefer not being limited to having a well-defined role. The remaining scores are all closely grouped near the mean and fall within the average range of scores of most persons taking the test. Social recognition apparently holds little interest for the ministers. This score is in keeping with other scores which suggest that much of the motivation in performing their duties provides them with intrinsic rather than extrinsic value.

---

[5]Johansson, p.iii.

With such a high score on Autonomy on the ACL, it is a little surprising to find the Work Independence measure only at the average range. Future research could provide additional information in this area.

Philosophical curiosity is the next highest score which likely reflects the curiosity these ministers have about human nature and/or groups in action. As might be expected, Leadership and Social Service hold the highest reward value for ministers in these churches. Their desire to lead and provide social service to others can easily be combined in the unique position that they have as a minister in a growing church.

To Dream the Possible Dream

Henry Kissinger has said that leaders must invoke an alchemy of great vision. Those leaders who do not are ultimately judged failures, even though they may be popular at the moment. That always makes the difference between mediocrity and greatness in pastors, too—a dream. Church growth quarterbacks are dreamers of the possible dream. God seldom calls a committee in order to make a church grow. He calls individual leaders, who in turn motivate others to rally round the flag of their seminal vision. God didn't send a committee to Asia Minor. He sent Paul. He didn't send a committee to Pharaoh. He sent Moses. He didn't send a committee to clean up the promised land after the Babylonian captivity. He sent Nehemiah. He didn't send a committee to stake out a new nation. He sent Abraham. Committees and boards can help to sharpen the details of a great vision. They can flesh out the skeleton of a grand idea. But finding that idea in the beginning—catching the first glimpse of the vision—dreaming the big dream—that is always the province of some pastor-leader-quarterback.

A Leader but Not a Dictator

Two other qualities set pastors of growing churches apart from their peers—leading and caring. Not one without the other, but both at the same time. The neglect of either blunts a church's ability to grow.

Dwight Eisenhower said that leadership is "the art of getting somebody else to do something you want done because he wants to do it." Pastors of growing churches are consummate Picassos of this craft. In contrast, many pastors have unfortunately interpreted "pastoral" as meaning "passive." They overlearned the Rogerian counseling model of "responsive listening." A listening ear cannot substitute for a thinking head, a zealous heart, and a working hand. Declining churches need a pastor who can lead them from where they are to where they haven't been.

The Protestant Reformation was, in many ways, a reaction to the problem of authority. It renewed and reformed the church—with special emphasis on democracy of lay leadership based on biblical authority.

This new democratic spirit brought many values to church life. It strengthened lay participation. It encouraged common folk to read and study God's word in their own languages. Only priests and scholars had been allowed to do this before. This was a healthy reaction against the Dark Ages, during which the authority of Popes and priests had been substituted for biblical authority. But mainline denominations sometimes push this "priesthood of all believers," idea to disastrous extremes. They overshoot the landing field and substitute the authority of a majority vote for the authority of the Bible.

Majority votes don't always reveal God's will. A majority built a golden calf while Moses was gone up the mountain to get the Ten Commandments. The majority screamed, "Crucify him, crucify him," when Pilate called for a mass opinion. The Protestant church probably wouldn't exist if Paul had waited for a majority vote from the Jerusalem Council. Hearing the cadence of a higher drummer, he struck out westward to set up gentile outposts at Corinth, Ephesus, and Phillipi. Nor do effective pastors today wait for a majority vote to lead a church out of its numerical stagnation.

Evangelistic leadership will not come from the church's evangelism committee. (Ironically, many growing churches do not even have an evangelism committee.) Such committees can nourish the vision once a leader gives it to them. But these organized groups seldom furnish the first spark that lights the blaze. As with Moses, Nehemiah, Paul, and Peter, God usually starts by inspiring some individual citizen of the Kingdom to say, "Let's go this direction, gang!"

Democratic church structures are fairly effective at protecting churches from financial stupidity and Jim Jones insanity. But they seldom lead a congregation to effective outreach action. The authority for strong evangelistic effort usually falls somewhere between the autocracy of a Pope and the kind of visionless democracy found in most mainline congregations. We call this pastoral *leadership,* and nothing can substitute for its power.

David McClelland, a psychologist at Harvard, feels that all ministers are motivated by one of three basic needs. Some are motivated by *affiliation.* These clergy are above all else concerned about the quality of their interpersonal relations. They make excellent pastors and counselors but not necessarily good program developers or parish managers.

A second kind of pastor is motivated more by *power* than anything else. She/he has a strong need to get recognition, command attention, and control other people, the primary concern being "Who's in charge?" Such pastors tend to busy themselves getting control of the channels of communication so that they are more "in charge of things."

A third group of pastors is by far the smallest. These persons are primarily motivated by the need for *achievement*. They would rather "get something done" than be rewarded in terms of success *per se*. They like work situations where they get specific feedback on how well they are doing. They are interested in and motivated by statistical results. Their ministry is likely to be marked by a great deal of change, especially in terms of programming.[6] Pastors of growing churches usually fall into this third category.

A Warm, Accepting Friend

The parson of a growing church is an umbrella person. He or she nurtures people without controlling them. A lay leader in one growing congregation put it this way: "He exhibits a number of positive qualities—dependable preaching and worship leadership; a Bible-centered approach to life; the use of Scripture to shed light on our problems, but always in an uplifting way; a good counselor, always sensitive and responsive to the needs of both church members and non-members."

The pastor of another rapidly growing small congregation was forced by his leaders to list himself as one of the reasons for their growth. "I am humbled," he said. "I do not consider myself a leader. But I do involve myself in things that I think are important in the life of our community. When I first came to town, I visited more than once every individual family in our church. Some of my visits are not necessarily pastoral calls. I am a friend to them. I am both their minister and their friend, and they have the confidence in me that allows me to knock at their door at any time."

One recent psychological study gives some scientific backing for the necessity of strong nurturing qualities in the leader of a growing church. Chana Ullman[7], an assistant professor of psychology at Wellesley College, found that converts to the mainstream religions (as well as converts to the newer sect groups) shared a need for a positive father figure to calm the emotional turmoil rooted in their childhood. More than 80 percent of the converts he studied reported anxiety, depression, and anger in the years before their conversion. So, Freud's theory that religious conversion represents a search for a substitute father (God) has at least some credibility.

In Ullman's study, neither new converts nor long-time members were concerned over big theological issues. Only 10 percent of them said they were interested in such concepts as the scientific notion of truth, the Trinity, or problems of racial and social injustice during

[6]From an article by Richard J. Kirk, "What Motivates You: Achievement, Affiliation, or Power?" *Alᵇan Institute Action Information,* Alban Institute, Mount St. Alban, Washington, D.C. 20016, Sept. 1979, pp. 8-9

[7]*Psychology Today,* August 1979, p. 25 "Newsline."

the two years prior to their conversion. But quite a number of them explicitly said that the appeal of a religious authority figure had promoted their change. "One look and you feel he totally accepts you," one person said. Others said, "The people were nice to me," or "The atmosphere was free of anxiety." The pastor's personality obviously helps to set these atmospheric qualities.

Every church member either consciously or unconsciously asks, "Does my pastor like me?" If the answer to that question becomes blurry, uneasiness enters the member's mind. When this answer becomes blurry in the minds of *numerous* laypersons, uneasiness turns to mass discontent. People begin to nitpick about their pastor's use of time, the programs he or she does or does not start, the quality of sermons preached, or the caliber of administrative ability.

Pastors need to lead as well as nurture people. But nobody will give them a chance to lead for long if they lack the knack of extending genuine concern, appreciation, and downright liking to that multitudinous variety of individuals who inhabit every church. The Bible calls this quality "grace," and indicates that God is very good at it.

Nor can this pastoral trait be merely an intellectual attitude of the heart, mind, and words. It must show in the face. A recent study at Brigham Young University reports that only 7 percent of the information about our attitude comes from message content; 38 percent comes from vocal qualities and 55 percent comes from facial expression.[8] These statistics speak volumes about the minister's manner—in the pulpit, on evangelism calls, when meeting with committees, or interrupted by a drop-in visitor at the office. Facial expressions and vocal qualities are the big communicators. If pastors fail in communicating warmth, friendliness, and acceptance with their face, what the mouth speaks will become irrelevant. Pastors of growing churches know that feelings cannot be hidden—they *will* out. So they concentrate on getting the feelings right so that what they communicate with the face will be friendliness, acceptance, warmth.

Theologically Firm, but Not Narrowminded

Twenty-three pastors of fast-growing churches filled in a twenty-five item questionnaire entitled "What Is Your Theological Position?" Composite results showed a mean score of 74.7 and a median of 68, both falling into the overlapping categories of liberal and neoorthodox. The mode (most common score) was 92, falling into the borderline between orthodox and fundamentalist. But the range ran all the way from liberal to fundamentalist—indicating that church growth is *possible* with almost any type of theology in the pulpit.

---

[8]*Family Weekly,* May 18, 1980, "Does the Face Speak Louder than Words?"

One hundred percent (twenty-three) of the respondents answered the following questions in the affirmative: "I believe in God the Father Almighty, Maker of heaven and earth. God loves each person and seeks to win his or her love in return." "Our lives are incomplete if we do not have a vital relationship with God. Persons are ultimately responsible to God." Growing church pastors love people, but they don't try to substitute human relationships for God relationship. They don't just point to themselves; they point to the Father. Twenty-two respondents agreed with these items: "I have a duty to help in spreading my religious faith to peoples and cultures that have not heard about it and/or have not accepted it." "Attendance at worship services is of vital importance in one's religious life."

A Student but Not an Egghead

An active layman in Denver summed it up accurately: "Ministers in growing churches all have one thing in common. They are always asking questions. They are forever trying to learn how to do it better. Pastors of declining churches," he said, "stay busy rationalizing about why their congregations can't grow." Growing church pastors are already the most skilled evangelism leaders in their denomination. But they are the first to sign up for evangelism seminars. They read books on the subject. They pick the brains of pastors in other growing churches. They continually study to find a better way.

After World War II, higher education became more highly valued and sought after by Americans. In this social milieu of educational appreciation, many mainline seminary students embraced *above all else* the values of intellectual scholarship—often absorbed from seminary professors who have never served a congregation. In so doing, they lost their potency for leadership in the church. Pastors of fast-growing churches do not fall into this category. They are not egghead scholars. Their study is directed toward practical parish ends—not toward intellectual philosophizing.

A Preacher, but Not an Orator

Studies in various denominations have noted that the *style* of pulpit work seems little related to church growth. W.A. Criswell, a Southern Baptist, credits expository preaching as the major factor in his Dallas church's growth to 18,000 members. But Robert Schuller, whose Garden Grove Community Church in California exceeds 9,000, rarely preaches expository messages. He communicates "possibility thinking" through topical preaching.

Nor is the quality of oratory a significant factor. A committee decided to produce a book entitled *Sermons from Growing Churches*. (They assumed that great preaching must be happening in growing churches.) After much effort, they scrapped the project. "These are good, average quality sermons," they concluded. "But they are not so exceptional that people would buy a book of them."

Works Hard, but Knows What Not to Do

Colleagues often accuse growing church pastors of being workaholics. Sometimes this accusation is accurate. Sometimes it isn't. The pastor of a 1,000 member growing church did a time study on himself. (This included counseling, studying, visiting, administration, every aspect of a pastor's work.) In the average week he worked 70.4 hours. That seems a great deal to most laypersons. But other studies show that the average Protestant minister in the United States works 64 hours per week.

The big differences between pastors of growing and nongrowing churches lies not so much in hours worked but in the kind of work done. Pastors of growing churches are more than efficient. They are effective. Efficient workers do things right and quickly. Effective workers do the right things.

All pastors have difficulty discriminating between *important* matters and *essential* matters. Many suffer from "detail fatigue" because they try to do both. This frustration grows out of the natural pressures that go with every minister's territory. In a survey of Protestant pastors regarding the most essential functions of their ministry, the clergy listed in order of their perceived significance: preaching, pastoral calling, teaching, counseling, administration, evangelistic calling, social concerns, fund-raising. Why does evangelism come so far down the list? Sometimes the minister does not really believe in it. But along with this, no environmental forces push him/her into doing it. The sermon must be preached. Hospital calls must be made. People who come to the office for counseling must be seen. But the pressure to do evangelism must come from *inside* the pastor, or it doesn't come at all. Since evangelism is not the squeakiest wheel in the church, it usually gets greased last. If the pastor is not thus inclined, most laypersons will not complain if it isn't greased at all.

As well as working in a pressure cooker profession, each pastor consciously or unconsciously adopts a particular *model* for ministry. All clerical duties are then fitted around that particular model or way of doing ministry. Every veteran clergy watcher can think of pastors whose ministerial activities cluster around one of these fifteen central cores: The sociological model, the psychological model, the biblical studies model, the administrative model, the Holy Spirit model, the teaching model, the recreational model, the church renewal model, the social action model, the world outreach model, the fund raiser model, the evangelism model, the fellowship model, the music model, the scholarship model.

What causes a pastor to choose a particular model as ideal? Several things: Cultural trends, personal aptitudes, early experiences of success in ministry, what the pastor *likes* to do, the things for which a pastor receives frequent praise, the environment and needs of the first church served. These ministry models change with the times. Some are "in" during one decade and "out" in another—which is why some preachers are called old-fashioned. When they adopted their model, it was in.

No pastor escapes adopting a particular model. No mind is large enough to see *everything* as having equal importance. But pastors must—if their church grows numerically—prevent that particular model from crowding out the task of evangelism. They must rise above their pet aspects of ministry enough to answer God's call to go fishing.

Makes the Best of What Is

A great violinist visited Houston for a concert. The newspaper, however, used most of its space to describe his original Stradivarius violin. The morning of the concert, the paper's front page carried a picture of the great instrument he would play. That night, the hall filled with people, and the musician played extremely well. As he finished, applause thundered. After it subsided, he carefully laid the bow down and carried a chair over to center stage. Raising the violin over his head with both hands, he smashed it across the chair back. It splintered into a thousand pieces. The audience gasped. Coming back to the microphone, he said, "I read in this morning's paper about how great my violin was. So I walked down the street and found a pawn shop. For ten dollars, I bought a cheap violin. I put some new strings on it, and that's the violin I played this evening, then smashed. I wanted to demonstrate for you that it isn't the violin that counts most. It's the hands that hold the violin."

Some churches are built like a Stradivarius. You get the impression that they would do well in almost any minister's hands. Other churches look like they were constructed with an inferior grade of bamboo. But just as different kinds of violins are still violins, each church is still the Body of Christ. Each congregation has the potential for proclaiming his message and doing his work. Put that institution in the hands of a pastor who believes that God wants it to grow. You will likely hear some terrific music—even if that body isn't a Stradivarius.

Group Discussion Questions

1. What additional ways do you think your pastor could help your church grow numerically?
2. Do you think the pastors in your congregation have emphasized evangelistic outreach as much in recent years as in the years before 1955? Illustrate.
3. Name some programs and activities that you feel use up so much time that we have little energy left for evangelism.
4. How important do you think preaching is in relation to evangelistic success of a church?

5. Have you had experiences in which the evangelism committee gave strong leadership in evangelism? Have you had experiences where the pastor gave strong leadership in evangelism? Illustrate.
6. Ministers often become weary working at the tough task of evangelism. In what ways can they bolster themselves against that weariness that leads to lethargy and apathy about the unchurched? What are some ways church members can help with this problem?

Adjective Check List

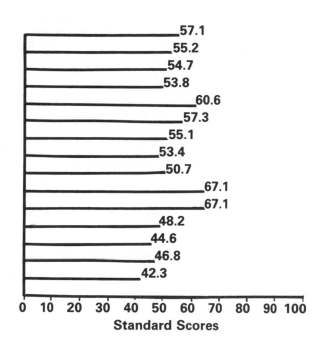

Figure 1

Temperament and Values Inventory

Personal Characteristics

Routine	49.2	_____X_____	Flexible
Quiet	49.1	_____X_____	Active
Attentive	49.4	_____X_____	Distractible
Serious	55.1	_____X_____	Cheerful
Consistent	43.1	_____X_____	Changeable
Reserved	55.0	_____X_____	Sociable
Reticent	54.0	_____X_____	Persuasive

```
        30     40     50     60     70
               Standard Scores
```

Reward Values

Social Recognition	51.0	_____X_____
Managerial/ Sales Benefits	43.6	_____X_____
Leadership	52.1	_____X_____
Social Service	53.9	_____X_____
Task Specificity	46.2	_____X_____
Philosophical Curiosity	51.7	_____X_____
Work Independence	51.3	_____X_____

```
        30     40     50     60     70
               Standard Scores
```

Figure 2

Determined leaders can make a crumb of experience go a long way.

3

The Core Corps

A company having trouble with sales called in an expert to give them an outsider's viewpoint. The consultant spent the day going over their problems and provided several good ideas. As he packed his briefcase to leave, the sales manager said, "Is there anything else you can tell us that might help increase our sales?"

The visiting pro thought a moment, then walked over to a huge wall map. Little red pins marked the location of company salespersons in several states. "There is one other thing you could do," the expert said. "Take all these little red pins out of this map. Then stick each one in a salesperson."

Zig Ziglar says, "One person with a conviction is worth more than 1,000 with only an interest." Raise that to the tenth power for evangelism. Jesus took twelve and changed the world. But they had more than a mild interest in this carpenter. Each died a martyr. They paid for a new world with the currency of blood. History redounds with examples of that truth. Fanatical leadership often succeeds against the heaviest odds. Growing churches are not 100 percent filled with that sort of leadership. But at the core you always find a few strong seeds of conviction about evangelism.

Axiom #3: Growing churches contain a core group of lay leaders who want the church to grow and are willing to work at it. Churches, like individuals, are much more likely to succeed at matters to which they give their attention. If you want a college education, your chance is increased by attending classes and studying a little. If you are unemployed, your likelihood of getting a job shoots up if you go out each day and hunt one. Accidents do happen. A few people find jobs without looking for them. But not many people hit targets they don't shoot at. Churches are the same. Most leaders want their congregation to grow, in a *vague sort of way*. But they often assume that this will happen by accident. Corporately, they have never really discussed the matter. But evangelism seldom occurs by indirection.

The words *homicide, suicide,* and *decide* grew out of the same root parent. *Sidere* means *to cut*. To *decide* is to cut off. Ministers and churches must *decide* to do evangelism or they are cut off from it: not deciding equals deciding negatively. This leads to ecclesiastical suicide and homicide against the kingdom of God. Churches which grow have at least a few leaders who believe in evangelism and work at it.

A few congregations, of course, consciously resist growth. The pastor of a small church in Texas tried to encourage his church board toward evangelism for three months. During his third appeal about this need, a "pillar of the church" interrupted him with, "You've been talking about evangelism for two or three months now, Preacher," she said. "I think we need to get one thing straight with you."

"What's that?" the pastor said.

"We really aren't interested in evangelism. This building we are sitting in is going to last just as long as most of us board members. And, Preacher, that's really all we're interested in." She was serious. They all were serious. Soon afterward he sought relocation in the greener grass of another pastorate. He didn't want to help the church commit suicide.

Leaders can block themselves from vigorous evangelism in a number of different ways. Some do this by the way they *define* evangelism. They overshoot Karl Barth and define evangelism as social action. Others assume that everyone in America has already heard about Christ—so evangelism is relegated to what we do on the mission field. Either definition pushes evangelism to a convenient, impersonal distance. Ironically, the denominations that blur and blend the definitions of these three activities—social action, foreign missions and evangelism—do poorly at all three. Denominations which make sharp distinctions among the three accomplish far more concrete results in each. (Only 4 percent of foreign missionaries, for example, come from ecumenical denominations; 96 percent come from non-Conciliar bodies of the church.)

36

Other church officers block themselves from evangelistic leadership with a new kind of religious synchrotism. "It doesn't really matter that people are outside of Christ," they philosophize. "After all, doesn't God love everybody, sinners, too, even if they haven't responded to him?" On the surface, this shallow universalism is the old idea that God is just too good to damn anybody—or that people are too good to be damned. This view is, of course, not modern at all. This is the Pelagian heresy against which Augustine battled in the first years of the fifth century—the idea that "human nature is indestructibly good." A church council set this idea aside as unbiblical and unchristian. Every few centuries, well-meaning people retrieve it from the scrapheap of theology. But it always returns there within a few decades. Underneath the surface, this universalism is a blatant agnosticism about the Great Commission—a way of calling unnecessary the Master's suggestion that we become fishers of men and reapers of wheat.

Some lay leaders can also block themselves away from evangelism by assigning the task to pastors. This phenomenon is more frequently seen in upper and middle socioeconomic class churches. These persons are accustomed to *hiring* their work done. So they naturally think of hiring someone to do the Great Commission for them. But American denominations who serve these sections of society have shown the largest declines in membership. No amount of money can hire sufficient staff to make a church grow. Churches only expand on the crest of mass enthusiasm by their participants.

Many mainline denominational offices are now suffering acute financial shortages. Their membership numbers have declined sufficiently to pinch their pocketbook. Several of these denominations are pushing for better stewardship programs, trying to squeeze more juice from fewer turnips. Others are finding that better stewardship methods cannot compensate for drastically reduced numbers of giving units. What they really need is a bureaucratic alchemy to convert dedicated apathy into fanatical enthusiasm about evangelism. Both local churches and entire denominations can sometimes, however, get their initial interest in evangelism from these "wolf at the door" circumstances. One pastor of a growing congregation said that a financial crunch was their first motivation. "Then, after we got serious about reaching out and growing," he said, "we discovered the joy and benefits that new people bring. After those experiences took hold, we began to work at growth for the right reason instead of selfish reasons."

Stewards of the Word

The national board meeting of one rapidly shrinking denomination discussed future priorities. Some board members stressed financial stewardship as the key to *all* priorities. In one sense, that is true. But money merely serves means to end causes. The church's *basic* stewardship is the Word (Christ). Jesus said that the work of

God is to believe on him whom God has sent (John 6:29). The intelligible proclamation and preaching of Christ—that is our primary stewardship.

Jesus described God's steward as a willing caretaker of what God has entrusted. He illustrated this with a story about three men given differing amounts of silver coins. One took his tiny allotment of silver and hid it in the ground. Jesus' condemnation of this man is accurate prophecy of denominations which bury their basic stewardship of the Word. "For I say to you, that to everyone who has shall be given but for him who has not, even what he has shall be taken away. Take from him the pound of silver and give it to him who has ten pounds" (Luke 19:11-27).

Numbers Are Important

Pastors of nongrowing churches often praise the importance of quality by saying, "After all, evangelism is more than numbers." That is true, but evangelism is certainly not *less* than numbers. Commitment to Christ comes in packages of *one*. Until you get that minimum *quantity,* you have no foundation upon which to build *quality*. These "ones" are called persons. When you put several of these *ones* together in groups, that collection of commitments to Christ is defined with a *number*. Leaders who say that their evangelism doesn't concentrate on numbers usually mean it has no concentration at all. Methods that don't focus on numbers don't focus on people.

The pastor of a fast-growing church says, "I have never played a game with numbers. Nor have I ever intended numbers as my motivation. However, to be very realistic, if you don't have numbers, you don't have anything. People are numbers, but they are very important numbers. . . I never use a sales approach to get people. Numbers is not a game. Life is the issue—life with or without Christ."

The New Testament is full of rejoicing about numbers. Paul reached the *whole* Praetorian Guard, not just a few. Throughout the book of Acts, the word *many* rings like a joyous bell pealing the news of a war ended—*many* cleansed of evil spirits, *many* believed, *many* baptized, *many* giving up their faith in magic. (Acts 8:7; 9:42; 17:12; 18:8; 19:18). Modern growing church leaders treat evangelistic numbers with the same seriousness as they do other kinds of numbers. Every church elects an official scorekeeper to monitor one kind of number. This is the treasurer. Counting dollar bills is important. Growing churches take people as seriously as dollar bills. They are not afraid to count them—to see how many are coming in, going out, why and why not.

Organized to Do Evangelism

Critics often accuse churches of over-organization. This is seldom true. More often, they are poorly organized. Well-meaning leaders siphon off member energy into organizational work rather than New Testament work.

Church organization structures exist in order to achieve two New Testament goals—making new disciples and nurturing present disciples into better disciples. Church leaders easily, however, shift their concentration to the nuts-and-bolts structure of their assembly line. When that happens, they forget the products that should roll off the end of that assembly line, and productivity diminishes to disastrous levels.

The boards, departments, and committees of growing churches concentrate on the product as well as the organization. They take evangelism as seriously as repairing the organ, fixing the roof, and painting the sanctuary. They know that buildings are never the most important temples of God; people are. God is always more concerned about persons than buildings. Growing churches therefore keep a sane balance between production workers and maintenance personnel for the assembly line. They remember that when Jesus called Peter and Andrew from casting their net into the sea, he didn't say, "Come, follow me, and I will make you net menders." He said, ". . . I will make you fishers of men" (Matthew 4 : 19).

The Pull and the Push

Several fire drills were held at an elementary school. The principal, not entirely satisfied with his results, decided to try one more. This time, all 900 school children trooped out of the building in four minutes and thirteen seconds. The principal was pleased. They had set a new record. But when the closing bell rang at the end of the day, the assistant principal decided to stopwatch that evacuation. The last kid cleared the building in three minutes flat. This speedy performance was powered by *motivation*. Key leaders in growing churches have that kind of drive for evangelism.

This motivation is increased by a strong pastor. But it does not come from his or her personality alone. Growing church leaders keep in touch with their basic *purposes* as a church. They are somewhat like a championship basketball team. When that group takes the court, what motivates them? Not just what's inside them. They keep in touch with their big objective as a team—winning the game.

The second quality that differentiates growing church leaders is *attitude*. If motivation is the pull, attitude is the push. A Scottish Highland minister met one of his parishioners on the road home from summer maneuvers with the army. The soldier was still wearing his fighting uniform and carrying a full pack. "How far can you march, Jock, with such a heavy load?" the pastor asked.

The weary Scot replied, "Maybe twelve miles." But then he added, "Fifteen with a good bagpipe band." Key leaders in growing churches are driven forward with that sort of attitude.

Every church has three kinds of leaders—rowboat people, sailboat people and steamboat people. Rowboat leaders must always be pushed or shoved along. Sailboat people move when a favorable wind blows. Steamboat people move continuously, through calm or storm. They have an inner *attitude* that drives them forward to great goals. Growing churches have at least a few steamboat leaders.

In any social grouping, the only quality more contagious than enthusiasm is apathy, and more contagious than apathy is negativism. Every congregation contains some of each. Growing churches do not exclude apathetic and negative persons, but they try to limit the number of them in key leadership positions.

Napoleon said that of the four basic elements which constitute an army—size, training, equipment, and morale—morale is worth more than the other three put together. Triple that principle for churches. And a positive attitude by key leaders *determines* much of the morale. Key leaders always influence churches toward the direction they themselves are going. Even the strongest of pastors have difficulty counterbalancing the negative influence of leaders who sound as if they were baptized in dill pickle juice.

Leaders of growing churches get clear about their *purposes*. They get *motivated* by their purposes, they get *positive* about their purposes, their church, and their future. And they get going.

Twelve Church Growth Inhibitors

Looking for a way to raise the consciousness of your leaders regarding factors which can inhibit the church's evangelistic effectiveness? The following exercise, called "Taking Your Church's Evangelistic Pulse," allows each individual board member to see what all the other leaders feel about their church in an anonymous, non-threatening manner.

Directions for using this exercise with local church boards: Give each person a blank sheet of paper. Have each individual write the numbers 1 through 12 down the left side. As you read the twelve church growth inhibitors aloud, ask each person (without discussing it with others) to place either T, PT or F beside the number on their sheet, according to whether they think this particular inhibitor is a true, partly true or false description of their congregation. After finishing, collect the papers and count the number of the three different answers that individuals gave on each of the twelve inhibitors. Place the totals on a flip chart and discuss.

1. Inadequate Visibility in the Community. Some churches provide fine personal faith experiences for the members, while becoming gradually invisible to the community around them. As the positive self-identity of the church declines, the members find themselves increasingly apologizing for its inadequacy with statements like, "We are just a small church, so we can't do much." This negative news does little to recruit new members.

40

2. Inadequate Pastor Tenure. Some churches have been "conditioned" to expect a short-term pastor and will refuse to cooperate with him because "he won't stay long, and the next pastor will just want to change everything around again." This problem is complicated by the fetish toward independent thinking commonly found in many rural areas where people have had to rely on themselves for so much for so long. The church members often reject outside ideas, even those that come from their pastor, until he/she has been there several years and is considered a part of the community. A pastor who arrives at such a church with a spirit of hope and optimism often gets to a state of disillusionment and moves on before creative change can come about.

3. Inadequate Spiritual Focus. In some churches, both the members and those who visit begin to sense that the church concentrates more on self-preservation than on serving God, people, and the community. During several years of effort to keep the church doors open by keeping financial expenditures to a minimun, the focus has subtly shifted from the spiritual to the materialistic. Over a long period of time, the whole church board loses its broad vision about the basic purposes of the church, and becomes instead a "building and grounds committee" for an organization which, to outsiders, looks like a hybrid between a mausoleum and a museum. Few people are inspired to full participation by the idea of preserving an institution.

4. Inadequate Programming. The basic bread-and-butter programming (worship opportunities, Bible study, fellowship events, service to the community, and interaction in wider denominational work) in some churches is so limited in volume and variety that it cannot meet the spiritual/religious needs of a broad range of people. Visitors see little evidence of programming that would attract them to return.

5. Inadequate Personality Appeal of Present Members. Many people have described their visit to a cold, unfriendly church. While first impressions are not always accurate, the second or third visit sometimes confirms that first impression. Personalities in some congregations appear to be set in their ways, stingy, suspicious, and clanish, a pattern which is unattractive to both newcomers and long-term residents. Since birds of a feather flock together, hummingbirds are not attracted to a flock of pelicans.

6. Inadequate Population Base. This can happen in a number of different ways. In many rural areas, population has dropped radically during the last three decades, leaving an over-churched community of mostly older adults. Some city churches experience an inadequate population base when a new interstate highway bisects the community and cuts off a large segment of the population in

41

such a way that they cannot attend without long and difficult travel. Other churches were originally founded to serve a particular language or ethnic group, whose size has not radically declined in that neighborhood. In some towns, residential neighborhoods are rezoned so that business or light industry moves in, creating a basic shift in population content. Slaton, Texas, a major railroad junction town, has seen its railroad facility cease operation and the community population cut in half while the number of churches remained the same. Another community already contained too many churches for the population base, but everyone said, "Our town is going to grow." So, a new church was established. But the town did not grow.

7. *Inadequate Evangelism Methods.* The line between an inadequate population base and inadequate evangelism methods is frequently fuzzy. A slothful congregation may claim that they have an inadequate population base, when their real problem is inadequate effort. Some large congregations get a false sense of security from seeing new members join fairly frequently, but do not notice that the annual number of those joining does not equal the number moving away or dying—thus, the church may suffer several years of decline before anyone notices it. Some new churches reach a "plateau" and do not grow beyond the small church category even though population is booming within blocks of them. This is often caused by overreliance on people transferring in automatically, without intentional outreach into the community. Other churches realize that the traditional week of preaching does not work for them as a method of evangelism, yet never venture forward to test other kinds of evangelism methods. In many towns, the church has relied for fifty years on community population growth or "biological evangelism" to provide all their members. But when these methods stopped working for them, no thought was given to a "Plan B." Since 50 percent of the population in American communities is unchurched, the fields are still white to harvest everywhere. While older people do not respond to church invitations as readily as persons in the twenty to forty age bracket, some do respond. Failure to see and take advantage of the remaining opportunities in each community is a form of inadequate evangelism caused by faulty leadership vision.

8. *Inadequate Openness toward Newcomers.* The fellowship glue that holds a church together is often the very thing that keeps new people from getting into it. Some churches are surrounded by invisible glass walls—invisible to themselves, but everyone else can see them clearly. They are friendly people, but mostly just toward each other. They are one big happy family—but a family that doesn't grow bigger, just older. One example of this is the farm area which has now merged into a suburban bedroom community. The conservativeness and clanishness of long-term members often means that

they overlook, ignore, or actually fear the newcomer group.

9. Inadequate Openness to Constructive Change. One of the most distressing examples of this problem is the "family chapel." The majority of the membership in some churches is interrelated because of long residency or ethnic background. So, it becomes a tight little enclave, calling a pastor who becomes a chaplain to the family group. Any change in programming becomes especially difficult because of the "clan" and their feelings for each other. Change cannot be instituted because it will offend significant relatives. This tendency to settle down to an inflexible pattern of organization, worship, and tradition is compounded if the community is presently undergoing severe economic or sociological change. Since stable features of community life may be disintegrating, the church becomes a refuge from the storm of change. Serious efforts are made to keep the church the same, for it is the last remnant of a world that was. The church becomes a place where people can turn for the security of having something remain the same—the old hymns, the old familiar building, and the traditional form of services. Unfortunately, such features also lead to a static or dying church. The Christian faith has made its greatest impact on people when it was untraditional, and stimulated them with old ideas in new ways.

10. Inadequate Opportunities for New Leadership. The overly aggressive personality can more easily dominate all decisions in a small church than in a larger church, where large boards and complex organizational structures create more checks and balances. In a few larger churches, however, some individuals—through skillful manipulation or extraordinary financial giving—are able to block the ideas of newer members. In rural areas the difficulty of protecting the church against a dominating leadership personality is compounded because rural people often have great fear of open conflict. They prefer not to deal with differences of opinion openly in committee and board meetings. So they often go quietly home and later complain vigorously to other members in private but continue to allow the dominating member to have his own way. This allows some churches to be captured and controlled by well-meaning persons who are concerned about "theological purity" and thus inhibit participation by anyone with a different viewpoint. Other churches are dominated by long-term residents with the finest of intentions, who feel that any newcomer must wait five years before speaking on an issue.

11. Inadequate Decision-Making Methods. Smaller churches often find that the traditional committees and democratic structures used in larger churches require too many people and produce more frustration than results. No other alternatives have been considered, so the organizational life quietly dies. The church board, generally a small, uncreative group dominated by older members who are dedicated to "not rocking the boat," becomes the only remnant of organizational life, while the real decisions are made by one or two key leaders in the vestibule before church or at the corner drugstore over coffee. Younger generations of leaders are thus blocked from leadership roles, and tend to drop out or switch to other churches.

12. Inadequate Planning and Goal Setting. Some church leaders feel that they are drifting into the future without a sense of direction or conscious effort to set clearcut goals. Such organizations are not thrilling participation experiences.

Group Discussion Questions

1. Can you name persons in your church who have a strong zeal for evangelism?
2. Do you think your congregation has ever given evangelism a top priority? When? In what ways?
3. Are the leaders in your church consciously opposed to growth? Illustrate.
4. Can you list any rationalization for not working at evangelism that your church members frequently share with each other?
5. Do you think your church's lay leaders feel that numbers are important? Unimportant? Illustrate.
6. In what ways do organizational matters in your church consume time that is needed for evangelism? How could you improve that situation?
7. Do you remember any lay leaders from other churches or the distant past who had strong evangelistic motivation? What personality qualities did they possess? Illustrate.
8. Are any of the twelve church growth inhibitors mentioned in this chapter present in your church? If so, how might you correct that situation?

What was, was. What is, is. What will be is up to us, and God.

4

Congregational Climate Control

A church board meeting argument in a small Texas town over-heated into a fist fight. Leaders called the sheriff in to quiet the disturbance. That drama happened several years ago and has not been repeated. But the controversial climate still lingers. Coffee-shop talk will perpetuate it for decades.

Irritation seldom gets that public in most churches. But the incident points toward another key factor which determines congregational growth patterns. *Axiom #4: Growing churches have a positive spiritual-emotional climate within their congregational life.* Paul reminds the church at Corinth that God gives the growth, not people (1 Cor. 3:6). But Paul didn't leave *all* the responsibility for growth on God's broad shoulders. He gave the Corinthian leaders "what for" about the poor environment they were giving God to work in. While God through the Holy Spirit moves people to become disciples of Jesus Christ, church leaders have responsibility for maintaining a climate conducive to such responses.

Dawson County, Texas, produces more cotton than any other county in the United States. But farmers north of Amarillo, only 180 miles away, seldom plant cotton. Why? Climate and soil conditions prohibit it. New members grow abundantly in some churches but are rare exceptions in others. Why? Not because of community population trends alone. While many rapidly growing churches are found in cities with escalating populations, other congregations are quietly dying in these same booming neighborhoods. Why then? For the same reason that the tropics drown wheat in a sixty-inch annual rainfall. Inappropriate weather conditions.

The congregation is not, of course, a sealed terrarium free from all outside influences. External climatic factors also influence a church's growth. The climate in the community is one of these: churches do not grow well in an economically depressed, population-declining town whose coal mine has shut down. The climate in the denomination: When top leadership asks members to set their greatest energies toward something other than evangelism, growth motivation goes down and most of that judicatory's congregations decline in size. The culture: National political leaders influence public moods. Jimmy Carter's "born again" ideologies encouraged more citizens toward religious thought patterns than did Lyndon Johnson's administration. The post-Vietnam War mood and the baby boom echo among young adults added to this cultural weather change. But the congregation's internal climate has far more influence on its growth pattern than all these other factors lumped together.

"Climate unlocks the doors to everything else," one pastor says. "Solve a church's climate problem, and you begin to solve all the other problems." Evangelism method manuals line the shelves of every religious bookstore. Do you want to increase spiritual maturity in people? Would you like to reach out a helping hand to the community's needy? Stacks of good ideas lie waiting. But the emotional-spiritual weather in many churches blocks pastor and people from using these excellent programs. If the right climate prevails, good methods will be found and utilized. If the wrong climate inhabits a congregation, introducing better methods succeeds like hailstones against a Sherman Tank.

Can congregational climates be changed? Absolutely. Unlike the weather, which few can alter, psychologists help people change their internal climates every day. Churches can also redecorate their emotional interiors. Once a diagnosis uncovers the present climate (which often comes as a big surprise, even to the members who live in it), changes in leadership direction can profoundly alter its future. These climate factors may have had little influence in drawing persons to the church for a visit (they were probably influenced there by friends). But after they attended, these powerful factors drew them back again, and eventually into membership.

Positive Enthusiasm

"When you bring them, they have got to come to something," says T. Garrett Benjamin, Jr., pastor of a large, fast-growing black congregation in Indianapolis. "The attitude of church growth should include enthusiasm. A lot of this enthusiasm has to be transmitted from the pulpit. The pastor has a tremendous responsibility in setting the tone for a church. I am excited about the Gospel and I think that's contagious. If you catch on fire, people will come to see you burn. Man is both cerebral and somatic. He both thinks with his mind and feels with his heart and soul. So, enthusiasm is a key in the ministry at Second Christian. People come here with all kinds of problems. Man, they want some enthusiasm. They want somebody to pick them up. And sometimes from our pulpits we have a tendency to depress people. If we can get excited about the Prince of Wales, can't we get excited about the Prince of Peace?"

Lay leaders of that congregation echo their pastor's views: "Second's explosive evangelistic movement is due to three broad thrusts: positive preaching evangelism, unstructured contagious witness by members, and structured evangelism. The enthusiastic participatory preaching is a contagious condition which has produced loving, friendly, warm, free-worshipping, unified, and 'turned-on' members."

The pastor of another fast-growing church in Ruidoso, New Mexico, says, "Our members make a contagious witness through their individual lives. They do this on an informal basis. I'm not talking about grabbing people by the lapels and saying, 'Are you saved?' But in their everyday lives they speak to people on a one-to-one basis—at work, social functions, civic clubs, wherever they are. They are excited about the meaning that is in their lives because of their church relationship and their God relationship. So they don't hesitate to share it with others."

Edward Rauff, in his helpful book *Why People Join the Church* (Pilgrim Press, 1979) describes a typical "magnet church." He says that such a congregation may scrape along in dreary fashion for years, making little impact on the community, then suddenly transform into a busy church, changing people within the fellowship as markedly as it changes those unchurched men and women it draws in. Rauff says that a magnet church has four characteristics: (1) *Quality worship,* a Sunday morning experience that makes God real; (2) a *minister* who attracts, emboldens, uplifts, and communicates God's love; (3) *People* who, by their warm welcome and their confidence in the worth of their congregation, convey its benefits to outsiders; and (4) *Programs* that build up and reach out. Enthusiasm is the silver thread that runs through all four of these pearls. Without that, they fall useless to the floor.

The flowering of positive enthusiasm is not determined by size of the church. Tiny congregations of thirty members can get it. Nor must *every* member of a church turn positive before a church becomes electro-magnetic. This enthusiasm often begins when the minister and a few leaders decide to "take it from the top" one more time with a new view of the future. Most of the big things in history were *started* by small groups or individuals—Columbus and his crew, the Declaration of Independence, Jesus and the Twelve. Churches can change from negative to positive tense when a few proper nouns start using active, positive verbs to predict the congregation's sentence endings. "Future perfect" is the grammar of faith.

Active Love and Acceptance

The climate of growing churches goes beyond the traditional "let's be friendly to visitors after church." As one new member of a growing black congregation described her first visit: "There was an aura of warmth in the place. The bond between congregation and pastor was openly loving and supportive. At the end of the service, we addressed our neighbors and firmly held their hands as we sang the benediction. No one shirked me."

New members of growing churches repeatedly relate this warm experience as a drawing point. The psychological feeling-tone is supportive, noncritical, reassuring. Visitors report a "feeling at home" quality which they say is absent from many other congregations they visit. Contrary to popular opinion, this love and acceptance that visitors so appreciate has nothing to do with the number of worshipers present. Some small churches have it; others feel cold and aloof. Some giant-sized churches have it; others are impersonal and staid.

Pastors of growing churches describe this love-acceptance element in various ways: A Kansas pastor says it takes four obvious forms: (1) They love Christ (people who don't love Christ seldom achieve much love at other places). (2) They love their minister (conflict at this point breeds conflict everywhere in the system). (3) They love each other (which means they tolerate each other's foibles). (4) They love the people outside the church (which means they express that love in clear-cut, active ways, not in passive, unseen forms).

Jesus puts these four qualities this way: "Love God and love people (Matt. 22:37-39). Then he goes on to specify exactly what type of love we are to have for each other: "This is my commandment, that you love one another as I have loved you" (John 15:12). That definition moves beyond friendliness into genuine acceptance and forgiveness.

From a New Mexico Church: "People tell us that we are a friendly, loving, and accepting church. Many people walk through the doors of our church fearful of being rejected—fearful because they have been leading public lives that they know have not been pleasing to the Lord. But one of our people has shared with them, made an impact on their life, and they are coming, seeking, searching, to see if it is real. They come expecting to be rejected and ignored, but they find themselves loved. We start with them where they are. Then we cultivate them through our programs. Quite often they begin by telling us that they have no intention of joining the church. They are only coming to see what it is like. I always encourage them to keep coming, to give it a try. If I hear that they are visiting other churches, I encourage them in that. But I always leave the doors open for them to walk back in and never feel embarrassed because they have visited around at half a dozen different congregations."

From a Louisiana church: "Remember names. Not just the adults; remember little two-year-old Johnny, who toddles in, and Melissa, the four-year-old—the one who keeps squirming during the service. Our elders and I work together on this constantly. They prod me and I prod them in this effort, teamwork. Another way we indicate our acceptance of visitors is by immediately putting them on our newsletter list—so they are advised about happenings in the congregation."

From a new congregation in Dallas: "I particularly appreciate some of the things the Catholic theologian Henry Nouwen is writing. You see in them a certain flavor about the evangelistic process:

> In our world full of strangers who are estranged from their past, from their culture, from their country, their neighbors, their friends, their family, from their deepest self and their God, we witness a painful search for a hospitable place where life can be lived without fear and where community can be found. It is possible for men and women and obligatory for Christians to offer an open and hospitable place where strangers can cast off their strangeness and become our fellow human beings."[1]

From a small town congregation in the South, pastored by a native of India: "According to our church people, an important factor in our growth is the loving and caring attitude within the congregation. The greatest thing that has happened in our church has not been the numerical growth but the growth of attitude. Someone asked me, 'How do you change the attitude of the older members?' I do not know. One thing I do know, God has given them the love for outsiders. The older people have accepted the younger, newer people and turned over to them their leadership and trusted them. In all our fellowship events, our pattern is to invite outsiders. And when outsiders attend a dinner, the church people accommodate them with a loving and friendly attitude."

From an Illinois congregation: "Jesus said to us, 'I was sick and you came to me. I was in prison and you visited me.' There is no place that we can draw the line. The pastor must do this, but he is only part of it. The members of the congregation must care for one another. We had an incident where one of our elders who happened

---

[1]Henri Nouwen, *Reaching Out: The Three Movements of the Spiritual Life.* Doubleday Books, 1975, p. 46.

to be a banker was found guilty of embezzling funds. During the time he was in jail, I visited him. The people of the congregation wrote to him. Every bank director was a member of our congregation—a built-in situation for disaster. We met together to determine what to do with this man who had been an elder. We decided that it was not time to eject him; it was time to support him. Even though some of these people lost money, they all agreed to do so. The man is still part of our congregation. He is today a deacon. And those directors and former directors receive the communion from his hands on Sunday morning.

"We have a church family in England today. He is an executive for Caterpiller, a large firm in our community. His wife had to have an operation. I called long distance. Many others in the church called long distance to assure her of our prayers and concern. Two groups in the church sent flowers. Many sent cards and letters. She wrote back to say, 'I did not believe it was possible for a congregation to minister to me halfway around the world, but you have done so.'

"Our people are involved in many community organizations. Our Masonic Lodge is quite active, and after they retired, some of our older men decided to go back and go through the chairs in the Blue Lodge. They encountered there a man named 'Good Brother Earl.' He knew every charge and every lecture in the Blue Lodge. He helped these men, and these men grew to know him and love him. Finally, they were saying to Brother Earl (who had never been a part of any congregation), 'We have a great church on that other corner down there. Why don't you come and be a part of us? We are very much alike.' And they said it so often that Brother Earl did show up. Brother Earl stayed, and at the age of seventy-five became a Christian man of God. Not because of what the pastor did, not because of programming, but because of the love, care, and concern of the people."

The world is full of desperate, lonely people who still respond to warmth and love. But many churches are so busy with their programs that they provide little of that caring-acceptance. Love is not God (even though God is love). But love is one of the principle avenues through which people find their way to God's front door.

Peace, Unity, and Tension

Growing churches thrive on two opposite elements—unity and tension. Both are necessary, yet an overdose of either is fatal. "No house divided against itself will stand" (Matthew 12:25). On the other hand, the only completely tensionless organism is a corpse.

Unity and peace cannot be manufactured in a vacuum. They grow out of the love-acceptance ecology mentioned above. A leader cannot create peace and unity among unhappy church members by urging them to be more peaceful. But if that leader helps people practice love and affirmation with each other, peace will come to the group. The peace of a growing congregation is occasionally broken, just as it is in *every* congregation. But as long as loving acts are encouraged by the leaders, peace will return.

Some of the tension found in growing churches arises from the continual changes precipitated by their growth. But another part of this tension comes from continual efforts to serve people better. An elder reported that he prayed with an eighty-five-year-old shut-in to whom he took communion on Sunday afternoon. In his prayer with her, he asked that she would have perfect peace. But after he had finished praying, she reprimanded him by saying, "Don't pray for me that I will have perfect peace. People who obtain perfect peace would have no concern whatever for their fellow man. There are some things we *do need to worry about and be concerned about.* If I started being at perfect peace with myself, I suspect I would stop being a Christian."

Do not see peace as the ultimate goal of a church. You might get it! The kind of peace that churches need is the cohesive unity found among people who work together to achieve the great purposes of God. That kind of peace always contains some tension. Those who seek peace for its own sake are falling down before idols. The next to the last thing they will achieve is lethargy. The last thing they will achieve is an ecclesiastical coffin.

Positive Self-Identity

The aggressive programs of ministry in growing churches lead them to numerous failures. Not everything they try works. But unlike declining churches, their failures do not destroy their will to try new ideas. When they fall down, they get up. Success records of growing churches are like Babe Ruth's batting record—mixed. He hit 714 home runs. But he also struck out 1,330 times—an all-time record. When you hit for the far walls, you occasionally miss the ball.

The Old Testament Jews had a strong sense of self-identity. They began their first book of scripture by identifying themselves as having originated from the first man on earth, Adam. They then tell the story of being freed from slavery by a God who expects big things from them. That strong, positive self-identity kept them plodding through the Babylonian captivities and Auschwitzes of history. Early Christians also established a positive self-identity. The first chapter of their first book of scripture, Matthew, leads off with a family tree. Their leader, Jesus, has his family roots in a royal family of the Jews, the house of David. He not only springs from Adam but from royalty. Thus, before Matthew ever begins to tell the story of what Jesus said or did, he states in unequivocal terms: "We are somebody. We Christians are a holy nation, a royal priesthood." This not only established Jesus as a good guy to the Jews to whom Matthew addressed his writing; it portrays church people as good guys to *themselves and the world.* "We are *somebody,*" says Matthew, "and don't you ever forget it."

Any church that intends to grow must operate from a similar launch pad. Without that positive self-perception, it's hard to find the courage to throw the ball of the Gospel against a world far more interested in playing Pac-Man or watching the Super Bowl than in catching the truth that makes them free.

Hope

Members of growing churches are hopeful about their future. They expect good things to happen to their church. This doesn't mean they are unrealistic about their problems. But they also know that realism without hope is less than Christian. When they think about their future, they fulfill Zechariah's "prisoners of hope" prophecy (Zechariah 9:12).

Paul advises the Roman Christians to "abound in hope" (Romans 15:13). He suggests the need for this quality at least once in each of his letters to other churches. In correspondence with his problem church at Corinth, Paul lists hope as one of their three big needs. Faith relates us to God in a positive way: love relates us to each other in a positive way; but hope relates us to our future in a positive way. Without that quality, we stop being Christians and start instead to become sour, cynical skeptics about what God can do with people who give themselves to his purposes.

Agricultural crops require the presence of three elements: sunlight, water, and soil. Churches require the light of faith (Sonlight), the water of love, and the soil of hope. No matter how much light and water they get, growth cannot occur without soil.

When individuals lose all hope, they eventually lose their life. Some instantly, through the suicide which results from acute depression. Others die more slowly, over a period of mediocre years, victims of a hope anemia that bleeds the iron out of human souls. Churches are the same. Without a vision, the parish perishes. Creativity withers. Good intentions paralyze into lethargy. The world's worst air pollution is the negative smog found in some congregations.

Among the citizens of antiquity, only the Hebrews stand out as a people who envisioned a golden age in the future as well as the past. Their *tikva* (hope) envisioned a positive future (not just in heaven, but here on earth). They anticipated this great future while at the same time passionately memorializing the great age of King David past. Today's growing churches share those qualities with their Jewish roots. While glorifying New Testament church days, they anticipate a positive future.

Churches (like nations) who become preoccupied with their past to the exclusion of their future stagnate quickly. Churches and nations that glorify only a need for change (without keeping their roots in a biblical faith or constitutional law) likewise come quickly to nothing. Growing churches and nations do not forget their heritage. But their hope keeps them anticipating great fruits ripening by God's power in the years ahead.

Joy

Personalities saturated in hopefulness usually show it. Joy rises to the surface of their face, manner, and conversation. This climatic quality hangs abundantly in the air of growing churches. People exhibit a contagious enthusiasm, a joyous excitement, and a sense of expectancy. They have something to celebrate, and feel good about inviting others to share it. "I was glad when they said to me, 'Let us go to the house of the Lord!'" said the Psalmist (Psalms 122:1). Members of growing churches feel the same.

After attending the worship service of a declining congregation, a pastor described his experience like this: "They sang 'Joyful, Joyful, We Adore Thee,' but acted like they were in a funeral. As I got better acquainted with them, that first impression was not dispelled. Their joy syllables are definitely not backed up by joy-full living."

Adults who work with youth notice that young people particularly need and desire joy experiences together. Is this why so many churches don't attract young people? Because they don't provide the joy experiences that meet the psychological and spiritual needs of this age group? Is this why charismatic and evangelical congregations draw so many youth to their activities? Whatever the answer to that frightening question, one fact is clear: congregations with large numbers of participating teenagers don't stop with providing the big three—opportunities for deepening *faith,* receiving *love* from others, and reflecting *hope*fully on the future. The events they schedule for youth are soaked with joy potential. In this kind of climate, young people go on to discover a deeper level of faith and a stronger personal relationship with God.

This need for joy is not limited to teenagers. The most common psychiatric malady of our current society is depression—characterized by a feeling of hopelessness and a joyless facial appearance. How can people who suffer from mild depression during the bulk of their days begin feeling better? Certainly not by spending time with gloomy and downcast people—sour saints. This doesn't mean that spending time with joyful Christians in a growing church eliminates depression. But the company of happy people can at least provide a recess from this inner hell.

Churches that offer this kind of time-out opportunity will find depressively-inclined visitors coming back to visit again because they received some personal help from the atmosphere they found in the place. This is one instance where "like does not attract like." Congregations whose climate is gloom and doom do not attract gloomy and doomy people; they repel them. "Let your hopes keep you joyful," Paul advises (Romans 15:13, paraphrased). Growing churches still do.

Strong, Clear Goals

Cavett Roberts said in a recent speech, "You have everything in life you *really want.*" Churches and individuals are identical at this

53

point. Setting strong goals does not by itself produce growth. But setting goals begins quickly to influence all the various factors that do produce growth. Those who aim at a target don't always hit it, but people (and organizations) seldom get what they don't shoot at.

The visitor in a New Mexico pastor's office was fascinated by the little wooden statue on the bookshelf. The tiny Norseman was holding a big spear and a giant shield, poised as if ready to enter battle. But the little man's hair was so long that it covered his face and half his body. He was well equipped for battle, but couldn't see a thing in front of him. Many church leaders—armed with the world's best weapon, good news about the kingdom of God's love—lack the vision to do anything with it.

The pastor of one static congregation asked people to fill in goal cards completing the following statement: "The goal I think our congregation should work toward accomplishing in the next twelve months is. . ." One respondent wrote "softer chairs." That near-sighted vision describes the goal orientation of many other church lieutenants. When called to carry a cross, they think of softer seats. Parishes that set those kinds of goals may not completely or immediately perish, but they rarely triumph.

Why then do churches not set strong goals and work toward them? Several reasons. An anemic belief in the Great Commission is one. If pastor and congregational leaders have no compelling vision that evangelism is the first business of the church, they set few expansion goals. Day after day Columbus entered in his ship's log, "This day we sailed west, because it was our course." Not because they saw land, but because Columbus was gripped with a compelling vision. Captive of a magnificent obsession, he had a goal that wouldn't let him quit. Churches held spiritually captive by Christ's call to win the world set solid courses in that direction. And they don't stop just because they don't make landfall the first week out.

Poor self-image is another big reason for weak goal-setting. Leaders who think negatively about their organizations are trying to drive a car with mud on the windshield. Their perceptual difficulties block them from seeing or arriving at a worthy destination. They continually overestimate the costs and underestimate the potentialities for ministry by that congregation. When pastors in growing churches are asked to rate the growth potential of their congregation, they tend to say things like "unlimited."

A strong congregational orientation toward yesterday is another cause of ineffectual goal-setting. This "rear-view mirror complex" causes leaders continually to reminisce about targets hit in the past rather than those still ahead. The glory of past achievements was so great that nobody in the present can imagine us ever doing that well again.

If a long-established congregation has plateaued in size, the setting and achieving of several short-range but significant goals is usually the best first step toward changing this congregational cli-

54

mate pattern. Only by experiential action can leaders with a strong fixation on the past begin shifting into a future orientation.

The Spirit Connection

Perhaps *this* climate factor should have topped the list. Some feel that its absence *causes* all the other climate problems listed above. The pastor of a growing black church says, "Power comes, not from program or from personality, but from the Holy Spirit. 'But ye shall receive power, after that the Holy Spirit is come upon you' (Acts 1:8, King James Version). Some of us are afraid today to talk about the Holy Spirit. But it is the thing that gives power, the thing that gives life, the thing that gives health. It is the presence of God in our midst. It's a yearning and a yielding unto God. That takes a praying church. We need to bow down and to pray and ask the Lord to anoint us. Power comes from the Holy Spirit *after* the Holy Spirit is come upon you. What I'm talking about is so old that it is ridiculous. It's so simple that I'm embarrassed. I don't have any fancy ideas. It's the old agenda.

"Let's be imbued and energized by the Holy Ghost. Let's get off our assets and get on with the Master's mission. Your church is like my church—not much different. We basically believe in the same things. But faith doesn't just believe. It acts. I'm not satisfied in my ministry until I can preach every Sunday morning to 5,000 people and see 3,000 come down the aisle. Crazy, huh? Bite off more than you can chew and chew it. Do more than you can do and do it. Hitch your wagon to a star. Take a seat and there you are."

Another pastor says, "One important cause of our growth is prayer. That's a power which we unfortunately may not say enough about. Maybe it's assumed and goes without saying. But if it goes without saying, it surely ought not to go without doing."

This most significant climate factor is thus the most elusive to describe and the most impossible to control. "The wind blows where it wills, and you hear the sound of it, but you do not know whence it comes or whither it goes; so it is with everyone who is born of the Spirit" (John 3:8). And so it is with churches born of the Spirit and borne on the Spirit to new levels of growth. Jesus did tell us how that Spirit power becomes available to a church: ". . .Ask, and it will be given you; seek, and you will find; knock, and it will be opened to you. For everyone who asks receives, and he who seeks finds, and to him who knocks it will be opened. What father among you, if his son asks for a fish will instead of a fish give him a serpent; or if he asks for an egg, will give him a scorpion? If you then, who are evil, know how to give good gifts to your children, *how much more will the heavenly Father give the Holy Spirit to those who ask him!"* (Luke 11:9-13, italics added).

Group Discussion Questions

1. Can you remember instances in which our congregational "climate" was described to you by other members of our church? Illustrate.
2. Did a casual visitor or new attender ever comment to you on the climate they experienced in our church? Illustrate.
3. How would you personally describe the climate in our congregation? Can you think of reasons why your personal feeling may be different from those illustrated in questions one and two?
4. Do our church members show real concern and love for one another? In what ways do you think we could improve that aspect of our climate?
5. The pastor of one growing church said that many people who come to a worship service for the first time fear being rejected. Do you think this describes the emotional feelings of most church visitors? Explain.
6. Most growing churches have a personality of acceptance regarding new attenders. Do you think such a label could be applied to our congregation? What are some ways we could improve our personality at this point?
7. Most growing congregations have a climate of warmth and caring. Would you describe our church in that way? State the reasons for your answers.
8. Is there or is there not a climate of joy in our congregation? Take a secret ballot vote and count the answers. Make a list of ways in which we might improve that climate.
9. Can you remember any individual in your life who seemed to love you with complete abandonment? Did that person have a positive influence on your life? What does that experience tell us about the type of climate in which evangelism is likely to happen?
10. List three goals you think our church should try to achieve during the next twelve months.

The best way to get something done is to begin.

5

Put Landing Gears Under Your Dreams

An oil company engineer who was serving as church board chairman sat down in his pastor's office. "I've been thinking," he said. "I believe our people really do want evangelism to happen in our church. But I don't think they know how to go about it." History took a new direction on the hinge of that conversation. The pastor and leaders recognized that they must start doing something *specific* about growth. They went looking for someone who could tell them what to do. He did, and they did. The congregation doubled in size the following year.

That experience illustrates another obvious contrast between churches that grow and those that don't. *Axiom #5: Growing churches use some kind of plan or set of methods to reach out beyond the walls.* Static congregations, on the other hand, expect their growth manna to fall from heaven. Their posture is prone. They lounge in the green grass of a summer day, watching the fleecy clouds roll over, waiting for God to do something wonderful with their church. Research in one mainline denomination turned up three major factors that cause growth in their congregations: (1) the pastor wants the church to grow; (2) the people want the church to grow; and (3) they have some kind of plan to make that happen. Many congregations have the first two but leave out the third. In evangelism, as in most things, God usually moves with those who act rather than those who watch and wait for something to happen.

Historian Arnold Toynbee was right when he said that apathy can only be overcome by enthusiasm. And the arousal of enthusiasm requires two factors: first, an ideal which takes the imagination by storm; and second, a definite intelligible plan for carrying that ideal into practice. Most congregations have high ideals but no concrete plans for action. Their dreams have no landing gears. They soar, but never land.

Jesus stopped one day by a temple pool where people came for healing. He started talking with a man who had laid there thirty years without success. This patient patient told Jesus that he could not get healed because no one would lift him into the water. But Jesus shattered his defense with a penetrating question: "Do you want to be healed?" (John 5:6). Any declining church (or denomination) which says it wants to fulfill its Jesus-assigned mission of going into all the world and making disciples must face the same question: "Do you really *want* to be healed of your non-growth?" How often crippled bodies of Christ lie around their population pool, helplessly waiting for someone to come and shove them into a growth pattern.

In dealing with another sick man, Jesus said, "Rise, take up your pallet, and walk" (John 5:8). Here, as always, Jesus inextricably links faith and action together. Only by standing and walking can the lame man learn that he is healed. Church growth is definitely a product of God's activity. Congregations don't heal themselves. But God's activity seldom becomes operational until God's people become operational.

Churches and business enterprises are in most respects as dissimilar as cucumbers and pears. Yet, both are trying to influence the thinking and behavior of human beings in new directions. Because of this common objective, church leaders may occasionally find it helpful to view their church through the lens of a business consultant's remarks. "The recurring crisis in all service-oriented firms stems chiefly from failure to generate a constant flow of new business," says Robert Agee, head of the New York based New Business system. "The first thing is to keep everything simple, Avoid complications that take your eye off the ball." Agee's six basics for business growth apply equally well to church growth. (1) Each firm should have a master plan aimed at getting *specific* new business, not just maintaining a specified volume. The plan must name target client prospects. (2) The plan must be based on "excellent" time management. Do first the things that have the most impact. (3) The firm must have a commitment to visibility. If you don't toot your own horn, it won't get tooted. (4) Maintain performance to present clients. You won't get new business if you don't, and you might lose existing clients. (5) Have a company philosophy and personality that presents a good image. Think about these things and exploit your strong points. (6) The action step. Maintain constant contacts with prospective clients. Develop precise techniques for wooing them and closing the contract."[1]

By coincidence, two grown-up twins ended up residing in the same town. One was a minister, the other a doctor. People were always getting the twins confused. One day a man stopped the doctor on the street and said, "Sir, I want to compliment you on the inspiring sermon you preached last Sunday."

"I'm afraid you have us mixed up," the doctor replied. "I'm not the brother who preaches; I'm the one who practices."

Growing congregations both preach and practice evangelism. They talk about going into all the world. And they go. They teach about fishing for men. And they fish. While a great deal of spontaneous evangelism always occurs in a growing church, it also has organized, systematic, concrete plans for reaching out beyond the holy moat.

These plans take countless forms. The evangelism commission chair in one fast-growing congregation says, "Evangelism at our church is both structured and unstructured. It flows from the dynamic Christ-centered, people-oriented pulpit and through the members to visitors and the unchurched. A core of lay, trained evangelism ambassador volunteers represent an extension of the pastor's arms. After a letter has been sent to registered visitors, these ambassadors provide the essential follow-up contact. Names provided by members are also followed up by these evangelism ambassadors. This organized approach helps our members get free from their hang-ups and gain more confidence in witnessing for Christ, thus enabling them to become more effective, spontaneous evangelizers."

The pastor of a tiny congregation in a small Texas town organized and motivated his people (most of whom were past sixty-five) to make repetitive calls on every unchurched home in the community. The church tripled in size the first year. They continued this system each spring by a well organized and highly publicized Easter program. Both plans reached out repeatedly to invite numerous persons who had not previously attended church.

The pastor of a fast-growing congregation in Oklahoma City (who does his ministry from a wheelchair) says, "We stress the need to contact visiting people that very week. We have done that a lot of different ways. We have assigned church school classes to calling in particular weeks of the month. We have assigned groups of people

---

[1]From an article by Leroy Pope, *Lubbock Avalanche-Journal*, December 6, 1978, page 10-B.

to particular Sundays. In recent years, we have hired a retired layman who served on the staff of the regional office for our denomination in Oklahoma. As our church grew and my time became less available, he did all the first-week calling. That has been an essential part of our ministry and growth. The salary we pay him is the best money we ever spent.

"The minister cannot back out of evangelistic calling. But I think lay people should visit visitors the first week. If they continue to worship with our congregation, then I call and make an appointment . . . But the first home contact is always someone other than myself."

Using one of these methods will not guarantee instant church growth. A concrete plan is only *one* of nineteen factors in growing churches. As the pastor of a fast-growing church in El Paso, Texas, says, "Evangelism ideas are worthless when they remain on paper. But where these ideas are studied and carefully followed, they are worth everything we can put into them and more. The Gospel is *not* God's power unto salvation (Romans 1:16) when it is not preached; when it is not believed; when it is not obeyed. But where it is preached, believed, and obeyed, it *is* God's power."

Why don't church growth consultants crate up these methods for shipment all over the country? While certain principles, like personal contact, repetition of contacts, and large volume of contacts, apply everywhere, the specifics for these universal principles must be worked out by trial and error in each community. If there is any *one* specific universal formula, it might read: Find a method. Try the method. Analyze the method. Revise the method, or eliminate it and try another method.

Why Johnny Churchperson Can't Learn Methods

In spite of all the data which points toward the need to find and use concrete methods, many churches don't. Why? Perceptual blocks! The mental equipment of members filters out the grand ideas that work in colleague congregations. While the following list of these cerebral blocks is not exhaustive, it illustrates the problem.

The Numbers Game Block. Two decades ago, mainline Protestants started criticizing the "numbers game." Embarrassed at their own success in the religious, cultural wave following World War II, they started saying, "Numbers don't count. It's *quality* that really adds up." Careful scrutiny will show, however, that church leaders are very selective in their condescending application of this cliché. When working with dollar bills, they continue to show interest in quantity as well as quality. Stewardship campaigns remain important. Mission giving is another place where the numbers game seems to cause little embarrassment. Percentages are meticulously reported on each church. Conference giving records get close tabulation. Awards are given. Judicatories print recognitions in their monthly papers.

But these same leaders may turn to the subject of evangelism and say, "Let's not play the numbers game!" What does that defense really mean? A failure of apostolic nerve. Churches who don't take numbers seriously aren't taking the Great Commission seriously. In church work, the numbers game is the only game in town. So you had better learn how to win it. Reaching people with the Gospel means reaching *numbers* of people. The real question is never, Will we play the numbers game? The real issue is, Will our numbers be smaller or larger?

The Busy Member Block. A church in Corpus Christi, Texas, did a self-study in which they identified their lack of evangelism efforts as stemming from the following sources: members are too busy, young marrieds especially too busy; couples go to lakes and beaches on weekends; active members already over-involved (with two or three nights each week committed to church work); overemployed; need rest. Churches far away from the balmy Gulf raise similar objections to evangelism tasks. Many Christians are just too busy doing church work to do the work of the Church. Others feel they are too busy doing their own personal vocational work (or rest). One wonders what response the sharp-tongued apostle Paul might have made had he received a Xerox of such a self-study from his church at Corinth.

Architectural Evangelism Block. "Aren't the other people in this town adults, just like the rest of us? They do know where the church is, don't they?" Another variation of architectural evangelism goes like this: "If we build a beautiful new sanctuary, people will be attracted to our church." But church buildings do not build churches. Church people build churches. Can you imagine Paul saying to Barnabas, as they are sitting in the Holiday Inn coffee shop in Antioch, "Barnabas, I've got a great plan. We're going to hire the best architect money can buy. We're going to build the most beautiful church here in Antioch that you have ever seen. From all over Asia Minor, people will come here to learn how to build great churches in their communities."

Paul's method for building churches wasn't carpentry. He sailed and walked through the Roman world, planting churches everywhere. After about 300 years, these congregations began to house themselves in special buildings. But the church's most rapid expansion came *prior* to the buildings. These structureless Christians literally took the world by 325 A.D. (the known world), when Emperor Constantine decreed Christianity the official Roman Empire religion. This peaceful conquest didn't succeed through an architectural witness. A small, determined group exploded a spiritual revolution that drew in the masses—to a church without walls.

The Biological Evangelism Block. In cultures where the birth rate runs four or five per family, churches grow quickly, especially if people rarely move to other communities. Prior to World War II, this system built mammoth churches across the United States. With children and grandchildren of large family units living out their lives in the same town, churches expanded rapidly. The Catholic Church understands this biological system well. Without the invention of birth control pills, they might have taken the world by geometric progression within a few hundred years. In fact, since 1947, Catholics have gained 3 percent of the U.S. church population pie through this method alone. But times have changed for both Catholics and Protestants. Americans are now highly mobile. Nearly 20 percent change their residence each year. Most of a church's children grow up to become adult leaders in some other congregation. And since 1960, the birth rate has dropped to almost two per family.

Now, twenty years after it stopped working, most denominations have noticed that their Evangelism Plan A—based on sexual promulgation, sectarianism, and low mobility—is no longer operable. So they are looking for a Plan B. Hence, the increased interest in evangelism methods found in most mainline churches across the continent.

The Ecumenical Block. "There's nothing wrong with joining another denomination," many mainline members say. "We're all Christians." And they act on that belief. Fifty percent of church members who move to a new community join a different denomination than they previously attended. While that is a positive advance in theological thinking, it is a built-in, self-destruct mechanism for membership loyalty. Denominations with the most open ecumenical stances lose more of their young people to other denominations after they grow up. The Christian Church (Disciples of Christ) and the United Church of Christ furnish the best examples of this phenomenon.

The Christian Education Block. The essential proclamation of the early church was called *kerygma*—a preaching synopsis of the core message. Faced with the task of winning the whole world, Christians had to communicate with people who knew nothing about them or their Christ. "How can we explain the whole history of redemption in a very brief way?" they must have asked themselves. "We can't spend years telling people the entire history of the Old Testament and giving them a course in the life of Christ." So, in their initial evangelistic preaching, the Apostles tried to reduce the basic message to its central nucleus—so that people could have something to which they could make an initial response. All the recorded New Testament sermons follow this kerygmatic pattern. They attempted to proclaim the basic fundamentals of Christianity.

After new converts made their initial response to the central thrust of the Gospel, they were placed in classes for continued instruction. The teaching content of these classes was called the *"didache"*—the foundation catechismal instruction for new converts.

But today, how many modern Christians could articulate the core message of their faith—the twentieth-century *kerygma?* Why not? Because of a subtle reversal of the way the church approaches new persons. Now, we tend first to expose new people to a massive Christian education program in a very broad way—so broad, in fact, that they don't quite find the main point of it. But rarely does anybody get around to articulating for them the core concepts of that to which they are being asked to respond.

Mainline churches have in this manner blurred their *didache* and *kerygma* together. They expect that Christian education will in some vague way do their evangelism for them. But that lack of sharp focus about how one becomes a Christian (what beliefs are essential) has blunted their evangelistic ability. They ask people to espouse a faith that has never been concisely explained to them. They ask them to join an organization whose purposes have not been clearly defined.

The Hyperactivity Block. The wastebasket is one of the most useful pieces of office equipment. As an ancient Chinese sage, Lin Yutang, said, "Besides the noble art of getting things done, there is the noble art of leaving things undone. The wisdom of life consists in the elimination of nonessentials." Burdened with the twin diseases of American activism and ecclesiastical peer/authority pressure, church leaders have trouble learning this. They decide what to do more easily than they decide what not to do. And when they decide to do too many nonessential things, they lose the option for deciding to do evangelism. Like the glutton who took three servings of rice on the first course, no space remains for the Cherries Jubilee.

The Apathy Block. You can stand absolutely still on roller skates, while moving toward a brick wall at high speed. Not deciding to take action lets action decide to take you. Doing something in evangelism—almost anything—is better than doing nothing. In World War I, someone asked a French general, "Which side will win?" He replied, "The side that advances." Successful churches rarely sit and wait for things to get better. They act.

The Revival Meeting Block. An old legend tells about a pipe on which Moses played when he was a shepherd. The pipe was handed down for several generations. It became so venerated that someone decided to goldplate it. That enhanced its commercial value, but its ability to produce music vanished; it could no longer be played. The spring revival meeting is a Moses flute for many churches—especially in the South. Long enshrined as an annual ritual, only the oldest members can remember when anyone had a conversion experience at the event. In evangelism, as in stewardship, you can tell when a method works. It produces numerical results. If a particular method doesn't work, smart people scratch their heads and wonder why. Then they try something different.

The Materialism Block. After Christian people win the struggle for such basic needs as an education unit and new sanctuary, their energy level and interest drops. Having reached some great goals, they become relaxed victims of their own achievements. But this same materialistic success paradoxically breeds a virus of spiritual discontent in rank-and-file church members. People seldom remain happy for long after they get what they want. Leaders of growing churches learn how to redirect this materialistic drive for bricks and mortar into a zeal for ideals and persons.

The Fear Block. Some pastors fear any sort of aggressive evangelism program. They subconsciously feel threatened by the possibility of losing political control of the congregation. Strong evangelism efforts necessarily involve large groups of laypersons. What will happen if church members start taking charge of these endeavors? Who knows, they might decide to take over other things in the church.

But the other side of this coin involves the danger of losing control when irritation about the congregation's obvious decline turns to scapegoating the pastor. People who see their church dying always find someone to blame. The direct object of that sentencing is seldom themselves.

The Blindness Block. A group of foreign manufacturers was touring an American plant. They watched in awe as a huge machine took a piece of sheet steel and in one operation stamped, punched, and shaped it into a finished product. After gazing at it for several minutes, a bitter argument broke out in the group. In the midst of much arm-waving and finger-shaking, the guide asked the interpreter what all the shouting was about. "Some of them," replied the interpreter, "insist that it can't be done." Many church leaders take the same attitude to evangelistic growth. Such a possibility is far removed from their perceptual horizons. The success of nearby growing churches cannot penetrate their blindness.

The Logical Discussion Block. "If it were possible to lose weight by reading diets," quipped a woman in Borger, Texas, "I would have achieved my ideal weight by now. I just love to hear about new diets. If it were possible to tighten and tone sagging muscles by reading about exercising, I'd be trim and fit. I clip all the articles on exercise for future reference. But stick to a diet? I'd rather talk about it! Exercise daily? I haven't the time."

How quickly a high-moment inspiration can dim to one-watt output when perspiration breaks out on it. Evangelism is easy to talk about—sometimes even mentally stimulating. How equally easy to allow talking about evangelism to substitute for doing it. (And the more educated and rationally oriented a denomination becomes, the more it tends to substitute thinking and discussion for action.) That's why most great leaders are action types who influence people to *act differently* and then arm them with rational reasons for doing so.

The Theological Discussion Block. Numerous fantastic theological observations can be made about why and how to do evangelism. In some denominations, that sort of discussion becomes a substitute for the correct answer regarding what actually works. Paul gets good marks as a theologian, but he didn't stay home in Antioch discussing the relative ideological merits of how to deliver the Word to the Gentiles. He set sail for Asia Minor and tried by every means to win some. When he found methods that worked, he used them

64

again. When he used a wrong methodological answer (as in his "unknown God' sermon at Athens), he discarded it. Paul didn't discuss evangelism. He did it.

The Questionnaire and Survey Block. Not knowing exactly what evangelism methods to use—or lacking the courage to use the ones they do know—some church leaders busy themselves with surveys, questionnaires, and psychological instruments. They expend much energy and money in data collection regarding congregation and community. But after assemblage, these materials often lie dormant on office shelves. The "scientific" gathering of facts substitutes for evangelistic activity—often leaving leaders with the delusion that they actually did something. Surveys and questionnaires are excellent aids—unless they become anesthetics. Analysis and self-evaluation can make church people feel better. But they can as easily camouflage the fact that nothing has been done.

The Complex System Block. Soren Kierkegaard, the Danish philosopher of another century, used to tell the story of a man who wanted to jump a ditch. He backed up and backed up in order to get a long run at the ditch. But he backed up so far that when he finally got to the ditch he was too tired to jump. Some pastors are "perpetual preparation machines." They always have a plan that they predict will produce great moments in evangelism. They invest much energy in organizational machinery. Immense time is consumed in evangelism committee meetings. But when all is said and done, what was said is all that was done. The church's available energy was consumed in backing up to make a run at the ditch.

The Inflexible Method Block. Some pastors become fixated on a particular method, perhaps because they have always done it that way. Nobody told them that evangelism methods may need to vary with each culture, community, and church. So, these otherwise rational leaders go on using a particular nonworkable evangelism formula for years—without asking whether this works in this church.

The Sincerity Block. A traveler sat beside a man from India on a flight from Fiji to Calcutta. The man was completely baffled by the breakfast which the smiling stewardess brought him. He began by pouring his coffee into the cornflakes and eating them. Then he mixed the milk and the sugar and drank it. Next, he licked the butter from the small paper square. For a chaser, he ate the marmalade. Sincerity is important. And food quality is certainly important, just as it is in church life. But no amount of sincerity and quality substitutes for the knowledge needed to put it together in palatable form. Christians don't need a seminary degree to do evangelism well. But they need to know some basic principles and methods.

Obsessive-Compulsive Management Block. A psychiatrist once observed that many members of a particular mainline denomination are obsessive-compulsives—that is, they are people determined to do things in a repetitive manner, regardless of the results. While no data is available to prove that hypothesis, many Christian leaders are clearly frozen into decades-old repetitive patterns of evangelism methods.

John the Baptist condemned the Sadducees and Pharisees who came to him for baptism. He said that no amount of ritual washing would make up for the need to change their ways. He also warned them that the ax was at the root of the tree. If their tree did not bear fruit, he said, it would be destroyed (Matthew 3:10). His admonitions apply to modern churches. They either learn how to bear fruit in reaching others for Christ, or they lose their tree.

The Form Without Function Block. Driving to work one morning, a passing car piqued a pastor's imagination. It carried a large sign on the side and a tiny light on top. The sign said, "Yellow Cab." The car, however, was bright blue. Six blocks later he saw another car with the same sign. This vehicle was white. How strange for a company to advertise one thing by its name and another by its equipment. Not much stranger, however, than churches which proclaim certain words on their lawn signs but show little evidence of behavior like that of their idealized leader, Jesus. He spoke of fields white to harvest, searching for lost coins, sheep strayed into bramble bushes. He spent his life reaching out to lepers by the roadside, sexually errant women, self-righteous teachers, and people of questionable conduct among the scattered villages and solitary seashores across his native land.

One New Testament book, James, devotes most of its paragraphs to condemnation of players who talk big games but never show up on the field. "Be doers of the word, and not hearers only, deceiving yourselves" (James 1:22). Putting a sign on the lawn doesn't equal doing evangelism any more than putting a sign on a cab makes it that color.

The Hard Work Block. "Doc," said the man who had come in for a checkup. "If there is anything wrong with me, don't give me a long scientific name. Say it so I can understand it."

"Very well," the doctor agreed, "you're lazy."

"Thanks, Doc. Now give me the scientific name so I can tell my boss."

Some churches seek scientific names for their nongrowth. But the pastor of one fast-growing church said, "A lot of our poor evangelism comes down to just plain laziness. I am constantly amazed at the people in whose homes I call who say to me, 'You are the first pastor who has ever been to see us.' We apparently have lots of boats rowed by sailors who never put their oars in the water." Kim Linehan set a world record for the women's 1,500 meter freestyle. A dedicated worker, she practiced by swimming seven to twelve miles each day. Someone asked her what the hardest part of her regimen was. "Getting into the water," she replied.

The Jealousy Block. The more successful a pastor becomes in evangelism, the more other pastors begin to resent him/her. Their overwhelming sense of inferiority breeds resentment against the superior model. And the greater their jealousy, the harder they find it to learn the successful methods.

The Mission Giving Block. During the past two decades, many denominations have urged their churches toward increased money for mission/benevolent works. Many medium-sized and larger congregations have responded by achievements of 25 to 40 percent of their income sent to denominational coffers. Twenty-year membership charts on many of these churches show terrible declines. Why? Two reasons: first, their pride in mission giving allows them to relax in other matters, like evangelism. Having taken the tranquilizer that said, "God will bless unselfish churches with growth," they relaxed into the tranquillity of that false assumption. Second, rather than spending part of their increased money on additional staff to serve additional members, they were consistently understaffed. Decline followed as a natural result of this erroneous thinking/behavior.

The Unwillingness to Learn from Other Denominations Block. Jesus says that a bad tree cannot bear good fruit (Matthew 7:18). Thorn bushes don't grow figs. As usual, Jesus tells us that the heart is the heart of religious matters. A thorn bush is in its heart a thorn bush. A fig tree is in its heart a fig tree. Each inevitably produces a harvest of that heart. Agricultural scientists, realizing Jesus' basic truth, began changing the cornstalk by changing the genetic heart of the corn seed. They succeeded. Taking two different varieties of cornstalk, they overruled mother nature by performing a genetic marriage. Through this agricultural intercourse, agronomists produced a completely new variety of corn, with a new heart. When they planted this offspring the following year, its per acre productivity often more than doubled that of either parent.

Church history has recorded similar events for twenty centuries. John Wesley rode a boat to America as an Anglican missionary. On the way, he was profoundly influenced by observing the religious pietism of the Moravians who traveled on the same ship. When that cross-pollenization occurred, nothing happened immediately. But after seeing such slight results from using his own personal theology among American Indians, Wesley returned to England and started a whole new variety of cornstalk—the Methodist Church.

Similar hybrids are seen in all of history's renewal movements. Most denominations don't do better just by trying harder. They more often blossom and flourish with productivity when cross-pollenated with other denominations than when they build high walls around their theology and plant the same ideas year after year. Wise people learn from the experience of others.

Find a Different Organizational Pattern

Another big block to evangelistic growth in many congregations is the traditional evangelism committee. Most churches that decide to grow will need to organize their evangelism efforts differently than in the past. This necessity becomes obvious by examining the way churches usually structure their evangelism planning. At the beginning of the year, they appoint a new evangelism chairperson. He or she takes office with high enthusiasm and hopefulness. Next, the chairperson collects committee members to help make decisions and expedite the work. Three or four persons show up at the first meeting and consume a large chunk of time trying to figure out why some committee members didn't attend. Discussion develops about how we can get them to come next time. In the minutes remaining, everyone shares perceptions about why evangelism is *not* happening in our church. Following this discussion, the group usually concludes with: "We can't possibly solve the evangelism problem in this church. We're just a committee. Evangelism is something the whole church must do." Having arrived at this valid observation, the committee goes home feeling much better. Rational people find great solace in identifying the *source* of a problem: it makes them feel as though they have actually done something!

As the year proceeds, the committee meets again. This time, they decide to give the church board a lecture on the need to be more friendly with visitors after church. This is not a bad idea, unless it becomes the congregation's only plan for evangelism. They are not organized to *do* evangelism; they are organized to discuss it.

This situation is a bit like the couple who live on a large country acreage with a big lawn. He travels a lot in his business, so getting the mowing done is often troublesome. One summer they bought a riding lawnmower to help resolve this matter. The first time he was gone on an extended trip, she thought, I'll surprise him by mowing the lawn. The machine started easily. She wheeled it out of the garage onto the grass. How good she felt about herself, until she looked over her shoulder. The mower wasn't cutting grass. Stopping the machine, she fiddled with the levers, then started again. It still wasn't cutting grass. After ten more minutes of frustrated failure, she gave up and drove it back to the garage. When her husband arrived home later in the week, she said, "I tried to mow the yard for you, but I couldn't get that silly lawnmower to cut grass." His face fell. "Oh, I took the blade off that thing to sharpen it the other day," he said. "I guess I forgot to put it back."

Evangelism committees in most congregations run. They operate. But they seldom cut grass: form without function. Why? The motor is not attached to a blade. The committee is not hooked up to the power. The congregation definitely does have the responsibility and strength to do this task. The committee is accurate in that assessment. But where is the concrete method for connecting that power to the intended result? Conclusion: Most evangelism committees do not work very well!

This does not, of course, mean that every single person in the church must become an enthusiastic evangelist. People are different from each other. They have different gifts and interests. No point in trying to teach a bird dog to sing. It wastes your time and annoys the dog. But if evangelism happens in a church, the power of numerous people must be harnessed to the cutting edge of evangelism methodology.

A church cannot organize for evangelism simply by urging every member to be a personal witness—*whenever*. Such urgings are never the total answer. Protestants rate higher than Catholics on their willingness to make personal evangelism contacts, and evangelical Protestants will do this more than ecumenical/social action Protestants. But personal witness isn't the only answer either. Congregations are different and approaches must be different. Evangelism requires planning and preparation.

Find People Who Are Evangelism Possibilities

Jesse Bader, for more than two decades Director of Evangelism for the National Council of Churches, was fond of saying, "Evangelism begins where the old recipe for rabbit stew begins. Right there on the card it says, 'Number One: Catch a rabbit!'" More than eighty million American people are unchurched. Perhaps more than one-hundred million, depending on whose statistics you quote. This translates into almost half the population in every city and town. Approximately every other person you meet on the street is an evangelism possibility. In spite of this obvious truth, dedicated church attenders have difficulty thinking of anyone they know who does not attend church. Growing churches figure out how to transcend that mental block. They develop ways to isolate the names, addresses, and phone numbers of the unchurched masses.

Part of the difficulty in telescoping down to the finding of evangelism possibilities may arise from biblical misinterpretations. Sincere Christians look at the early chapters of *Acts* and see Peter preaching at Pentecost. (He apparently had a fairly decent sermon that day. Three thousand people came down the aisle when he finished.) It's easy to read that and conclude, "Evangelism comes from preaching." There is a sense in which that's true. But we tend to extract more meaning out of that text than it actually contains.

In another familiar scripture, we read, "And how are they to believe in him of whom they have never heard? And how are they to hear without a preacher?" (Romans 10:14). This makes excellent material for the installation service of a new pastor. Great sermon mileage in those words. But we tend to take more ore out of this mine than it contains. True, the preached word has power to transform human life in ways that nothing else can. But if the spoken word is going to accomplish something in the human mind, you must get the preacher within earshot proximity of the preachee. If unchurched people are on the other side of town as the sermon is delivered, few results accrue from the message.

Congregations that grow develop concrete methods for finding unchurched persons and attracting them toward the church. Some experts label these methods "preevangelism" rather than evangelism. But that makes them no less essential. As Charles Allen, the distinguished Methodist pastor, has said about the Bible, "Not one time in this book does Jesus command people to attend church. Do you remember one instance? I don't. But he had a lot to say about people going out into the highways and hedges and finding people."

Specific Programs to Attract the Unchurched

Churches which grow execute definite programs whose unabashed purpose is to draw in the unchurched. They, more than their declining neighbors, tend to recognize the function and significance of various types of groups within the church. The small primary group is always *people*-centered. These building block groups are acute need-meeting for their participants. Examples of such groups include the charter members of a small, new church and the tight-knit executive committee of a large congregation. The next concentric circle away from the middle of the church fellowship pool is the *activity*-centered group. Examples include the choir and the usher core. At the greatest distance from the center, we find *event*-centered groups. The annual bazaar committee and the spring fish fry workers fall into this category.

As congregations grow larger and contain more older people, the number of primary people-centered groups diminishes as a percentage of the whole. And it is precisely this type of group that has the greatest evangelistic pulling power. That's why a congregation that increases beyond thirty-five in Sunday morning attendance and sixty-five in total membership must stop relying on primary group pulling power alone. It cannot grow without organized procedures to attract and incorporate new members.

An Aggressive Sales Force

Measured by objective standards, communism is a bad system. Its industrial productivity is low, and how many communist countries can feed their own people? Yet, this has been one of the fastest growing forms of government in the world. Why? Because its proponents fervently believe in their system. They enthusiastically sell their idea. The merits of merchandise do not always control its salability. Enthusiastic, dedicated, committed sales people can often sell inferior products.

Several American religious groups with weird, irrational-sounding theologies have experienced significant growth patterns during the past twenty years. Despite adverse publicity, Rev. Sun Myung Moon's Unification Church continues to swell with new recruits. A Gallup Youth Survey shows that as many as 500,000 teens may be involved in the Unification Church, or two percent of the total United States teenage population.[2]

A traveler eating lunch in Cloudcroft, New Mexico, noticed on the bottom of his lunch ticket the words, "It has been a pleasure." What could be more impersonal than that sort of warmth? Nothing, except a church newsletter inviting you to worship, or a piece of stationery urging you to attend our warm, friendly church. Such persuasion reaches the power levels of a mass mail piece addressed to "occupant."

The Word Requires Words

The portable marquee in front of a sandwich shop said, "A good example is a lesson anyone can read." That sign speaks truth, but only some. Studies show that very few people are influenced toward Christ by the shining light of Christian example in church-person lamps. A solid 95 percent of new disciples were influenced not by exemplary living but by some form of verbal communication. Christianity must, of course, be *more* than verbal. Word pushers should back their church invitations with the integrity of a life lived for God. But a Christianity that totally depends for its spreading on the good example of a lived life will reach very few, very slowly. Members of growing churches find a way to make the Word verbal. They invite people to church, share their faith, say a good word for God, or in some way touch the ears of unchurched friends.

People who use words to help the Holy Spirit are not really producing new Christians. Only God can do that. But people can help. That is what Jesus meant when he said, ". . .you shall be my witnesses. . ." (Acts 1:8). He was suggesting that we get on with the business of helping God get on with his business. That requires more than words. But it does not require less than words.

[2]December 1981 *Emerging Trends,* Vol. 3, No. 10, published by the Princeton Religion Research Center, P.O. Box 310, 53 Bank Street, Princeton, New Jersey 08540.

Group Discussion Questions

1. Review the list of "Why Johnny Churchperson Can't Learn Methods." Which of these do you think applies to our church?
2. In what ways has the traditional evangelism committee system been effective in our church in recent years? Ineffective?
3. Does our church have any effective method for identifying names of that approximately 50 percent of our community that is unchurched?
4. What, in your opinion, have been the best methods for attracting new members to our congregation in the past few years?
5. Does our congregation depend mostly on individual Christians working by themselves to do evangelism? What percentage of the congregation do you estimate actually tries to do evangelism in this way?
6. One pastor says that his denomination tends to take very narrow stands on certain public issues, then implies, "If you don't agree with us, you must not be a Christian." He feels that this adversely affects evangelism efforts. Do you agree or disagree? Are there any ways in which you think this is true of our denomination? Of our local church?

In the aerodynamics of institutions, small changes in wing design can produce radical redirection.

6

Introversion Is a People Repellent

One of the best fishing guides on Florida's west coast entertains his clients with endless, tall fish tales. After someone came back from a first-time trip with Charlie, a friend said, "He's a real pro, isn't he?"

"Yes," said the tourist. "He is so good that I was home for an hour before I realized that we didn't catch any fish."

Many mainline congregations know that feeling. Programmatic activities like Sunday school, once designed for extroverted mission to the unchurched, now do more story-telling than fishing. Leaders place great emphasis on a "quality educational experience" but almost no emphasis on the quality of effort put forth to draw in new people. Part of this introverted stance comes from "overlearning." Christian education specialists during the past two decades increasingly used public school methods as an idealized role model. They blended the finest in educational theory with the best in Christian ideology. Teachers were urged to get on board with plans that would

73

produce "quality learning." While this new medication has much to commend it, concentrating on education technology caused many Sunday school teachers to develop a "shop-keeping mentality." Being a good teacher began to mean opening the classroom door at a certain time on Sunday, closing it an hour later, and using good didactic techniques in the time between. Increasingly, experts told teachers and pastors that quality student experiences attract more learners. "If attendance is down, look for the cause in faulty curriculum and poor teacher training," they said.

Ironically, the rise of the Christian education movement among professional clergy since the 1950s has run concurrent with the numerical decline in mainline church schools. Based on a hypothesis that proved insufficient to bear its weight, its appealing logic overlooked one important fact: the law of the land says you must send your child to public school. No such law impels parents to send their youngsters to church school. Even superlative instruction methods do not ensure that bodies will arrive on Sunday. Unless attendance is worked at directly and intentionally, the finest curriculum will fall on absent ears. This doesn't mean that churches shouldn't strive for high-quality education. They should. But even if they do achieve that, it won't be enough.

Do the Sunday school teachers in your church see the task of reaching new students as an important part of their teaching responsibility? If so, their classes are probably growing larger (and so is their church). If not, both are declining. *Axiom #6: Growing churches have reaching-out oriented Sunday school classes, youth work, children's choirs, etc. (as contrasted with programs geared only to meeting the educational, social, and spiritual needs of persons who have already joined the church).*

In many nongrowth churches, evangelistic reach-out has been thrust into the organizational/educational machinery and lost there. As the Australian United Methodist, Alan Walker, observed in a recent address: "For over fifty years the church, especially in the West, has been a maintenance rather than a missionary church. Seminaries have concentrated on counseling and Christian education rather than preaching and evangelism. Pastors have been maintenance people, spending all their time shepherding and nurturing the gathered flock of Christians. Local congregations have been introverted, complacent, stoking up the grace of God rather than pouring it out for a lost world."[1]

A group of Southern Baptists was touring Westminster Abbey in London. After seeing the many graves of notable people buried inside that great monument, one man asked the guide, "This is mighty impressive, but has anybody been converted here lately?" That traveler was raising a question of balance—the same kind of balance

---

[1]Alan Walker, address at the 1980 World Convention of Churches of Christ, Honolulu, Hawaii.

question that church leaders must perpetually ask themselves. Any church, anywhere, must accomplish four principle tasks. Failure to execute one or more of these puts it out of balance. And eventually, out of business. The first task is *koinonia:* to develop a loving community of people with shared religious faith. The second task is *didache:* to develop and nurture religious tradition and pass it on to succeeding generations. The third task is *diakonia:* to prepare members for service in the world. The fourth task is *kerygma:* to reach out and share the faith with outsiders. Growing churches work at each of these goals intentionally. They never assume one is more important than another.

Draw Larger Circles

Adult classes and groups form a significant part of the propellant in growth churches. Leaders in these congregations know that children don't drive cars or make decisions about how the family spends Sunday mornings; adults do. So they concentrate on drawing larger circles which take more adults in, rather than emphasizing youth and children's activities only. But what causes the growth of adult classes in these churches? Not just the educational quality of the curriculum. These adult classes grow because they reach out instead of in. They are convinced that Jesus does not call them to be keepers of a Sunday aquarium but calls them to go out and be fishers.

Take a poll of the adult classes in your church. Ask the class members to write their feelings on a slip of paper regarding why they enjoy attending their class. Hand these answers to the class leader. Read them aloud. Now, ask the class whether it is larger, smaller, or about the same size as five years ago. For those classes that are plateaued, raise a third question: "If we like this class so much, why isn't it growing larger?" An honest answer will involve the admission that we never consciously intended for it to grow. We have been organized for meeting with each other but not for drawing larger circles that take outsiders in.

Many adult classes stay the same size for the same reason that most small churches remain static. The warmth of their fellowship locks strangers outside. "We are such a friendly church," they proudly exclaim. But to whom? Mostly to each other. To outsiders, they seem like a closed shop. Until "invisible introversion" is dealt with, significant church growth is seldom possible. Every prospective adult class member looks for one thing above all others: active acceptance. They hope class members will care about them and want them in their social group. Adult classes that systematically provide this acceptance grow.

Growing classes don't make the mistake of overconcentrating on the church's hard-core, inactive member list. They know that congregations don't grow larger by seeking to attract people who have already fallen in and out of love with them.

The newest members are among the most likely candidates for

adult class attendance. But most churches fail at this, the easiest form of reach-out. How can you reverse this particular form of invisible introversion? Try the "Magic Three" formula. Begin by enlisting the aid of all your adult teachers and officers. Explain the system and ask for their cooperation during a one-year trial period. Then, every time someone joins the church, the pastor and Sunday school superintendent decide which adult class might best fit that person's needs. The superintendent then contacts the teacher or designated officer in that class, giving the name and address of the new member(s). During the following three consecutive weeks, three couples or individuals from that adult class make a visit to the new member's home. Each couple or individual communicates three things during this brief call: (1) We are happy that you joined our church. (2) We wanted to stop by and get acquainted with you. (3) We invite you to attend our Sunday school class. During this visit, they tell the new members how to find the classroom. They may offer to meet them in the foyer if the building is large and confusing.

Once people get to the building, four ingredients are particularly significant for increasing class extroversion: (1) A gregarious greeter. Always early, he or she remembers names and faces and has the social knack of making strangers feel like home folks. (2) Name tags. Every Sunday, for every class attender. This makes newcomers feel equal and reduces the social awkwardness of feeling that everyone is acquainted except you. (3) Coffee, tea, etc., in each classroom. The coffee urn distributes more than caffeine. Everyone knows how to fix and drink a cup of coffee. This gives strangers something specific to do with their hands. (4) Occasional class social events. Invitations to picnics and parties are much more personal than to a Sunday school class, and hence increase feelings of acceptance.

A young educator says, "When people come to Lion's Club or a civic club they are always a somebody. Older members pay attention to them, count them present or absent, notice them, etc. But people come to Sunday school and we make them nobodies. We fail to understand that people don't come so much to learn things as they come for acceptance, fellowship, and affirmation." His criticism may be slightly overdrawn, but he has put his finger on a mega-truth: those whom we seek to educationalize we must first socialize.

Another significant factor in growth churches is the frequent organization of new adult classes. Growing congregations usually have six or seven adult groups (choirs, prayer circles, women's groups) per one hundred worship attenders. Growing churches of moderate size form one or two new adult groups each year. This provides new doors through which potential new attenders can enter. A number of psychological factors make new groups far more enticing than older, established classes: (1) everyone has equal opportunity for leadership in a new group; (2) the invisible walls of introversion are not yet present in a new group; (3) the new group was designed to meet a particular need rather than a general need; hence, persons attracted to it are coming because they feel that need will be met; and (4) it is more fun to get in on the ground floor of any endeavor, rather than trying to fit yourself into a social system already frozen into inflexible relationship patterns.

The Youth Work Illusion

Growing churches usually have strong programs for junior high and senior high youth. Casual onlookers often make the mistake of assuming that these are the *cause* of growth rather than one of the *characteristics* of a growth church.Congregations do not grow because of strong youth work; growth comes from strong adult work. But one of the first things strong adult work churches do is develop strong youth work.

Eighty-five percent of persons will not become Christians unless they do so before age eighteen. Growth churches keep many more of their own youth and through peer influence draw in some extra young persons from the unchurched community. But active efforts to evangelize the parents of youth is a far better way to strengthen youth work than the reverse procedure—trying to attract the youth and thereby hoping to appeal to their parents.

As with adult classes, the factor of extroversion is far more important in youth work than the curriculum used or the group activities. But not just any sort of extroversion works. Many churches invite youth to parties and trips, hoping they will drift into church life. Most of these fringe types never make the transition. A better approach: take reservations for a Sunday morning youth breakfast just before Sunday school. This relates guests to the church's program rather than to a party.

If you are trying to attract college students, identify as many as you can who have your denominational background. Start in the fall with some kind of college-age event. A Sunday morning breakfast can focus together incoming students. Freshmen and sophomores are the most receptive since they have the greatest need to establish a secure place in college social life. From that beginning event, start rolling up your snowball of participation. Create a class that meets together during the Sunday school hour or has a snack supper on Sunday evening. If the group numbers above twenty, divide it into smaller support groups that meet at other times. As in all other age levels of evangelism, the "birds of a feather" principle helps determine the success of group development. Students fighting their way through the graduate school jungle don't have much in common with high school youth or senior citizens. Adult singles have little in common with college freshmen.

But despite the value of youth programs, remember that youth evangelism does not cause a church to grow. Expanding congregations do youth evangelism as part of their Christian mission.

Singing in the Sheaves

Most growing congregations have strong youth and children's choir programs. Music participation draws in many youngsters who will be attracted to no other church activity. And on the Sundays when these special choirs sing, their parents (even the unchurched ones) will attend worship. Thus, you have achieved the double goal of pulling new adults toward the church and exerting a positive influence on the lives of their children.

One growing congregation of approximately four hundred members has a dynamic, graded choir program which they describe like this: "People today usually visit among various denominations in town before joining a church. They look into the programs offered, especially those for kids. Children's choirs provide attractive pull. New residents think to themselves, 'My child is going to receive spiritual concepts as well as musical training.' That means a great deal when you make evangelism visits. You can tell them about the choir fellowships and their value for youngsters. Young adults in our society have increased by 40 percent, due to the 1950s baby boom reaching child-bearing age. They don't have as many kids per family as people did four decades ago, but the totals are just as great. And these parents seem much more intensely concerned about what their kids get in quality of life.

"Every fall, we hold a beginning festival in which children and youth register for the choirs. The last two years, that has been a carnival. We now have about ninety children and youth in our singing program. Many non-church members in the community have begun to enroll their kids in our choirs, so the evangelism aspect of the program has started to snowball automatically. Every time one of our children's choirs sings in church, attendance takes a tremendous jump. It helps get the adults in the church door.

"The choir director doesn't handle the fellowship part of the choirs. Laypersons take care of that. A choir mother arranges the refreshments. She contacts the other mothers and schedules their duty dates. The director just comes in and does the music at the appropriate time in the schedule. Professionals in the public school music program often feel that this can be part of their ministry. Instead of teaching Sunday school, they work with the choir program.

"Music programs are not inexpensive, financially speaking. In our church, the music ministry costs about 5 percent of the total budget (which doesn't count the salary for the youth/music minister). The materials are expensive, but we feel that the offering income generated by people who would not otherwise have joined our church far more than repays the cost.

"What if you are a small church without a music staff person—perhaps a church of 150 members? What can you do in that situation? Look at qualified people in the community who could direct the music ministry on a part-time basis. First, check with your high school choir director. That may limit you, because he or she usually prefers to take responsibility for the adult sanctuary choir only. In that case, look around for someone else, like a music teacher in the public schools. Say to this person, 'I'd like to talk with you about starting a new ministry in our church—something that would really help the church—something which perhaps you and you alone can do.' Some persons will do this without pay in a smaller church. And if you can't have anything but a choir involving grades one through six, that is far better than doing nothing.

"Begin where you are and improvise with what you have. It will surely pay off in big dividends for evangelism. Whatever you do, don't wait until you grow before you add some kind of music staff— full-time or part-time."

Motivational Target Building

Growing congregations set specific numerical goals each year. Setting goals focuses our attention in a positive way and helps priorities for evangelism compete with all the other church activities. The following technique is a good illustration of such an approach. Use it for a one-year period or for the remainder of the current church year. After the initial goal-setting procedure, ask each church school class to set a specific number as their share of the total church goal.

The annual business meeting provides an excellent scenario for people goal-setting. Most of these sessions are so dull that they need sharpening anyway; no real participation and few surprises. New officers are elected, but everyone already knows who the nominating committee has asked. A new budget is approved. No excitement there, either. The stewardship committee has been putting it together for weeks. Neither officers nor budgets are the primary tasks of the church (they are tools to achieve the primary tasks). Why not get back to basics by letting the congregation talk about people-goals? The Great Commission has not been repealed. Nor is the Great Commission the "great suggestion." Fifteen minutes of setting goals in that direction helps reeducate a congregation to that fact.

The leader can introduce this section of the business meeting like this: "Good Christian people give their time, attention, and money to a lot of meritorious things in church life. All of these are important, because each in some way contributes to our worship of God and our concern for people. But there is one task upon which everything else we do depends. Do you know what it is? Evangelism! Without successful evangelism, all the other things we do in the church eventually stop happening.

"Some things are important in church life. But some things are crucial, utterly essential. Evangelism is one of those things. Churches that don't do evangelism eventually lose all their options for doing anything else they're doing. Because the fuel base upon which the church runs to do its mission is people."

The leader can then explain that the average church in the United States loses about 10 percent of its participating membership each year by death, transfer, and moving to inactive status. This means that our church must have annual additions equaling 10 percent of our participating membership in order to stay even. A church of two hundred members, for instance, must have average additions by baptism and transfer of twenty persons each year to avoid slow death. A good analogy to use as an explanation: "Every church is like a large water tank with a pipe running out the bottom. That pipe is letting water out all the time, and there is no way to shut it off. So we must have a pipe of at least the same size running into the top of the tank in order to keep our church from shrinking each year. A one-inch pipe running out the bottom requires a one-inch pipe running in the top."

After giving this analogy, ask everyone at the meeting to help set a numerical addition goal for the year. This goal should be at least 10 percent but not more than 15 percent of the present participating membership. (More than 15 percent is unrealistic, except in a very few metropolitan areas with extremely high turnover rates, such as those found near military bases.)

The actual goaling can be done in various ways. One is to divide people into groups of ten or twelve (around each of the tables if they are seated at tables). Have each group spend ten minutes deciding what they think the numerical addition goal for our church ought to be this year. Then ask a reporter from each table to read to the total gathering the suggested goal, while the leader lists each figure on a blackboard or flipchart. Have someone add these up, divide by the number of tables, and you have your goal for the year. Educate people about this constant need to do evangelism. Give them a part in the decision-making, and they much more eagerly help with the reach-out work later on.

Do this goal-setting annually. People forget and become preoccupied with other matters. Then, too, the congregation constantly changes as new members come in and old members move away, making the continual education process a necessity. Think where most churches would be if they didn't have an annual stewardship campaign to remind people of the best and highest things they already know. Stewardship levels would gradually decline. The same is true in church growth, but since failure in this work produces no dramatic instant readout on a bank statement, leaders easily overlook the need for education.

A man ran a hardware store in a small town for several decades. But as he moved into retirement years, he grew weary of being confined by specific store hours and having to stay open on Saturday. He also became irritated at dealing with customers, so he gradually restricted the number of days per week he opened for business. In all his spare time, he concentrated on rearranging the remaining stock in his store. Eventually, he stopped unlocking the doors at all.

80

Having the merchandise well displayed became more important to him than letting people in to see whether they might like to take some of it home with them. Congregations which fall into that pattern inevitably decline. Churches which grow don't allow that to happen. Their life orientation is extroversion. They have something that everybody in town needs one of. So they try to stay open for business.

Group Discussion Questions

1. Do you think our church is basically extroverted or introverted? Why?
2. Do our Sunday school teachers see the work of growth as an important part of their teaching responsibility?
3. What concrete things are we doing to encourage new attenders in our Sunday school?
4. Do we have a youth choir? Children's choir? Name some people who might be able to lead such a choir or choirs.
5. What first attracted you to our class or group? What two things do you like best about this class or group? Have class members write their answers to these questions on a slip of paper. Collect the.answers and read them aloud to the class. What do these answers imply about how we can attract new people?
6. This chapter mentions four tasks that every chuch must do: *koinonia, didache, diakonia,* and *kerygma.* In which of these four areas do you think our church is strongest? Weakest? Illustrate on a flipchart the various things we do to accomplish each of these four tasks.
7. How long has it been since our church organized a new adult class or group? What does this tell us about when the next one should be started? What target group should the next class seek to serve?
8. Has our church been setting numerical goals the past few years? If not, when and how do you think we should begin to set goals as a congregation?
9. How do our youth programs enhance or detract from our church's evangelism work?

An airplane propeller may have four blades, but its power depends on the strength of the metal at the point where they all come together.

7

The Main Thing

For three solid weeks in 1757, a mounted messenger was dispatched from Berlin to Prague every day, a distance of 160 miles. Although engaged in bitter military combat with the Austrians, King Frederick the Great of Prussia insisted on daily bulletins concerning the health of his pet greyhound. The king's dog was certainly not unimportant; no pet is that. But compared to the broad sweep of history being decided on that battlefield, the greyhound was secondary. In that same way, mainline churches often neglect the main thing they went out to do while furiously majoring in minors.

The New Gnosticism

Several greyhounds compete for the attention of church leaders. One of these is *knowledge*. The heresy of gnosticism appeared in the second century A.D. and died out by the fifth century. This skewed theology taught that salvation comes by acquiring special knowledge rather than by faith. Therefore, only those who achieved certain levels of knowledge could relate to God effectively. Gnosticism has reappeared in contemporary denominations, masquerading as intellectual sophistication and often clothed in the teachings of some particular theologian. Dedicated enthusiasts try to sell it to the mass public in packages like the following: "You really don't understand the Gospel until you understand Martin Heidegger (or Bultmann, or Tillich). Those Baptists (or Assemblies of God, or Pentecostals, or Charismatics) just don't understand the New Testament. They take it literally instead of grasping its deeper meanings."

But what passes for "true knowledge of the faith" to the Christian intellectual often comes through as "mental fog" to the average person in the street. By making the Christian faith a matter of knowledge, its concepts are placed on a high shelf beyond the reach of ordinary people. They have no trouble grasping their need to love God and their neighbor, but are thrown into confusion when somebody tries to explain between-the-lines meanings of some obscure European theologian.

Such pseudo-sophistication is an insidious form of "intellectual good works." The Gospel is not complex; it is simple. It is not obscure, but clear. It does not require long hours of concentrated study, but rather a quick leap of faith toward a living, loving Christ. We do not come into his kingdom by education, but by affirmation of his leadership in our lives. Jesus certainly challenged the intellect by daily teaching in the temple and expounding the truth about God. But when he called his disciples, he did not demand from them the intellectual acceptance of complex propositions. He invited them into an experience of friendship. He did not say to them "Believe this," or, "It is written." He said, "Follow me."

Jesus' principle teaching method was not informational; it was "formational." He seemed not so much interested in making persons knowledgeable as in making them different. Formation, not information, was his motive. He called for a change of heart: repentance, a change from concentration on self-will to a concentration on God's will. But he focused not nearly so much on intellectualizing as on action.

A graffiti wall at St. John's University displayed this inscription: "Jesus said unto them, 'Who do you say that I am?' And they replied, 'You are the eschatological manifestation of the ground of our being, the kerygma in which we find the ultimate meaning of our interpersonal relationship.' And Jesus said, 'What?'"

When the apostle Paul arrived in Athens, the intellectual center of his world, the scholars said, "May we know what this new teaching is which you present? For you bring some strange things to our ears; we wish to know therefore what these things mean." The author of Acts adds, "Now all the Athenians and the foreigners who lived there spent their time in nothing except telling or hearing something new" (Acts 17:19-21). Paul soon recognized that pseudo-intellectuals can hang around the Areopagus fringes of church life forever—anxious to debate everything in general but committed to nothing in particular. So he gave up that game and got on to the main thing: "But far be it from me to glory except in the cross of our Lord Jesus Christ . . ." (Galatians 6:14). Paul had every right to glory in many other things. His intellect, which was considerable. His philosophical background, which was extensive. But he recognized these for what they were—greyhounds of the faith, something less than the main thing.

Churchianity

Another greyhound of the faith: *social churchianity*. Reduced to its raw sociological elements, a church operates on tracks identical to other social organizations. Churches are often accused of a country club or civic club mentality because at certain points they are similar. Like a hydroplane floating on a layer of air, they can survive only on a cushion of warm, friendly fellowship. Because of this, Christian leaders are tempted to work at evangelism as if socialization were the only currency with which they can buy growth. When this happens, what Fred Craddock has said comes true: "I know some churches that spend every day manufacturing fun, manufacturing enthusiasm. Why? So nobody will notice how empty the house is!"[1] Jesus did not work hard to bring people into a new social organization. They already had the synagogue. He tried to bring them into a new life.

A Lutheran campus minister in Maryville, Missouri, finds it helpful to ask students the question, "How important is Jesus Christ in your life?" He says this probe always leads to deeper conversations—not necessarily conversations with positive conclusions for Christ and the church, but they do help the discussion reach a level otherwise impossible. Successful evangelism work among adults has taken a similar trend in recent years, away from the old style of trying to relate people to the church. It tries to relate them to the Head of the church rather than just the local body of the church. That trend will surely continue. Americans are definitely interested in social relationships. But they also look for something much deeper than social connections.

Charles Allen, the distinguished United Methodist clergyman from Houston, says, "I live around the corner from a man named Allen Shepard who walked on the moon. And every so often when I'm at home, I'll get out and walk in the evening. Sometimes, I'll go by his house and he'll be out in the yard and he and I talk. And I think, here is a man who has walked on the moon. And that's great. But the greatest thing that ever happened was not that a man walked on the moon. The greatest thing that ever happened was that God walked on the earth. You and I have the privilege of proclaiming the glories of Jesus Christ."[2]

[1] From a speech at the National Evangelism Workshop, Amarillo, Texas, May 1980.

[2] From a speech at the National Evangelism Workshop, Amarillo, Texas, May 1980.

We can bring people into the church without first bringing them into Christ and his kingdom. But when we do that, they don't fit, don't feel at home and soon fall out. Church leaders work at two tasks simultaneously: helping people into the church and helping them find new life. But these two similar things produce very different outcomes. And one of them is not the main thing.

Psychologianity

Another deceptive greyhound of the faith: *psychologianity*. The discipline of psychology has provided the church with important helping instruments, especially for pastors educated within the last two decades. Unfortunately, some clergy overrated these new counseling skills and started defining every aspect of the church's work through this perspective. This insidious idolatry makes the counselor god instead of God and sets up psychiatric technique as religious ritual.

Mainline denominations find this bad trip a particularly luscious temptation. Already suffering from a severe identity crisis, they no longer believe what they originally believed at an earlier point in their historical development. They were once convinced that Christ brings salvation (wholeness) to the human lives that turn to him in faith. Now, they are not quite sure what salvation means and aren't utterly convinced of what good it does for people. This identity crisis causes a loss of self-confidence not unlike that found in senior citizens who can no longer depend on the physiological parts to function in the same reliable way as before: stomachs become undependable food-conversion systems; knees begin crumpling on the seventh step of the stairway; ears begin blurring sentences into indistinguishable tone blobs. What a fearful loss of self-assurance these failures start producing! And when the former apostolic successes of a denomination's expansionary era start withering, we cast about for something that might substitute for the lost powers of a vigorous ecclesiastical youth.

But effective evangelism cannot be built on the foundation of behavior modification, counseling skills, and Freudian analysis. These tools are helpful—but still human, horizontal systems. The church, in every period when it grows expansively, works from a transcendent, vertical connection. It understands what Paul meant when he said, "Remember that there are men who [have plenty to say but] have no knowledge of God" (1 Corinthians 15:34, Phillips).

The writer of John's Gospel concludes by saying, "...but these are written that you may believe that Jesus is the Christ, the Son of God, and that believing you may have life in his name" (John 20:31). Churches are set in the world for precisely the same purpose: to help people find life in his name. If they do not achieve that goal, they and their denomination fade.

Social Actionianity

Studies of growth congregations indicate that their volume of social helping activity in the community is greater than that of declining churches. But these growing churches do not see their social action as the main thing. They see social action as a *result* of evangelism, rather than a cause of it. They understand that when a farmer confuses fruits with roots—tries to fertilize and water the apples on the tree rather than the roots of the apple tree—he eventually loses both. Start with social action as the primary goal of church life and you usually achieve more social talk than social action. Eventually, your tree withers and you lose a chance at both social action and evangelism.

When the Central Committee of the World Council of Churches convened at Lucknow in the 1950s, the members were shocked when a high official of the Indian government said condescendingly that while his nation had benefitted from the schools and hospitals established by Christian missionaries, this sort of cultural imperialistic proselytizing had to stop. The late Dr. Franklin Clark Fry, chairman of the Central Committee, replied graciously. He told the official that the mark of a Christian is a feeling of compulsion to share his best with his friends. Clinics and colleges are good, he said, and American Christians have been glad to give them. But as valuable as these are, the minds which they train will be empty and the lives they preserve will be a mockery if it all ends there. "The very best thing we have to give is the fruit of joy, peace, and hope which grows only on the vine of a living faith in Jesus Christ," he said. That is still the *best* gift that church friends have to offer.

"So faith comes from what is heard, and what is heard comes by the preaching of Christ" (Romans 10:17). Note that Paul doesn't say faith comes from seeing Christians doing good deeds. It comes from *hearing* a witness. Paul didn't go to Asia Minor to do good deeds but to *say good news*. In his excellent book, *A Song of Ascents*[3], E. Stanley Jones reports what a Hindu principal of a college said at one of his meetings: "Jesus has stood four times in history before the door of India and has knocked. The first time he appeared in the early days he stood in company with a trader. He knocked. We looked out and saw him and liked him, but we didn't like his company, so we shut the door.

"Later he appeared, with a diplomat on one side and a soldier on the other, and knocked. We looked out and said, 'We like you, but we don't like your company.' Again we shut the door. The third time was when he appeared as the uplifter of the outcasts. We liked him better in this role, but we weren't sure of what was behind it. Was this the religious side of imperialism? Are they conquering us through religion? Again we shut the door. And now he appears before

---

[3]p. 110, Abingdon, 1968.

our doors, as tonight, as the disentangled Christ. To this disentangled Christ we say, 'Come in. Our doors are open to you.'"

A woman who had been sick for many years had spent all she had but was in no way improved. Having heard about Jesus, she pushed her way through the crowd in order to touch him. In an instant, her health improved (Matthew 9:20-22). Denominations that seek a cure for their numerical decline must touch the disentangled Christ. Political and social action are necessary in the living out of Christian discipleship. They just aren't the main thing.

And Finally, the Main Thing

Axiom #7: Growing churches emphasize the importance of God, Christ, and the Holy Spirit (as contrasted with a merely social, psychological, or community agency orientation to helping people). "The most important thing is the centrality of Jesus Christ in the program of the church," says the pastor of one growing congregation. "The centrality of Christ when you are singing in the choir; when you are repairing the sewer; when you are preaching; the centrality of Christ in the elder's meeting; the centrality of the Good News, Jesus Christ, crucified, dead, buried, resurrected from the dead. We do not forget who is the Lord. We do not forget who is the leader. We do not forget who it is that we glorify and serve."

How is this centrality of Christ maintained? How do these churches avoid slipping off-center? Primarily through a high concentration of biblical teaching. The pastor of another growing congregation says, "Our Sunday schools are Bible-centered, as are our women's study groups and prayer groups."

"Any one who goes ahead and does not abide in the doctrine of Christ does not have God..." says John (2 John 9). Philosophy focuses on ideas. Psychology focuses on human behavior. Theology focuses on God. Some critics of mainline church decline think we need to improve our theology. Probably not. We need to be certain that we preach a theology that actually is a theology. Philosophical messages draw people to ideas. Psychological messages draw people to introspection and self-improvement. But new life in Christ requires turning to God, not just turning to a good idea.

Church history provides numerous illustrations of how easily Christians lose their focus. Resting totally on the authority of a book leads to bibliolatry (fundamentalism). Excessively resting our case on the authority of an institution leads to ecclesiasticism. Excessively resting our faith on the authority of reason leads to rationalism (the positive rationalism of the 1950s). Resting on the authority of experience tends toward mysticism (the charismatic temptation). Resting on the authority of a creed tends toward dogmatism (a temptation of the late 1700s).

"But woe to you, scribes and Pharisees, hypocrites! because you shut the kingdom of heaven against men; for you neither enter yourselves, nor allow those who would enter to go in" (Matthew

23:13). Mainliners like to fling the truth of that text against the narrowness of fundamentalism. But how easy it is for rational discussions about the faith to become more prominent than our faith in the centerpiece of the faith. And when we can't quite step across the line from logical analysis into the main thing, we keep others from stepping over, too.

According to one of the laws of physics (the second law of thermodynamics) God, or something like God—a prime mover, a matter producer, an energy giver—must exist. Our world and universe cannot be accounted for in any other way. Jesus agreed with that. He never tried to prove it; he merely accepted it as an operational fact. Building on this "given" without trying to explain why or how it might be true, Jesus moved on to describe the *nature* of this God force. He said it is basically *relational,* basically love-relational toward human beings, basically like a good father type of relation. He said that we can do nothing to manipulate God into relating to us in a positive manner; all we need do is accept that positive relationship and act on it.

Jesus did not concern himself about whether this relationship should be more rational than emotional, or vice versa. What he said about God had both rational and emotional content. For Jesus, God was not just intellectual; God was *experiential.*

A radio transmitter sends out beams around the clock. Indiscriminate, it fills the airwaves of every city street, every home, every room. It doesn't ask whether the people in those places actually want to hear that station. It is omnipresent, always available. But how do people get in touch with this station? First, they must turn on their radio. Second, they must turn it to the right frequency in order to eliminate all the other stations that are competing for their attention. This is called free will. Even though that station is always available and within reach, they must *choose* to relate to it. Whenever these two factors come together—the everpresent love of God and the personal accepting response of an individual—a new presence fills that person's life circuits. Jesus called this "entering the kingdom of God." Today, we might call it entering the experience of God or entering the consciousness of God. Whatever we call it, it is definitely the main thing. Growing churches remember that.

Group Discussion Questions

1. In your opinion, are there any things the members of our church tend to substitute for "the main thing"? Illustrate.
2. List all the ways you can think of that our church is currently trying to help people find "the main thing."
3. Do you have any suggestions regarding how our church might move toward a more Christ-centered and biblically-centered orientation to the faith?
4. A pastor says that he asked a group of older women when they last experienced "communion with God." If someone were to ask you that question, how would you answer it?
5. A seminary's preaching professor says that he always assumes that the listener has a yearning, a hunger, a need for God. Do you agree or disagree with that statement as it would apply to the average Sunday morning church attender? To the unchurched?

"Search men's governing principles, and consider the wise, what they shun and what they cleave to."

—*Marcus Aurelius Antoninus, A.D. 121-180*

8

Which Jesus?

As shepherds washed their socks by night. Give us this day our jelly bread. Lead us not into Penn Station. Harold by thy name. Deliver us from people. These child-revised versions of cherished hymns remind us that our greatest religious truths are sometimes misunderstood. Communication is a difficult business. The sign in a Texas restaurant window said, "Wanted: Man to wash dishes and two waitresses." Applications poured in from thirteen counties. A church newsletter announced, "Tuesday afternoon there will be meetings in the north and south ends of the church. Children will be baptized at both ends."

Communicating the Gospel is even more complex than writing clear hymnody or printing posters. We sing "Jesus, Jesus, Jesus, Sweetest Name I know" with united gusto. But different singers interpret those words differently because they have different needs. The spiritual-cultural background of persons in one community call for a different approach than the same pastor would use in another town. New generations require a shifted emphasis. We keep shooting at a moving target. Every church tries to communicate the gospel message of Jesus Christ. But which message? Which emphasis? Which Jesus?

A doctor suddenly found himself overrun by patients. A line extended all the way out into the street. Soon, he knew each diagnosis before he saw the patient. They had all sprained an ankle stepping into a deep hole in the sidewalk outside his office. Had he not been so busy treating patients suffering pain from sprained ankles, he would have gone out and filled in the hole. Consultants who are called in to help reverse the nongrowth in churches eventually recognize a similar problem. The theological sidewalks over which a church's preaching and teaching travel can create numerical sprains that no amount of corrective evangelism technology alone can fix. Church growth comes, not just from doing things the right way but from saying the right Word. *Axiom #8: Growing churches have a theological stance indigenous to the spiritual perceptions, psychological needs, and cultural mindsets of current members of society.*

Jesus' Twenty Faces

Keith Minolta was confused. A college junior majoring in English literature, he had experienced extreme stress during the past few months. His parents unexpectedly divorced. Then his mother died from a brain tumor that snatched her life in three agonizing months. But the breakup with his high school sweetheart really finished him. Deeply depressed, his emotions had to stand on a stepladder in order to reach the pits.

During that grim period he searched for straws to keep his sanity afloat. Perhaps religion would help. Why not give it a try? So he started shopping. The first week he slipped into an Episcopal Church down the block from his dorm. It seemed like another world. The liturgy fascinated him, but more in the way a child feels when seeing a merry-go-round for the first time than as a spiritual experience. The sermon dwelt on the need for Christians to do serious thinking about the nuclear energy question. Delivered with eloquence, it was as relevant to his problem as a course in anatomy.

The next Sunday he attended the Christian Science church down on Center Street. What a radical contrast! The semi-sermon talk spelled out the value of mind control over physical ailments. Interesting. The idea sounded plausible, in a science fiction sort of way. Maybe they were right. But he wasn't physically sick, and he couldn't figure out how the theory applied to his mental turmoil.

Then he tried a Pentecostal church urged on him by a young man down the hall in his dormitory. That was more mystifying still. He liked the warm informality of the service. He certainly liked the hugging, having been fortunate enough to be seated by a cute blond. But the sermon ascended into clouds of irrationality. He came away wondering whether he had just participated in a group insanity session.

What perplexed him most was how every preacher could start in the same place and end up at such opposite destinations. Didn't they all begin with the teachings of Jesus? Perhaps he should go back to the basic material and see for himself. So Keith began a careful study of the red word sections of an old New Testament he had received from the Gideons in grade school. But that research increased rather than diminished his puzzlement. Yes, he found some ammunition for each church's theological position. But he also found numerous other points they had left out altogether.

Millions of persons, both Christian and non-Christian, share Keith's bewilderment. Why do sincere Christian spokespersons sound so different from each other when they describe Jesus' teachings? Why do the doctrines of various denominations come out so opposite from one another? But Keith, unlike those other millions, found the simple answer to that question. Using determined study, two cheap Bibles, and a pair of scissors, he began to pile Jesus' teachings into different stacks according to subject matter. Soon, what had at first appeared as a complex question dissolved into crystal clarity. Jesus had said so many different things on so many different subjects! His utterances fit neatly under twenty headings! And even when Keith tried to press these twenty into clusters, he still got eight distinctly different groupings. What some described as the "simple gospel" was simple all right, but it was more like a cafeteria of instruction than a one-course meal!

Why did Jesus have such broad appeal to the people of his day and those of every century since? His teachings about God and the human condition were all-inclusive. He touched on every human need of every kind of person at every life stage. And this breadth in his teachings explains why various denominations differ so much from each other: different sociological groups inevitably concentrate on different points among Jesus' twenty teachings. This also explains the differences among ministers *within* the same denomination. Each pastor centers in on some of Jesus' teachings more than others. This explains the differences between theological conservatives and liberals. Evidence for both viewpoints—and all in-between—can be found in Jesus' teachings.

Which Jesus Do You Believe In?

Take a simple test. Look at Jesus's twenty teachings listed in short form below. Pick out with a check mark the ten you feel he stressed the most. From those ten, circle the five that are most important to you personally. Disregard the ones to which you think Jesus gave little emphasis. Have a friend take the same test. Compare your answers. Have two friends, or ten friends, take the test. Have two pastors from your denomination take the test. Have ten ministers from ten different denominations take it. No wonder we cannot agree on matters of doctrine and practice! Yes, we all start from exactly the same source. But we all select a different emphasis from the material—then promptly wonder why other Christians can't see things as clearly as we do. (See Appendix for a longer list of New Testament texts which illustrate and support each of these twenty points.)

ENTERING

1. God is here and you experience him by entering what Jesus called "the kingdom of God"—a new level of consciousness that makes possible new ways of thinking and behavior. Example: "Jesus answered him, 'Truly, truly, I say to you, unless one is born anew, he cannot see the kingdom of God'" (John 3:3).

AIDS

2. You are able to enter this "kingdom of God" or new level of consciousness only by a changed attitude of the heart, not by following a list of religious rules. Examples: "You hypocrites! Well did Isaiah prophesy of you, when he said: 'This people honors me with their lips, but their heart is far from me; in vain do they worship me, teaching as doctrines the precepts of men" (Matthew 15:8-9). In Luke 18:9-14, Jesus contrasts the phony righteousness of the Pharisee who followed all the religious rules with the obvious virtue of the tax collector who had followed no rules, but changed his heart.

3. Concentrating your mind's attention on Christ strengthens your ability to enter this "kingdom of God" or new level of consciousness and experience it in greater fullness. Example: "Again Jesus spoke to them, saying, 'I am the light of the world; he who follows me will not walk in darkness, but will have the light of life'" (John 8:12).

4. Prayer strengthens your ability to enter this "kingdom of God" or new level of consciousness and experience it more fully. Examples: "Ask, and it will be given you; seek, and you will find; knock, and it will be opened to you" (Matthew 7:7). In Matthew 6:10, Jesus teaches his disciples to pray for the Kingdom to come.

BLOCKS

5. You are blocked from entering this "kingdom of God" or new level of consciousness unless you turn away from [repent of] self-centeredness. Examples: "From that time Jesus began to preach, saying, 'Repent, for the kingdom of heaven is at hand'" (Matthew 4:17). In Matthew 7:13-14 Jesus' metaphor about the narrow gate teaches that those who enter God's kingdom must make a clear choice between two alternatives.

6. Those who take pride in their religious achievements find it difficult to enter this "kingdom of God" or new level of consciousness. Examples: "Whoever humbles himself like this child, he is the greatest in the kingdom of heaven" (Matthew 18:4). In Matthew 18:1-4 Jesus elaborates on the need for erasing religious pride in order to enter the kingdom.

7. *The financially wealthy find it difficult to enter this "kingdom of God" or new level of consciousness because their money brings a false sense of power that distracts them from seeking something better.* Examples: "It is easier for a camel to go through the eye of a needle than for a rich man to enter the kingdom of God"(Mark 10:25). In Matthew 6:19-34 Jesus urges us to seek *first* God's kingdom rather than riches, since putting something else at first priority can block us from our God relationship.

REWARDS

8. *Entering this "kingdom of God" or new level of consciousness paradoxically gives you rich rewards.* Examples: "If any man would come after me, let him deny himself and take up his cross and follow me. For whoever would save his life will lose it; and whoever loses his life for my sake and the gospel's will save it" (Mark 8:34-35). In Matthew 5:1-12 Jesus lists among the beatitudes numerous rewards for those who enter the Kingdom.

9. *Those who enter this "kingdom of God" or new level of consciousness find a sense of security that comes from believing that their personal needs will be cared for.* Examples: "But even the hairs of your head are all numbered. Fear not, therefore; you are of more value than many sparrows" (Matthew 10:30-31). In Matthew 6:25-33 Jesus says that we should not be anxious about our need for food and clothing; God will care for us.

10. *Those who experience this "kingdom of God" or new level of consciousness find a new power released in their lives and thought processes that transcends the normal cause and effect patterns of their environment.* Examples: "And whatever you ask in prayer, you will receive, if you have faith" (Matthew 21:22). In Luke 9:1-6 Jesus sends the twelve disciples out with the power to heal the sick. In Luke 10:9 he instructs the seventy to heal the sick and informs them that the Kingdom has come to them.

11. *Those who experience this "kingdom of God" or new level of consciousness live and worship joyfully, not in sadness with long faces.* Examples: "These things I have spoken to you, that my joy may be in you, and that your joy may be full" (John 15:11). In John 10:10 Jesus says, ". . . I came that they may have life, and have it abundantly."

12. *Those who experience this "kingdom of God" or new level of consciousness continue to live in that consciousness beyond the time of physical death.* Examples: "My sheep hear my voice, and I know them, and they follow me; and I give them eternal life, and they shall never perish, and no one shall snatch them out of my hand" (John 10:27). Similar statements appear in Matthew 19:29, 25:46; Mark 10:30; Luke 18:30; John 3:15, 16, 36, 4:14, 5:24, 6:27, 40, 47, 54, 10:28, 12:25, and 17:2-3.

BY-PRODUCTS

13. If you enter this "kingdom of God" or new level of conscious-ness, you experience increased love and concern for other people.
Examples: "And he said to him, 'You shall love the Lord your God with all your heart, and with all your soul, and with all your mind. This is the great and first commandment. And a second is like it, You shall love your neighbor as yourself'" (Matthew 22:37-38). In Luke 10:25-37 Jesus used the parable of the good Samaritan to connect loving God with the qualities of neighborliness and mercy.

14. Those who experience this "kingdom of God" or new level of consciousness are not judgmental about other people. Examples: "Judge not, that you be not judged" (Matthew 7:1). In Matthew 13:24-30 Jesus illustrates the principle of leaving judgment to God instead of trying to do it ourselves.

15. Those who experience this "kingdom of God" or new level of consciousness have a forgiving spirit." Examples: "Then Peter came up and said to him, 'Lord, how often shall my brother sin against me, and I forgive him? As many as seven times?' Jesus said to him, 'I do not say to you seven times, but seventy times seven'" (Matthew 18:21-22).

16. Those who experience this "kingdom of God" or new level of consciousness work to help other people to enter it too. Examples: "Go therefore and make disciples of all nations, baptizing them in the name of the Father and of the Son and of the Holy Spirit, teaching them to observe all that I have commanded you . . ." (Matthew 28:19-20). In Matthew 18:10-14 he tells a parable about the urgency of finding lost sheep.

17. Those who experience this "kingdom of God" or new level of consciousness live their lives in a spirit of self-giving. Examples: "If any man would come after me, let him deny himself and take up his cross and follow me" (Matthew 16:24). In Matthew 20:26-28 Jesus says that the person who wants to be greatest among his followers must be the servant of all the other servants.

CONTINUING

18. You cannot continue to experience this "kingdom of God" or new level of consciousness unless your thinking and actions remain consistent with this new state of mind. Returning to self-centered-ness causes a loss of the new consciousness experience. Examples: "Not every one who says to me, 'Lord, Lord,' shall enter the kingdom of heaven, but he who does the will of my Father who is in heaven" (Matthew 7:21). In Matthew 7:15-27 Jesus illustrates the need for *continued* right attitudes and actions by saying that a tree is known by its fruits and by telling a story of two different kinds of house builders.

19. If you do not enter this "kingdom of God" or new level of consciousness, you experience negative results from your failure to do so. Examples: "So it will be at the close of the age. The angels will come out and separate the evil from the righteous, and throw them into the furnace of fire; there men will weep and gnash their teeth" (Matthew 13:49-50).

FUTURE HOPES

20. Your "kingdom of God" or new level of consciousness experience will at an unspecified future time become more fully and obviously manifested in the whole of creation. Examples: "Jesus said to him, 'You have said so. But I tell you, hereafter you will see the Son of man seated at the right hand of Power, and coming on the clouds of heaven'" Matthew 26:64). In Matthew 24:3-44 Jesus deals extensively with an end time when the Kingdom will become apparent and vividly real to all.

The Origin of the Sect Groups

Our universal theological selectivity (which can be scientifically validated by comparing which of Jesus' twenty points are usually checked by persons of different denominations) is most obvious when viewed in its *extreme* form among the small religious sect groups of every century. In fact, *all* Christian splinter movements can be classified in their *beginnings* (later they become more pluralistic) by a dogmatic emphasis on one or two of Jesus' twenty points. They then accuse the mother church of "neglecting these most important of Christ's words." Sect leaders overstress these particular teachings for one or more of four reasons: (1) the psychological and environmental needs of people in their contemporary society call for an emphasis on these points; (2) their Christian peers have deemphasized that particular part of Jesus' teachings; (3) they experienced in their growing-up years a serious lack in parents and church life of the teachings which they now feel are more important than all the rest; or (4) they are mentally deranged religious nuts.

New Testament Roots of Our Selectivity

This theological selectivity phenomenon is not, however, a late-blooming weed in the annals of church history. It can be spotted at the very beginning of the Christian era. The best-known and most prolific writing disciple, Paul, covered all twenty of Jesus' subjects. But even Paul dwelt more on three of them than on all the other seventeen put together.

3. the need to concentrate on Christ (Holy Spirit) as a means for entering a relationship with God
5. the need to turn away from sin (repent of self-centeredness)
12. the eternal life beyond physical death aspect of Jesus' teachings

But because Paul's emphases squarely met the cultural setting, psychological needs, and spiritual understandings of the people with whom he worked in that century, his approach met with wide public acceptance and the church grew admirably.

Selectivity Across the Generations

The church of every era has within its treasury a currency that will buy allegiance to Jesus Christ. In one period this is the Holy Crusades. In another time it is a call for pietism. In still another, the demand for an educated, rational approach to faith. But just as paper money replaced gold coins and the Lincoln penny displaced the Indianhead, the face of that verbal currency changes with the generations. Its value and power doesn't change; just the manner in which we express and communicate it.

Erasmus, a teacher who influenced Martin Luther, wrote in a tract: "In being fascinated with the contemporary interests one forgets some genuine insight of the past. That has to be recovered, and so there is a sort of oscillation in this fashion. Insights are thrown out now by one generation, now by another, which seem to contradict each other, to give a discord. There is no discord; there is more concord. This suggests that truth is to be expressed in a coincidence of offices." Erasmus was wrestling with the fact that different generations embrace apparently contradictory insights which overall contribute to a unity not visible all at one time.

Close scrutiny shows a variegated emphasis among Christians traversing the eighty years of our own century. During the first three decades, American society was grappling with the evil of alcoholism and the enormous moral issues that become important when any culture explodes from a rural, agricultural setting into an urban, industrialized society. In meeting this situation, Christian leaders emphasized the moral by-products of Christianity and tended thereby to promote the idea of a judgmental God who demands firm conformity to his laws from behind a stern supreme court bench.

But in the three decades from 1930 to 1960, American society changed radically. Religious leaders began to be shaped by and needed to give spiritual leadership to persons whose childhood and youth experiences involved the deprivation of the Great Depression, the horrible human tragedies of World War II, and then the need to correct great social ills such as racism, prejudice, and poverty—which became obvious in a mobile society no longer preoccupied with fighting a war against external enemies. Is it any wonder that by 1955 ethical mandates and the "love your neighbor on the Jericho Road" aspects of Jesus' teachings began to be touted by most mainline denominations as Christ's *real* message to the world?

Then, in the middle sixties and early seventies charismatic leaders began to grasp intuitively (or inspirationally?) the fact that our society was once again shifting on its axis—culturally, psychologically and spiritually. The overwhelming loneliness of our mass existence, the anxiety and downright fearfulness of a people detached from the secure roots of their small town childhoods, the obvious emptiness of the once bright philosophy of rational positivism and the dead dream of salvation through scientific advancement—this new day called for a new emphasis. So charismatic leaders came down hard on four neglected teachings of Jesus:

3. the person of Christ as a life-changing force (person of Christ now interpreted as the Holy Spirit)
9. the personal sense of security in material matters which comes from relating to God
10. the power of God to intervene in human circumstances (called the miraculous by some)
11. joyfulness as a part of the Christian life (in contrast to the long-faced religious approach that comes as a result of overconcentration on morality or working hard at remedying social ills that seem forever beyond our control to change completely)

The Rise and Fall of Denominational Empires

This ever-shifting, need-meeting, theological selectivity also explains why Christian movements and denominations increase and later decline across the march of decades and centuries. When first launched, they match the cultural settings, psychological needs and spiritual perceptions of a great many people (not *all* people, of course; no movement does that). But because they meet the needs of *most* people, great masses gladly give their time, attention, and money to help the movement thrive. But then, as the decades go by, people's needs shift and the old emphasis that launched the movement with such immense popularity no longer matches current situations. So even when leaders put redoubled effort into recapturing the original ideals of the movement and espousing these ideas with great fervor, the movement continues to decline.

Shortly after the upsurge of new theologizing during the Protestant Reformation in the early 1500s, pastors began settling back into these now familiar ideas (taken from Calvin, Luther, and a reenergized Roman Catholic Church). Rather than moving with the *current* people in the *current* world situation, as Luther, Zwingli, and Calvin had, their theology began once again to smell like an antique store. Today's mainline denominations can easily repeat that mistake without recognizing it. Their insecurity causes them to fall back on the thought patterns of John Wesley, Thomas Campbell, or whoever led their movement in its heyday. By so doing, they stop relating God to the contemporary world scene. The converse of this pattern can be seen in the popularity of people like Robert Schuller. He, and others who catch the popular mind, use a fresh theology that speaks to contemporary people. They speak "as one with authority," not as one whose thoughts depend for their validity on what others in their denomination have thought in the past.

But why do leaders of declining denominations and movements not see their problem and take steps to arrest their decline by updating their mummified theological focus? Because these leaders are now in the middle and latter part of their life-spans. The movement continues to meet their needs, so they can't perceive why it does not meet the needs of the new generation. This, of course, is why the reformers and leaders of new religious movements are usually young people, generally in their twenties and early thirties. Only the younger leaders can perceive experientially what meets the needs of the generation currently coming into the productive years of their life-span. Examples: Martin Luther was thirty-three when he nailed his Ninety-Five Theses to the Wittenberg Church door and started the Protestant Reformation. Zwingli, the Swiss reformer, had by age thirty-six become one of the most noted preachers and leaders of the Reformed Church movement. John Wesley, founder of Methodism, was twenty-six when he organized his first Methodist Society.

In a few cases, church bodies can flex their emphasis sufficiently to meet the needs of younger persons in their society. When that happens, the denomination achieves a shift that stops the numerical decline. Like a self-cleaning oven, it moves into new phases of renewal, usefulness, and perhaps even expansion. But this, unfortunately, does not come without great internal strife and dissension among leaders. The most notable historical example of such a "catching up with the times" shift was the Roman Catholic Church following the birth of the Protestant Revolution in Germany. In their reaction to and defense against Luther's "radical" ideas, Catholic leaders slowly set their theological house more in order. During succeeding centuries they returned to an effective role in world mission.

Few Christian movements have avoided this "theological time lock" in their presentation of the gospel message. Consequently, few groups experience enough renewal and currency of thinking to avoid biting the dust of historical obscurity. In our own day, charismatic leaders, like all great reformers, think they have reached the penultimate in the exposition of true Christianity. That is, of course, not true. Even now, a new generation is growing into adulthood. They will discover that the latest and greatest understandings of the Christian faith which we have achieved seem terribly old-fashioned. The current emphasis will no longer match their cultural circumstances, psychological needs, and spiritual perceptions, and they will call for theological reform.

Whither the Future?

Who can predict the emphasis needed for the next generation? No one! Its theological selectivity will depend on environmental factors that are not at the moment totally predictable. But here are a few guesses regarding the teaching focus of the next two decades: (1) *Christological*—far more emphasis on what Christ taught (as contrasted with what Paul taught), mostly because Paul often spoke to concrete problems in a straightforward language, while Jesus taught in parables, a method that allows continuous interpretation and application of principles to changing problems; (2) *Relational*— a high concentration on the importance of teachings that help people relate positively to one another; (3) *Biblical*—a high concentration on Bible study, as people seek for firmer roots in a time of emotional insecurities and become more conservative in a time of rising median age levels; (4) *Spiritual*—a high concentration on the transcendence of God and his ability to provide insights and solutions to problems through revelation.

Our task as Christian communicators is to proclaim the message of Jesus. In doing this, as in all types of communication, the *medium* is assuredly a big part of the message. But the *message* of the Gospel is also a big part of the medium. We must present the message in ways that meet current human needs.

Nestled back in the mountains of eastern Pennsylvania is a tiny town where the front of an automobile dealership still has a gigantic sign proclaiming it the local Kaiser-Frazer distributor. Driving past that building makes a visitor wonder if this business is waiting for a shipment to arrive. This seems doubtful. Nor should we expect floods of new customers to move through these salesroom doorways. Congregations that promote a 1955 model theology get the same results.

Group Discussion Questions

1. Copy the twenty teachings of Jesus. Using the directions in this chapter, ask each class member to take the test. Have someone list on a flipchart the total numbers of checks for each of the twenty teachings. Discuss the results.
2. Beginning with teaching number one and moving to number twenty, have group members who checked each teaching as one of their top five give the reasons that they think it is important. Ask people who feel comfortable in doing so to share any early childhood experiences or teachings that they feel cause them to make this kind of choice.
3. Do the class members feel that their parents would have checked this list in a different way? Illustrate.
4. If your current pastor has been with the church for some time, have the group guess from the content or his/her preaching which of the twenty points he/she thinks is most important.
5. How do you think our denomination fits into this chapter's description of the shift in emphasis from one generation to another? Are we on target theologically with the present generation? If not, which of the twenty points do you think we should emphasize more?

> "Men must be decided on what they will not do, and then they are able to act with vigor in what they ought to do."
>
> —*Mencius, ca. 372-289 B.C.*

9

Sixty Minutes

The flying instructor was guiding a minister through landing practice in preparation for his solo flight. As they came in toward the runway, the pastor "stalled out." The plane almost stopped in the air, fifteen feet above the ground. It would have fallen like a rock had the instructor not grabbed the controls and zoomed them away. "Try the approach again," he said. After their second near-crash, the instructor pointed grimly at the panel in front of them and asked, "What is that instrument?"

"That's the air speed indicator," the budding pilot replied.

"And what is this other instrument?" the teacher asked."

"That is an altimeter," said the student.

"Pay attention to those, will you? If you don't, you are going to kill us both."

Churches should pay similar attention to what happens in their worship services. Poor quality here seldom causes an *instant* crash, but it is another crucial determiner of numerical rise and fall. *Axiom*

#9: Growing churches have worship and preaching that meet the spiritual needs of community residents. Everyone who attends a church has needs that can only be met through public worship. If the services help meet those needs, he or she wants to attend again. Regular worshipers who drop out are sending invisible air speed/altimeter readings that say they don't find these needs met.Visitors who don't come back are sending the same signal.

Looking back across American church history, we see successive waves of denominations that displace those falling slack on the beaches ahead of them. At first, each denomination did well because it met the unspoken, spiritual needs of its particular era. When it stopped meeting those needs, it began to do poorly. In colonial days, the big three need-meeting mainliners were the Congregationalists, the Presbyterians and the Church of England (later called Episcopalians in America). This triad was shortly supplanted by the nineteenth-century revivalists: the Baptists, the Methodists and a miscellaneous family that included the Church of Christ, Christian Churches, and Disciples of Christ. But as the twentieth century dawned, this successful second wave was also dissipating. The flood of immigrant arrivals from Ireland and Europe were mostly Roman Catholic and Lutheran. By 1981, America had fifty million Catholics and only thirteen and one-half million Southern Baptists. The Lutherans had outpaced everyone but the Baptists. But a new kind of wave was emerging. Charismatics and evangelicals were drawing adherents from all the major denominations. Without changing the sign on the lawn, many congregations began to reshape themselves around a new focus.

Part of the success behind each of these waves obviously lay in its ability to meet ethnic and socialization needs. But the real genius of each popular movement came from matching the mental-emotional tone qualities of its generation. At the right time in the right way, each walked into a spiritual vacuum with the right ideas. They found a need and filled it. Consequently, people filled up the churches. Worship services were not the only way each delivered these better ideas, but they were the main way. And that is still true. Growing churches understand that.

What Hurts Need Healing?

The five greatest inner stresses from which Americans suffer are loneliness, hopelessness, purposelessness, fear, and emptiness. Growing churches do a better than average job of healing these anguishes. They understand that worship ritual, interpersonal sharing, reassurance, affirmation of identity, and participation in meaningful activity are not just old customs passed across the threshold of generations. These are the purposeful medications by which churches carry the healing ministry of Jesus to the hurting masses. People don't go to church because attendance is a societal nicety, but because they *need* what religious institutions have historically provided. Why are conservative churches growing? Not just because they are conservative but because they meet these deep needs. Why are liberal churches in numerical difficulty? Not just because they are liberal, but because they do not as adequately meet these needs.

Loneliness. For eight dollars per hour, you can now rent an ear to help combat your loneliness. A San Francisco suburban coffeehouse called "Conversation" rents twenty "nice people to talk to" and fourteen soundproof booths to do it in. An elegant display of jewelry in a fashionable Kansas City shop contains several items with identical words. A cigarette lighter is stamped with "I am loved." A sterling silver bracelet carries the monogram "I am loved." These commercial ventures reflect one of the deepest yearnings of our age. If we have to rent someone to talk with and wear jewelry that tells us we are loved, we must need that love very badly. But can you really feel loved by reading the words of endearment to yourself, or wearing them? Love only happens between live people. Romance and marital love meet part of that need. But they are never enough. We need the love of God and a loving relationship with several other people. That's why the worship services in growing churches encourage members to reach out to new people in a warm, friendly, accepting manner. They promote by every means the opportunities for positive contacts between worship visitors and present members. They understand that one of God's most powerful tools for evangelism is a caring human personality.

Hopelessness. In its extreme form, this pain is a psychiatric disturbance called depression—the most commonly treated emotional maladjustment of the seventies. Anti-depressant medicines now run a close second in sales to Valium, the anti-anxiety agent which bloomed in the sixties. Fifty years ago, the most common human pain American Christianity tried to heal was guilt. During the 1950s and 1960s, this shifted to a mood of religious doubt and anxiety. But today, people are more likely to feel an acute sense of discouragement regarding their ability to cope with the chaos life throws at them. That kind of pain drives them to search for *security* and *hope*—which in turn requires a search for *authority*. This explains the renaissance of biblical truth-seeking among young adults in our culture. It also tells us why mainline ministers whose theology inclines them in that direction get such a positive response to biblical preaching and teaching.

Purposelessness. Communism has flourished on a world scale by meeting the human yearning to join self to a larger purpose. It offers an opportunity for actively engaging a larger portion of one's moral energies than routine life allows. It provides a subordination of ego to a great purpose, small private goals to larger ends, individual personhood to a collective structure. This brings a sense of inner harmony which in the past was achieved through religious experience. Because Americans have been protected by affluent materialism, communism didn't flourish here. But other movements based on *spiritual* rather than *economic* ideals have. The Moonies and other sects demand "everything" from believers and get it. Why? Because people have a deep need for the feeling of "wholeness" and well-being that comes from giving small life to big goals. Shy young people who join exotic religious groups find an instant, strong sense of self-identity.

Fear. A poor man in Louisiana was arrested for being a flim-flam artist. When brought before the bar of justice, the bailiff announced, "The State of Louisiana versus Joe Brown!" The accused softly muttered under his breath, "Lord, what a majority!" A lot of people feel that way when the cup of life overflows with problems—inflation, divorce, alienation, self-doubt. The popularity of can-do/motivational/goal-setting/confidence-raising/positive thinking/success cultists like Zig Ziglar tell us how frightfully insecure and fearful of failure are people in our society. Crystal Cathedral theologies yield well in the eighties, not because they are slick, commercial manipulations but because they meet deep needs. The enormous pressure to succeed in school, college, and work has trussed the psyche with stresses that scream for relief. One way out is through big antidotes of "I can." Religiously based, positive hypnosis can have immense healing effect on persons who fear failure with the same sort of intensity that citizens in the Middle Ages feared the Bubonic Plague.

Flip the New Testament pages. Were not the persons who most readily received the Good News those who were most aware of their need for it? The poor, the maimed, the halt, the blind, the sinners heard him gladly. Those in good health who carried heavy life responsibilities and knew they were not adequate for their burdens also responded. Individuals who received the Gospel most quickly were not the self-confident optimists of their time but those who lived with sobering, perhaps desperate, experiences. Growing churches of today know those persons are still out there, and they work at meeting those needs.

Emptiness. People in a society riddled by drastic change are torn away from their identity roots. When that happens, they seek a strong framework of authority that can provide an anchor of continuity to keep them from falling apart on the inside. The electronic evangelists seem to understand this need. They know that the world is filled with empty people who feel ignored and unneeded. Workers who feel like commodities in the employment world. Citizens who feel like pawns of politicians. Parents who feel helpless in the face of a drug culture that can kidnap their youngsters without their permission. The evangelical, biblically-based theology of hope, which seems better than anything else to turn on the masses today, does not derive its power from the manipulative ability of a Schuller or Roberts, but from the unpredictable, pothole-ridden highway of history through which Americans must pass on their personal journeys.

Islam, a religion of the sword, made excellent progress among the people it defeated in Asia and Africa. Christianity, a religion of love and meekness, succeeded among the warrior tribes of Europe but made slow progress among the world's meeker millions. But is not this paradox consistent with Christian evangelism in our own day? Don't people always wish to be very different from what they are at present? Do not fearful persons respond best to a theology of courage? Do not depressed individuals always respond best to a theology of hope? As Jesus said, "Those who are well have no need of a physician. . ." (Matthew 9:12).

The Word Among the Words

What happens in the pulpits of fast-growing churches? Is the sermon a significant precipitating factor in their expansion? Paul, a notable leader of growing churches, ranked it high. "And how are they to believe in him of whom they have never heard? And how are they to hear without a preacher?" (Romans 10:14). But how should *we* rank it? Is it everything? Nothing? Crucial? Peripheral? Do inspiring sermons cause church growth? Or, are they a tasty frosting on the *real cause* of church growth—need-meeting programmatic life?

Preaching may not be as important a growth factor today as in the 1920s. But neither is it that triviality we judged it in the sixties. A church must have its act together in *other places* besides morning worship; but the pulpit will be *one* of those obvious places where that together act is viewed by the public.

Brevity. The pastor of one large-growth church preaches an average of thirteen minutes each week. Brevity in that extreme is rare, and the sermon length in most other growth congregations runs near the standard twenty minutes. Worship seldom exceeds sixty minutes. Many people who attend mainline churches, especially males, find their anger point rising toward ignition as the clock moves past twelve noon. The oral tradition in their heads says Christian things should take about one hour. Anything beyond that adds up to grand larceny of their time schedule. Preachers who break in and steal, regardless of their profound insights, will meet passive/ aggressive resistance. The saints stay home and stare at the tube or hit the golf course with increasing frequency. When recriminated by their consciences or spouses, they usually say, "He just goes on forever." When Paul preached too long one night, Eutychus went to sleep and fell out the window (Acts 20:9). When modern pulpiteers disregard the clock, people fall out of church.

Biblical. When members of a small church in East Texas were asked to list the causes of their church's rapid growth, the number one factor in the collated tabulations was "Bible-centered preaching." The evangelism chairperson for a rapidly growing black congregation in Indianapolis says, "One of our major evangelistic

105

strengths is the pulpit. In a celebrative service each week, members and visitors are filled with pointed, powerful, positive, spirit-filled, enthusiastic preaching. 'Teaching nuggets' [study questions] from the sermon are printed in the prior week's bulletin. Each formal Bible class—junior high through adult—studies and discusses these. The people-oriented, Christ-centered sermons appeal to the needs of people who are met and accepted where they are and for what they are and looked upon in terms of what they can become. Positive attitudes produce positive self-images; thus, the person in turn raises his own level and by so doing raises his respect and concern for his fellow man. Our new members frequently attest to the drawing power of the pastor's sermons. One person said, 'My nephew, a young adult of twenty-three, came to my house and excitedly preached Dr. Benjamin's sermon, quoting the scriptures used. I felt I wanted to find out more about anything and/or anybody who could excite him in this manner. So I came, found out, and joined.'"

In the 1950s, a *philosophical* style of preaching was popular. High in life-situation content, it often contained a low percentage of biblical material. Pew residents of the 1960s began hearing a new mix. Sermons often contained a high percentage of *psychological* content. Everything changed in the seventies. Young adult churchgoers led the way in demanding a higher percentage of *biblical* content in sermons. The same pastor who used only 10 percent biblical expository content in his 1955 model message began discovering that his people wanted a sermon mixture containing as much as 50 percent biblical paragraphs.

Belief in the Efficacy of Preaching. Pastors of growing churches believe that preaching helps persons find healing and wholeness. They understand that the Word has power to create people who are doers of the Word. Pastors who do not believe this soon falter in their pulpit preparation. They never give preaching its rightful priority in their time schedule unless they perceive the mysterious potency in the spoken word.

A United Methodist pastor, Theodore W. Loder, puts it this way, ". . .the whole intent of my ministry here is to touch you in some way so you will decide to live! Forever! What I have for the touching is not a sword but words, finally only words: words not only in this pulpit but in meetings, in offices, in homes, hospitals, on the street; words to carry ideas, challenges, dreams; words to bear whatever truth they can; words to open the mind, reach the heart, steel the will; words to move you, enable, encourage, enlarge you; words to set you *free*—set us free."[1]

Christ-Centered. Beginning preachers in conservative denominations usually emphasize the theme of morality. In theologically

---

[1] From a sermon by Theodore W. Loder devoted to interpreting how he sees ministry. *Clergy Talk*, Vol. 1, No. 2, mimeo by Colbert S. Cartwright, Trinity-Brazos Area Minister, Christian Church in the Southwest (Disciples of Christ).

liberal denominations, beginning preachers often stress social action. Why? Because a young preacher is usually making up his or her own mind about these issues at this stage of life. In the second phase of homiletical development, usually during the pastor's first few years out of seminary, sermons dwell much on the meaning and nature of the church. Why? Because the preacher is still trying to work out his own understanding of the church and its purposes. At the final, more mature phase, preachers emphasize Christ and his significance for every human being in every life situation. This "adult phase" of the evolving homiletician wears best over the long haul.

Faith-Oriented Rather than Academic-Oriented. The science of biblical "higher criticism" on which so many mainline pastors cut their teeth may have strengthened scholarship but it has done little to strengthen faith. No society is improved by disillusionment about its holy writ or its most precious institutions. Men and nations are empowered by having something great to look up to—some grand illusions of potential perfection from which they can draw their hope for rising above mediocrity. Biblical scholars in mainline denominations have, in the name of scholarship, tried to improve the quality of common faith by spotlighting imperfections in the cornerstones of that faith. While these imperfections certainly exist, examining them carefully with a pulpit microscope does not improve the sturdiness of the building or the sense of well-being in those who have chosen this house for their home.

The intellectuals in graduate seminaries shouldn't give up scholarship. Academic knowledge is important and necessary. But it can weave such a spell over people who enjoy it that they get trapped in it. Thus mesmerized, they can easily forget that academics are like the spade with which you dig a trench. You don't put that spade upon an altar and worship it; you dig with it. Jesus was a scholar, but not for scholarship's sake. He used his learning to help people. Paul was a scholar, but not for scholarship's sake. He used this tool to preach the Good News to a world lost in dark idolatry.

The dark moods of the masses stem from struggles to protect their children against drugs and personal disaster, from the inflation that eradicates all hope of financial security, and from the personal sense of isolation and nothingness in a faceless society run amuck. When they come to worship, they seek words that might help them in these matters.

Denominations with more fundamentalistic and dogmatic theologies are presently showing greater numerical growth than mainline churches. As others have noted, this fact has multiple causes. But one of the reasons they succeed is because they are clear in communicating their ideas about the faith. Others, who pride themselves on theological and intellectual honesty, often succeed in sounding muddleheaded and confused about what they believe. An unchurched man with whom a mainline pastor worked for six years without success joined a local Church of Christ (non-instrumental). A friend asked him why. He replied, "They told me what to do. They said, 'Do one, two, and three.' I could understand that." Mainliners can easily write this off as a simplistic, dogmatic approach. Perhaps so. But if you are in the message business, having a stack of them on your desk is never enough. They ought to be delivered.

People-Centered Rather than Scholarship-Centered. A little girl returned from her first day in school and proudly exclaimed, "Mother, I was the brightest one in my class!" "That's fine, Janie," her mother said, "But tell me how it happened." "Well," Janie replied, "the teacher told each one of us to draw a picture on the blackboard, and then the others were to guess what the picture was. Mine was the only one no one could guess—but I knew exactly what it was all the time!"

Pastors can be simultaneously erudite and out of touch with their people's reality. During a most unsettled period of history in Europe (1775-1825), a number of German philosophers whose towns lay in the middle of battlefields were totally absorbed in producing thousands of pages of abstruse philosophy. Drunk with words, most of them were convinced that they alone had a handle on ultimate truth.

The preacher's greatest danger is not that members of the congregation will murmur, "He isn't very intelligent." More often, they will criticize him for having lost the common touch. He does not connect with where they hurt and what they fear out there in the trenches. There is a place in the cobwebbed, ivory towers of seminaries for conversations about high criticism, apocalypticism, and *Heilsgeschichte.* But people who walk into the Sunday morning pulpit should attempt communication with normal folks. That is not accomplished by battering them with scholastic double-talk.

Indigenous Worship

A judicatory executive attending an ecumenical worship service in Kingston, Jamaica, was impressed by the music being developed among the congregations there. A Jesuit priest had composed music for the complete Roman Catholic Mass in Jamaican rhythmic style. These indigenous music and worship materials are seen and applauded everywhere the church flourishes on the mission field. Less well recognized is the need to make worship indigenous to the various cultures in different communities across North America. Growing churches have a knack for sensing what feels right to their community residents. Rather than trying to impose ideas gleaned from their seminary setting, they go with the flow of what works *here.*

"Our worship service visitors are looking for something meaningful," says a Rocky Mountain pastor. "Most people don't move to this tourist-oriented, resort community with the idea that they are going to find a church home. Many of them come here in order to escape their past. They would often prefer to leave their church relationship behind, too. So it is very important that they find meaning in our worship."

The pastor of a growing church in the western edge of Oklahoma City says, "One of the most important factors for evangelism in our congregation is the Sunday morning worship hour. I do not have the audacity to believe that I am a great preacher. Most of us will never become that. But with discipline and good study habits we can become good preachers. Think of the opportunity we have in that hour. If we preach to 300 people for twenty minutes, that's 100 hours of personal influence. Not that the sermon alone is important. During the years when we have had good leadership in the choir, we have had good growth. And the worship department gives me the privilege of changing the order of worship. We add new ideas occasionally and do some creative things. One Sunday I preached a sermon entitled 'God's Lollipops'—the idea that the special things in life give it sweetness and tastefulness. We handed out lollipops to everyone in the congregation. On another occasion, we had a Bach Sunday. All the music we sang—the responses, the prelude—all were Bach. It is important that the worship service be new and fresh, creative and subject to change."

The pastor in a small Texas town says, "In the beginning, we did not have a choir. With only twenty-eight people attending, you don't have much of a singing program. But we make the most of that hour. I pray for that hour and prepare for that hour. Apart from the sermon itself, the children's sermon, the pastoral prayer, good singing, and the communion meditation are highlights of our service. Our invitation hymn is not so prolonged as to make people feel uncomfortable, but it is very important. The service is formal but not cut and dried. During the informal moments, people can reach out and shake hands with each other."

One growing congregation uses the following formula to be certain they are providing indigenous music for all age groups in the church: Variety, not purely classical—a mixture of modern responses and anthems. The opening hymn is classical and stately, like "God of Grace and God of Glory." The second hymn is often from the gospel music era, like "Amazing Grace." The third hymn is usually something contemporary, like "I Am the Way" by M. Wynne (copyright 1967 by Louisville Area Council of Churches), or "In Remembrance," from *Celebrate Life* by Ragan Courtney and Burl Red, or one of the many fine pieces from Richard Avery and Donald Marsh. Many of the responses use modern words set to a familiar tune like "Edelweiss" that everyone can easily sing.

Whatever is done in worship, visitors should get the feeling of life and creativity rather than six-foot-deep ruts that never change. Worship should arouse some enthusiasm (the word *enthusiasm* means "filled with God"). Worship in many static churches seems "filled with sleepiness." Few people make major life commitments in a semicomatose state. Strong singing doesn't *automatically* connect human

109

experience to the God experience, but it increases the chances.

According to historians, one of the reasons for Calvanism's rapid spread in the sixteenth century was the tremendous way Calvinists sang their psalms in worship. James H. Nicols, a scholar especially interested in Reformed worship, has observed: "For over a century, representative Reformed spokesmen in this country and in Great Britain have been confessing that one of our most conspicuous weaknesses is in public worship. We are often commended for our theological scholarship, our intellectual vitality, and contributions to education. Of the churches dating from the Reformation, we have probably the best record of defending church independence of state control, while at the same time maintaining an active stance of social and political responsibility. No other modern church tradition has produced more consistently solid and powerful preaching. But who has ever converted to a Congregationalist or Presbyterian church by the expressiveness and reverence of its common worship? Whether it is cause or effect or both, this one-sided character of Reformed worship seems to be related to certain sociological limitations in the Reformed churches. These churches are predominently middle- and upper-middle-class churches. . . . Our worship is characterized by its highly intellectualized form, its poverty of imaginative suggestiveness, its emotional reticence. . . . For much the same reason, I suspect, in missionary outreach we find it very difficult to establish any self-sustaining Presbyterian congregations among Negroes, Italians, or Slavs. They just don't seem to feel really themselves when they are asked to worship like British-American business and professional people. . . . Is it perhaps possible that we have allowed our definition of Reformed worship to be narrowed unduly?"[2]

This historian is noting what would be obvious on the mission field but is not so easily seen at home—failure to establish indigenous worship. Rapidly growing denominations in America have not suffered from this inflexibility. They *still do* what Methodists and Presbyterians did in their earlier growing days on the American frontier—fit the music and worship to the people instead of trying to remake the people's tastes to fit their own personal choices. Jesus put it this way: "Neither is new wine put into old wineskins; if it is, the skins burst, and the wine is spilled, and the skins destroyed; but new wine is put into fresh wineskins, and so both are preserved" (Matthew 9:17).

How long will churches need to keep revising their worship in order to meet the needs of people in their community? That task is never finished because a new generation keeps coming on.

---

[2]*Theology Today,* July 1954.

Group Discussion Questions

1. Do you feel our worship services are indigenous to the people who live in our community? Illustrate your answer by comparing our church with other congregations.
2. What is the average time length of our worship service? How do the class members feel about that? Pass your opinions on to the appropriate decision-making committee or department in your church.
3. What concrete changes or improvements would you suggest for our worship service? If the class has a consensus about any of these needed changes, pass them on to the appropriate planning group in your church.
4. Do you know of other churches in town that seem to be growing rapidly? If you have personally attended one of their worship services, describe the ways in which you feel it is different from ours.
5. Do you think our service best meets the needs of younger people, middle-aged persons, or older people? Why?
6. What are your feelings about the hymnbook we use? About the songs we typically sing? Why do you feel this way? Is there a difference of opinion in the class on this matter? What do you think causes these viewpoint variations?

Beware the man of one book.
—St. Thomas Aquinas, 1227?-1274

10

Overcoming Hobbyhorsitis

A serious illness pervades the cerebral system of numerous church leaders. Most of them don't know they have it. Nor are their pastors aware. In fact, clergy often unknowingly disseminate and exacerbate this disease. Now for the good news: this infection is treatable. You can think your way out of it. Light applications of common sense kill the bacteria that spread it.

Do you want to find out whether leaders in your congregation have this ailment? Interview several individuals, asking them this open-ended question: "What do you think makes a church grow?" The first person you interrogate may say, "I'll tell you what it is. It's the preaching. We just don't have preaching like we used to. I don't know what they're teaching the students over at that seminary, but it isn't public speaking! If we had better preaching, we would have more people coming down the aisle!!" This man has now grown vehement. He will probably clinch his argument with the story of some pulpit giant who served the church with distinction in years gone by.

Ask another person the same question: "What do you think makes a church grow?" That individual may say, "You've got to have a strong youth program. You can't get the parents there if you don't get the kids to come. Why, I remember when Rev. Perfect Youth Worker was here. The young people came to church and youth programs in droves." Then you get a story from the good old days, ripe with the flowery distortions of rose-colored hindsight.

The next person you poll may answer like this: "That's simple. We are not a praying people. If we got all our members involved in prayer groups, things would start happening around this church."

Ask another person. She may say, "We don't study the Bible in our church. Get everyone into solid Bible study and you attract more visitors." By this time, you should not need to continue with more interviews. You can see the shape of this distorted thinking: hobbyhorsitis—the tendency to say that a complex result arises from one particular, simple cause. Growth may involve all or several of the above, but it never comes from one of them alone.

Axiom #10: Growing churches have a diversity of programming. Their life together contains multifaceted activity. They open many doors from the church into the world. They program to meet the needs of many different types of people at many different ages and stages of emotional, spiritual, and physical maturity. They recognize that people are different from each other—even Christian people. They don't all like the same things. And even those who do like the same things find their needs changing. The woman who needs a bowling league this year may need a prayer group next year—and vice versa.

The big attraction of a covered dish dinner is getting to choose what you like. That provides an excitement which the most elaborate of one-course meals can't give. Growing churches understand this principle. They do a very solid traditional program, but they don't stop there. They offer other options, from music programs for children, to singles groups, to softball leagues, to prayer groups, to Bible studies, to aerobics classes. Their style is conglomerate. A large number of small groups or classes designed to address a wide variety of interests meet regularly under the church's umbrella. Each congregation sets up some limits regarding the type of groups it will shelter (few would host a meeting of the Nazi Party), but they all make available a wide variety of options. In these diverse settings different kinds of people can enjoy a sense of community and common interest without demanding that all others in the congregation participate or agree.

Mulifaceted Adult Work

Growing churches are particularly proficient in providing for a wide range of adult preferences. The young citizens who overflowed suburban churches in the 1950s often selected a congregation on the basis of the Sunday school facilities. Young adults of the eighties still seek quality Christian education for their kids—which is one of the reasons why the children's sermon has become such an important component of the morning worship service: it symbolically proves that a church cares about the whole family. But members of the current parent generation look for something more than religious nurture for their children. They want to know what this congregation has going for adults. They are concerned about their own self-enrichment. Sacrificing their life for the future of the children is out as a lifestyle. For them, Christianity is not just for kids.

Studies by Warren J. Hartman identify five different "audiences" among the membership of the United Methodis Church: (1) The fellowship group. These individuals are looking for affiliation and support. This highly mobile, well-educated group contains young, old, and a large number of men. (2) The evangelistic concerns group. This extremely loyal group is concerned to win others to Christ. These are predominately older members with the lowest education and income levels. (3) The study group. This young, well-educated group supplies a disproportionate share of church leadership. They seek opportunities for involvement and education. (4) The social concerns group. Containing a high percentage of women, this group is eager to involve the church in community and world issues. This group has the poorest record of church attendance. (5) The mixed bag group. These persons share two or more of the above concerns. Fellowship is usually one of them.[1] Other mainline church members seem to fall into similar categories. So, when any denomination talks about "our kind of people," they are really describing numerous kinds of people with several different interests.

For Instance...

From a growing church in Houston: "We offer a full range of religious programming, so that people who visit our church will find something to meet their individual needs. Our adult Sunday school is a good example of this attempt to offer something of value to people who approach Christianity from widely divergent faith perspectives. More conservative members seem drawn to our Bible study class. Those with more liberal faith orientations seem drawn either to our "Read and Rap Class" (a book study) or our "Contemporary Christian Living Class," which seeks to bring biblical faith to a crossing point with the issues of today. This shotgun approach to adult Christian education is also reflected in other aspects of our church's program. We have an adult and a youth choir. The early service is much more informal, while the second service is more traditional in nature. We don't try to put everyone in the same box. We expect diversity, and program to meet it."

---

[1]Warren J. Hartman, *Membership Trends: A Study of Decline and Growth in the United Methodist Church 1949-1975,* Discipleship Resources, 1976.

From a growing church in Oklahoma: "We are a community, family-centered church. We've had a puppet ministry. We've had musical groups. We've divided our congregation from time to time into *koinonia* groups which met in various parts of our community for study. We've had ERA debates, Parent Effectiveness Training classes, Marriage Communication events. We developed a "Dinner for Eight" plan: these members meet in groups of four couples for dinners in each other's homes. We have organized talk-back sessions and cottage meetings throughout the community. A few summers ago we had a "Walk to Church Day" in observation of Earth Sunday. We encouraged our people to walk or ride bicycles. We arranged designated places—shopping centers and school parking lots—for them to park their cars so they could walk whatever distance they wanted to. Some even rode horses. We have tried to develop the kind of programming that appeals to people from all modes and styles of living."

A Kentucky church: "From the first time a young couple brings a new baby to the church nursery through the time that child becomes part of the senior citizen set, every congregation must provide programs which meet the particular needs of that age group. If a young couple returns from worship to find their baby with a messy diaper and obviously unhappy, they'll find another nursery the next time they venture out for worship. If a prospective family includes grandparents, parents, and children in the same household, they must find a church home with a program which nurtures all their needs. Attractive, clean, happy-looking facilities are also important aspects of programming. Persons aren't eager to leave a nice-looking, air-conditioned, comfortable home to worship in a run-down, unclean, drab-looking building. Parking is another essential part of the program. Studies indicate that people will walk a certain number of feet from their cars to the church building if they can see it from where they park. If they park around the corner where they cannot see the building, they will walk only half that far. That is why downtowns are deserted in major cities. The shopping centers offer free parking and easy accessibility."

From an Illinois Church: "A little bit of something for everybody. We do a lot of drama. When we built a new building, we constructed a stage area so we could put on plays. We've done everything from the old *Christ in the Concrete City* to things that we write ourselves. People love to act. They like to get up before others and perform. We have done several things with sports. You're going to lose your golf players in the summertime. So we have the Nineteenth Hole Golf League: men's golf league, women's golf league, mixed golf league. The church is the nineteenth hole. We have a basketball league in the winter. We have a senior citizen group of 136, which is more people than we have in the congregation at that age level. We have three choir directors and several choirs.

"And don't pass up the property committee. Men like to do things, and they like to do them together. Our property committee has been as evangelical as any group I know. They have won people to the church by spreading tar. Three weeks ago, we had to dig up the sewer. The chairman of the committee said, 'We can do it ourselves. We don't need professional help.' Sixteen men showed up to open the sewer and repair it. Their wives fixed lunch. All of these things happen not because of what the pastor does but because of what the people themselves wish to do. A growing church gives them the freedom and the opportunity to plug in where they are interested."

One simple way to increase your range of programming is to increase the number of worship services. It's always impossible to predict what will happen in a specific church, but two services generally attract between 5 percent and 15 percent more people than one service. Do you want to determine the value of this option for your congregation? Establish an experimental early worship service for six months. At the end of that period, evaluate the new service in three ways: (1) a questionnaire filled in by persons who attend the early service; (2) a comparison of the total number of people who attended worship services during that six-month period with the same calendar months of the previous year; and (3) an opinion from the financial secretary regarding whether the new service has produced any improvement in giving patterns. Generally speaking, persons who oppose an earlier worship service will feel more positive if it is conducted on this kind of experimental basis.

Board members who oppose a second service are often convinced that it will divide the church into two different groups. They are somewhat right about this. But a church is already divided into different groups: those who attend and those who don't—the active workers and the passive receivers—those who are well acquainted with each other and those who aren't. Members of large congregations never become thoroughly acquainted with *all* other members, nor is this necessary. The fellowship quality of a church's life does not depend on how many worship services it holds.

Another important quality needed in multifaceted programming is change. New programs need to be instituted each year as older ones become the norm or passé! Boredom is the root of much evil in church life. Sameness, sameness, sameness puts the mind to sleep. Something new grabs attention and recharges commitment. This "law of diminishing responsiveness to sameness" causes retail merchants to redesign their shelf displays. "If you want to change the response, change the stimulus," they say. This boredom syndrome applies in *all* aspects of church work. Most churches don't suffer from poor participation as much as from poor imagination. People need new opportunities and new possibilities. They need to feel they are moving forward rather than sinking into the muddy ruts of their own past history.

How Much Is Enough?

How much programming should a church organize? Ordinarily, more than they have at present. Additional programs, rather than working present members to death, usually attract new people who become a part of the leadership needed for the increased programming. Check your church for the following formula: count all the groups—Sunday school classes, choirs, women's groups, men's groups, cabinet, board, functional committees, etc. Then, divide the total participating church membership by the total number of groups. If the result of this division is larger than sixteen, the church does not contain enough primary groups. If your church fails to measure up to this "sweet-sixteen principle," it is short on fellowship and participation opportunities. People roll away before they ever get firmly related to the church, like apples off the top of a full basket. Ironically, the larger the church the greater the likelihood of underprogramming. The staff and leaders feel that "We are so terribly busy; this church is surely providing a very wide-ranging program!" Their own hectic schedule thus keeps them from seeing the program opportunities which, if instituted, would mean growth for the church.

Where to Begin?

"We are just a small church," the membership chair said. "We can't do everything a large church can do. Where should we start?"

Begin with a graded choir program. Launch as many youth choirs, and children's choirs, as you can get into the water. Use volunteer or part-time paid help if you don't have full-time music staff. Strengthen your youth programs. According to recent research, more than 75 percent of unchurched Americans would like to see their children attend a religious education program. The American pagan has many spiritual needs of which he is not conscious. But he has a few *conscious* needs. One of these is his children. While youth and music programs will not by themselves produce growth, the church is often judged by whether these programs are offered.

Get your adults involved in dreaming dreams. Bring them together in small groups in homes. Ask them to fill in an "I wish for our church" form. Discuss the kinds of programming they would like to see us try this year. Refer the ideas to the appropriate church committees for study. After much brainstorming input, make a decision to try two or three of these ideas the first year. Allow some of the persons who suggested these programs to help carry them out. At the end of the year, evaluate. Discard what didn't work. Brainstorm again. Launch some of the best-sounding ideas. New ideas and programs tend to breed more new ideas and programs.

A Sunday school teacher was using an Easter lily to illustrate the miracle of new life. "Now," she said, "who can tell me what makes this beautiful lily blossom forth from this drab-looking little bulb?"

"God does it," said the little girl promptly.

The small son of a farmer spoke up and said, "Fertilizer helps." Multifaceted, need-meeting, ever-changing diversified programs are the fertilizers of church growth.

Group Discussion Questions

1. This chapter defines hobbyhorsitis as the tendency to ascribe church growth to one single cause. What is the most frequent hobbyhorsitis symptom that you hear people in our church mention?
2. What new program has our congregation launched this year?
3. In your opinion, which of our church programs have the most significance for adults?
4. How does our church measure up to the "sweet-sixteen principle?"
5. Do you think our congregation contains the five kinds of persons discovered in the United Methodist study reported in this chapter? Illustrate reasons for your opinion.
6. In the section of this chapter that illustrates programs from growing churches, do you see any ideas you feel our church should consider instituting this year?
7. Does our church presently push some programs that have obviously lost their appeal to most of the members? Illustrate. Do you have any ideas for programs that might effectively replace these worn-out ideas?

Love your neighbor as yourself.
—Jesus of Nazareth

11

Helping Pick up the Pieces

A seminary student on an English bicycle was returning to his apartment from the grocery store. Clutching a large sack of groceries in one arm, his other hand was curled around the handlebars and the hand-brake lever. As he turned at a busy city intersection, the grocery sack split, spilling contents and dignity across the pavement. Scrambling to gather his lost edibles, he became aware of a man standing on the street corner with a bundle of materials under his arm. After watching the young cyclist's frantic grocery-collecting for a moment, the man stepped off the curb and handed him a religious pamphlet describing the values of salvation.

This street-corner evangelist wasn't doing something essentially *bad*. But his timing was off. He acted the right way in the wrong circumstances. Churches must, of course, recognize that a person is more than matter. Human transcendent aspects are our most important feature. And that has certainly been one of the saddest lackings among mainline denominations in recent decades—the failure to remember that life is more than bread. On the other hand, the opposite perception is an equally invalid half-truth. Life does require bread, along with a bunch of other nonspiritual items. And churches that pretend people's physical needs are not important seldom get a good hearing on spiritual issues.

Axiom #11: Growing churches try to serve the needs of community residents outside the church as well as those inside. These churches do not concentrate *only* on helping people pick up the fragmented pieces of their lives. Their leaders have advanced beyond that 1965 model naiveté. They take an interest in people's needs at the levels of both the Bread of Life *and* the bread of the body. This model is not new. Wherever he could, Jesus did both things. He met the paralyzed man's greatest need: "My son, your sins are forgiven" (Mark 2:5). But he also met his physical need:". . .rise, take up your pallet and go home" (Mark 2:11).

Many persons were attracted to Jesus' message about spiritual healing because he cared enough to provide physical healing. But Jesus never confused these two self-help activities. Nor did he say that either was sufficient without the other. During the temptations that prefaced the first chapter of his ministry, he rejected the high-sounding idea of feeding the body rather than the spirit: "Man shall not live by bread alone, but by every word that proceeds from the mouth of God" (Matthew 4:4). But he also said that failing to feed the hungry and clothe the naked is to neglect God (Matthew 25:31-46). Growing churches also hold these twin tasks in positive tension.

Evangelical churches have been accused of letting the world go hungry while they massage their complacent souls with a warm spiritual backrub. The mainline ecumenical side of Christendom has been accused of letting the world go to hell with a full stomach. If accurate, both criticisms would be scriptual. Jesus says the big test of our spirituality is what we do to help troubled people on Jericho Roads (Luke 10:30-37). But he also repeatedly addressed the need for spiritual work: "The harvest is plentiful, but the laborers are few; pray therefore the Lord of the harvest to send out laborers into his harvest" (Matthew 9:37). When Jesus says, "You shall love your neighbor as yourself," he doesn't mean love them with bread or love them with the preached Word. He means both. As Alan Walker, the United Methodist leader from Australia, says: "A born-again Christian without a social conscience is a menace. On the other hand, a social activist Christian who imagines you can change life by changing structures—that man is a menace. For the gospel of Jesus is at once personal and social."[1]

---

[1]From an address by Alan Walker at the 1980 World Convention of Churches of Christ in Honolulu, Hawaii.

The Ultimate in Community Service

Cypress Creek Christian Church (Disciples of Christ) in Houston, Texas, is one of the most rapidly growing churches in its denomination. Because this new congregation was established during the 1970s, it had the option of developing a theology of evangelism prior to the time it built a building. The pastor, Dr. Glenn Wilkerson, describes the church's theological rationale in this way: "We found that three historic mission objectives have been in existence since the earliest stirrings of the church in the first century. First, *kerygma*—proclamation of the good news about Jesus Christ. Second, *koinonia*—Christian fellowship, the gathered body of Christ loving one another. And third, *diakonia*—Christian service, the congregation going out in the name of Christ to serve the larger community. While all churches engage in all three of these mission objectives, one will usually be emphasized a bit more than the others. Deciding on which emphasis one will use is crucial, because this dictates the church's self-understanding of its mission to its nearby neighborhoods. Publicizing the emphasis selected in the surrounding community becomes the theological rationale for making evangelism contacts.

"Our long-range planning committee decided upon a *diakonia* emphasis. We want to be known in our community as a congregation that serves. Jesus, quoting Isaiah, says, "The Spirit of the Lord is upon me. . ." (Luke 4:18). How does Jesus know the spirit of the Lord is upon him? Because it compels him to serve. This is *diakonia*, and this is the mission emphasis our church has chosen to lift up in the eyes of our surrounding community.

"A church in Dallas uses a promotional flyer which features a picture taken by a professional photographer showing an elderly woman, obviously a grandmother type, with a little girl (presumably her granddaughter) sitting on her lap. They are reading the Bible together. And then at the bottom it says, 'A Church Where Generations Meet.' That's a *koinonia* emphasis. The congregation I pastored in Fort Worth decided to emphasize *kerygma* and we became known as the bus ministry church. Here at Cypress Creek, we have decided to emphasize *diakonia*, so we are known as the community center church. And that's the theological rationale for making our evangelism contacts.

"Extending this theology into reality, Cypress Creek has assumed the stance that the church is not a building; the church is people. Church buildings should be looked upon as a tool of mission, just like a hymnbook or collection plate. We therefore call our congregation the Cypress Creek Christian Church. We call our building the Cypress Creek Community Center. We utilize our building during the week as a tool of mission to house nonprofit, community-service organizations whom we feel can assist us in ministering to our community. We believe that the church-community center concept enables us to elevate the quality of life, not only for our congregation, but also for all residents of our community. This high profile that the community center concept gives our congregation has been of inestimable value in our evangelism work.

"We have two permanent resident users of the building: Interface Counseling, a pastoral counseling service, and a Planned Parenthood Education branch office. All the Scouting groups use the building. Little Theatre is another regular tenant. We house Defensive Driving, which is a state program. The Justice of the Peace sends traffic-ticket holders to Defensive Driving instead of fining them. We house an organization called HOPE (Houston Organizations for Parent Education), a Lamaze childbirth group. All sorts of religious groups meet there—everything from Bahai faith to the Jewish Community North to a couple of Bible fellowships. They use both the sanctuary and our activity room at different times. The Seventh Day Adventists use our building every Saturday. We have a preschool and mother's day out four days a week. Various nonprofit groups use the building occasionally. For instance, all the garden clubs of the area, the NOW organization for women, a barbershop quartet group, and the astrological society.

"When organizations ask to use the building, we give them a fee structure for their particular group. One of our members did an accounting of what it actually cost us to put the building into use. Organizations pay about a third of that cost. The congregation picks up the remainder. But if an organization is without any funds whatsoever, they can request that the fee be waived. We have several organizations which don't pay for the building—for instance, all the Scouting groups. And we don't charge religious organizations for the worship services."

This congregation is not content to gaze through stained glass at the community and say, "How can we relate these people to our church?" They ask instead, "How can we relate ourselves and Christ's gospel to these people in this place?"

Service in Traditional Settings

Most growing churches can't build their building *after* they decide to engage in community service. They already have a building, and must fit the service work into it. But these more traditionally patterned growth congregations practice the same wide-open-door policy concerning their facilities. Many of them house long lists of community activities. They try to give meeting space to every group they possibly can.

These congregations are practicing a kind of evangelism retail merchants know well. They call it "increasing the traffic through the building." Why do some department stores house postal substations in their facilities? Not just as a gesture of public service. And do these stores place their mini-post offices conveniently right inside the front door? No, they are always at the back, where you must walk a long way. Why? Because you walk past much merchandise on your way to mail a package. *Increasing traffic flow through the building increases sales.* Churches that house community activities exercise that same principle. Some of the people who attend self-help activities return later to sample the spiritual goods.

A well-meaning property committee sometimes blocks this open-ministry approach. They see the highest goal of a church as protecting the paint and woodwork. Then, too, they may be concerned about the expense of broken glass, chipped paint, and dewalled walls. If this group short-circuits a service ministry, the best thing to do is attack. Say to them, "Studies show that more public availability of the church building automatically adds a few new church members each year. The extra offerings from these persons far more than compensate for any additional repairs and paint."

Another way most growing churches serve is through community involvements by their pastor. One minister in a smaller town reports participation in the following groups: board of directors for the Chamber of Commerce, founder and chairman for Youth Encounter and Solutions, board of directors for Lift, Inc. (a community improvement program), board of directors for the Department of Human Resources Mental Health and Mental Retardation Center, Lions Club member and chaplain for the state school. He sometimes feels a bit overextended but tries to relate where he can be helpful. We should warn, however, that the larger the community population the less the pastor's civic activities enhance evangelism results. And ministers who lose their balance in time commitments don't have enough clock left for other evangelism necessities, such as personal visits in homes.

A small town church whose older members hadn't seen children in church for twenty years developed this idea: "We gave a baby shower for two expectant mothers who had moved into the community. They were strangers. We gave them the shower not to indebt them or bribe them to join the church. In fact, they never did attend our church. But from that day on God brought expectant mothers, children, and youth. Right now, we have forty-six children in our church family. Through this ministry of contact, members who were secluded in their attitude changed their minds. They began to have a deeper interest in the unchurched people all around them."

The minister in another growing church says, "In my twelve years as pastor, there has been at least one personal tragedy in some family in our immediate area every year. Our church has responded beautifully. For example: A family's home burned down on Saturday night. They are not part of our church. The next morning the treasurer came to me and asked if we could write them a check for $500. Other board members quickly agreed. That afternoon we took the $500 check to them. While we were doing that, the women were busy gathering up clothing and food and finding them a place to stay. This personal involvement and caring is nothing more than our commitment to Christ being put into action. If you don't have that in a church, I'm sure not very much else is happening. That has been a factor in our church growth. People in the community see that personal caring."

Pastoral work and counseling with the unchurched is another service provided by many growth congregations. "Through hospital calling and nursing home visiting, you make a lot of contacts with friends and relatives," one pastor says. "You also call on some patients who are not part of your fellowship. Most of these don't lead to actual evangelism results, but a few do. And even if they don't, this is an important part of the church's service ministry."

Another pastor says, "I expend much of my personal life with people outside the church—often those whose marriages are in difficulty. I become not just their minister but their friend. They trust me. So in moments of frustration, they contact me. The people in our community are our field, not just the members in our building."

These human service efforts are not done in place of the primary spiritual mission of growing churches but as an accompaniment to that task. The church in every era is tempted to become too much like its culture. When that happens, it loses the power to call people to redemptive relationship with God. We see this problem most clearly in historical periods when the church loses its moral footing. During the Renaissance (the early 1500s just before Luther called for reform), almost every priest kept a concubine, as one writer of that era described, "to the glory of God and the Christian faith." We can see why that sort of secularization would cause churches to lose community influence. We do not so easily see the secularizing of the church which comes when it copies the social helping agencies around it and neglects its distinctive spiritual contribution. Sect and renewal groups are apt to become *so* unlike the people in their culture that no one will listen to them. Growing, evangelistic churches strike a balance between these two extremes. They penetrate the culture aggressively with many "love your neighbor" acts of kindness. But while doing that, they do not let the culture penetrate the church in ways that eliminate its unique spiritual change agent role.

Where to Begin?

Goethe said, "If Christians had their way, they would turn the world into one great hospital where everyone went around nursing each other." That cynical statement fell short of the truth. The world already *is* one great hospital. The big question is whether anybody is looking after the patients. Every human being on the face of the planet has deep needs that require nursing by friends, family, church, and neighbor. Each person we meet has hurts that can only be healed by someone else. Many just need a listening ear. Others need much more than that. The Family of God is the best equipment yet devised for meeting many of these needs. "As he went ashore he saw a great throng; and he had compassion on them, and healed their sick" (Matthew 14:14). If the body of Christ has real love for people, it still wants to do the same. Not just with mind and thought but in concrete actions.

Where to begin? Find one thing in the community that needs doing and do it. Find a real human need no other church is meeting and try to meet that need in the best possible way. This could be a singles program, mother's day out, day-care center, senior citizens program or any number of other things. Have your adult Sunday school classes, your church vestry, and your women's group brainstorm (without discussing the relative merits of each idea) the following questions: What human problems are other community groups already meeting? What problems are we able to meet through our church? What is the Spirit of God calling *us* to do?

"Where there is no vision, the people perish. . . ." (Proverbs 29:18, King James Version) When a church achieves a vision concerning people needs in the community, it begins basing its budget on helping meet these human needs instead of funding for institutional maintenance alone. This changed agenda is particularly helpful in smaller congregations. It moves their church personality from insecure introversion toward extroversion. This breaks up the sometimes legitimate suspicion that churches are interested only in themselves. Growing churches always have the reputation of being churches that really care about people—both inside and outside their walls. And they can't get that reputation without taking action. ". . . faith apart from works is dead," says James (James 2:26). And churches without works die, too, eventually.

Move Beyond the Lighthouse

One Christmas season when the ten-year-old daughter was not home, a little boy in her class called on the phone. The girl's mother answered and the boy said, "This is Mike Marshall. I just wondered if Beth still likes Curtis. Cause if she does, he wants to buy her a present." That may be a reliable approach for a grade-schooler but not for the church of Jesus Christ. Its people are in business to give love away—not just to persons who like them, but even to those who may not care for them.

Jesus could have said, "I am the light of the Jews," or "I am the light of Galilee." But he didn't. He said, "I am the light of the world . . ." (John 8:12). Jesus had no small dream. He was out to love the whole world! He might have said, "God so loved the Jews," or "God so loved the church." But he didn't. He said, "God so loved the world . . ." (John 3:16).

The doctor was puzzled. "You should be pretty well by this time," he said. "Have you followed my instructions?"

"Well, doctor," said the patient. "I've done most of them, but I can't take that two-mile walk every morning that you recommended.

I get too dizzy."

"What do you mean, 'dizzy'?" the doctor asked.

"Well, sir," said the patient, "I must have forgotten to tell you that I'm a lighthouse keeper."

Members of growing churches do not walk in circles in their lighthouse. Yes, they do remember to keep the lamp lit for a dark world. And that is their principle task. But they also climb down and man the lifeboats.

Group Discussion Questions

1. Make a list of the activities and programs you can think of by which our church has met human needs in the community during the past year.
2. Make a list of other community needs that you think our church ought to get involved in helping to meet. If the class has a consensus on any of these ideas, forward them to the appropriate church planning committee. Consider having the class appoint a committee to investigate doing this as a class project.
3. What community groups use our church building each month? What do you see as the positives and negatives of this relationship with outside groups?
4. In what ways is your pastor involved in service to the local community? Can you give illustrations of how this has at times been helpful to your church's evangelism work?
5. Do you think it is accurate to say that every person you meet has some deep needs? Make a list of those. In what ways can the church help meet these needs?
6. Someone has said that there is much more warmth and caring among members of some denominations than others. Do you think that is an accurate opinion? Illustrate your answer.

Whatever you can do, or dream you can, begin it. Boldness has genius, power, and magic in it.

— Goethe, 1749-1832

12

Going Public

Strict new noise rules keep the check-in area at the Phoenix Airport pleasantly quiet. During Christmas season, even the familiar Salvation Army bells are prohibited. But by the end of her first day, the faithful attendant had learned that failure to attract attention means financial drouth: the kettle was still empty. The following day, she improvised, and money began to flow again. Christmas travelers saw the uniformed fund raiser waving two signs in the air. One said "ding" and the other "dong."

Webster defines public relations as the art or science of developing reciprocal understanding between a person, firm, or institution and the public in order to achieve good will. Jesus said, "Let your light so shine before men, that they may see your good works and give glory to your Father who is in heaven" (Matthew 5:16). Public relations for churches, broken down to its most basic element, is *kindness*—letting people know where they can get light. *Axiom #12: Growing churches have high public visibility in the eyes of community residents.*

Outward Signs of Inner Spirit

A smile is the outward manifestation of something positive going on inside the organism. A frown denotes an opposite condition. Community image begins with the sign on the lawn. It describes the spirit of people in the building. A shabby sign with faded, peeling paint is a public relations frown. It says, "We don't care. Why should you?"

Take a tip from Denny's Restaurant. Build signs high off the ground and perpendicular to the street—so the eyes of fast-moving motorists catch them from a distance. One congregation gained great growth speed after erecting a tall bell-tower sign that will later become part of its new sanctuary. The public suddenly became aware that it existed. A congregation in Oklahoma had no sign at all. The visiting consultant asked why. "When we remodeled, the old one was torn down. The church board could not agree on the type needed to replace it. So we didn't. That was six years ago. Now we are known as that church downtown which doesn't have a sign." One growing church sponsored a special Easter program that involved building a large unusual sign on the front lawn. All during the Lenten season, this sign said to the world, "Something different is going on here. Come and see." Many persons did.

The pastor of a growing church in Kentucky says, "Another way to advertise visibly the church's presence in the community is by signs in every area of the parish or town. Metal signs which can be ordered from denominational headquarters are better than nothing, but they are often second best. If they are permitted to get dented and rusty, with peeling paint, they make more negative than positive statements about the church's welcome. Large, attractive signs which capable lay members paint and letter are often preferable to ancient, and more expensive to replace, commercial signs. Every time it gets knocked over by a car, straighten it up so that it says 'We are happy about our church home.'"

Activities around the building are another kind of sign. One pastor says, "If you don't have automobiles at your building during the week, you may want to rent a few cars and park them there." Use by various community groups says that this church cares about people. When personal needs arise in the lives of unchurched persons, a sign has already been planted in their mind. It says, "These people care. Why not go there for help?"

Say It with Radio

Opportunities to use this medium vary with each community and local station policy. The pastor of a growing church in Oklahoma City says, "We have a member who is a disc jockey. He offered me free time at 6:25 A.M., six mornings a week. I have a minute and a half each day. This devotion reaches 27 percent of the listening audience in our city. That has made a difference."

Radio works even better in small towns than in large metropolitan areas. Soon, everyone in town knows the sound of the pastor's voice. If the material is well done, radio pulls people toward the church on Sunday so they can hear more. Broadcasting the Sunday morning worship service should more accurately be called narrowcasting. This traditional approach reaches very few persons who do not already attend church. A helpful service to shut-ins, it is rarely a cost-effective evangelism tool for the average congregation. Spots, on the other hand, penetrate the unchurched population.

A breakthrough idea that many small-town stations run free of charge is available from a syndicated service which provides subscribers with 260 "Bright Spots" each year (enough for a new spot each day, five days per week, fifty-two weeks a year). The content of the spots flows with the seasons. Each local pastor-subscriber uses the printed scripts to cut tapes (in his/her own voice) at the local radio station. That "tail" at the end of each sixty-second spot is personalized to say something like: "From First Presbyterian Church in Fort Dodge, that's today's Bright Spot. I'm George Mercer."

The annual subscription cost for 260 different spots is $260 ($30.00 per month). Churches can subscribe by writing Bright Spots, 5001 Avenue N, Lubbock, Texas 79401. Scripts come two weeks in advance of the month in which they will be used, so pastors can tape an entire month of spots with only one trip to the radio station. Most subscribers air "Bright Spots" in early mornings when people drive to work or in late afternoon when they return home. Some small-town stations run them several times each day with no additional charge. Such a coverage makes the local pastor's voice as familiar as Earl Nightingale's (and most of the spots resemble his in content and quality).

The following is a sample "Bright Spot" script: "It was snowing. The children were sledding and I was shivering from the cold. As I walked inside to warm myself in front of the fire, my wife brought me some hot chocolate and doughnuts. As I devoured the tasty delicacies, I thought, why do these doughnuts have a hole in the middle? They taste so good, and I could have one or two more bites if there was no hole, I reasoned. Whoever said a doughnut had to have a hole in it, anyway? What purpose could it possibly serve?

"Then it dawned on me how foolish I was being. Rather than enjoying the delicious taste, I was complaining about the hole. Instead of taking advantage of what I had, I was objecting to what I did *not* have.

"We are fortunate people, indeed. Sure, we have our problems and our troubles and they are *real*. But the doughnut is there. Let's don't complain about the hole. . . . From First United Methodist Church in Shreveport, that's today's Bright Spot. I'm George Foster."

Whatever type of radio spot is chosen, the pastor must sound professional while reading it. If his or her voice sounds like lines

129

from a school play, the effect is worse than no publicity at all. Begin preparation two days in advance of going to the station to cut the tapes. Use the following four-point formula: (1) Get by yourself and read *aloud* all the scripts for the entire month. Don't try to put expression into them. Just read for an understanding of the content. (2) Several hours or a day later, get by yourself and read the scripts *aloud* with feeling, seeking to express the stronger nouns and verbs in a conversational way. Underline a few key words to help fix the emphasis points in your mind. (3) Several hours or a day later (preferably overnight), get by yourself and read the scripts again, *aloud*. This time, work hard to *visualize* every picture word or sentence on your brainscreen. Try to *see* what is happening with the movie projector of your mind's eye. (4) Go to the radio station's taping room. Put special emphasis on relaxing your hands, fingers, and facial features. Make a strong effort to *smile* while you read the scripts. Don't concentrate too much on reading the words with feeling. That can produce a "pulpit inflection" which sounds preachy. Instead, try hard to visualize every picture and action sentence in your mind. This brings you close to a conversational style and makes you sound like a radio professional.

Critics of church advertising often ask, "Can our congregation afford to spend money this way?" This is a classic example of asking the wrong question. Careful advertising investments inevitably draw in at least two or three new families each year. Total their annual contributions, and a more appropriate question emerges: "Can we afford not to advertise?"

Getting Your Name in the Paper

The cheapest newspaper ads are free. One pastor says, "Every time there's a picture-hanging at the church, we see that it gets in the paper." Another pastor says, "You've got to get the church in the papers and on the posts. People need to be visually confronted over and over again by the church's presence in the community. We organized an additional functional department that is responsible for getting articles about past and future church activities into local newspapers. They have arranged for me to write columns in a local paper and a monthly community magazine. Some of the church's most creative minds work on this task force. They are not like the old publicity committee that you find tacked onto so many functional department systems. This is an *aggressive* publicity committee."

If the church elects to use paid newspaper ads, make them big enough to cover at least one-fourth page. Otherwise, they get little attention. Focus them on the needs and interests of the reader rather than on programmatic aspects of church life. Avoid "stained-glass language." Zero in on contemporary feelings and needs of unchurched people rather than trying to appeal to church attenders' needs. A United Church of Christ congregation in St. Louis, Missouri, had great success with a series of personalized ads in the local newspaper that covers their part of the metropolitan area. One ad, for instance, is directed toward singles. It shows the picture of a young woman and reads something like this: "Hello, I'm Joan Smith. I belong to the singles group at Pilgrim United Church of Christ." The ad goes on to give some personal description of Joan Smith, such as her place of employment, hobbies, etc. The ad vividly communicates the fact that this older, inner-city congregation has a strong program for young adults. The other ads in the series communicate other equally significant items of information concerning the types of persons who attend this church. In all mass advertising, remember that people do not so much join an institution as they join other persons whom they perceive as similar to themselves, with similar needs and interests.

Most denominational offices prepare newspaper ad mats for use by local congregations. An excellent, inexpensive commercial source of such ads is Life Stream Evangelism, 7275 South Broadway, Littleton, Colorado 80122. A Saturday edition of the local paper is probably the best time to run them. If a Saturday edition is not published, Friday would be a second choice. Monday through Wednesday is too far away from Sunday.

In all types of mass advertising, a series of repetitive ads sequenced close together during a one-month period is far more effec-

LIFE TENDS TO GET SWALLOWED UP–DOESN'T IT... Sometimes we get so caught up in the day's activities, the week's agenda, the month's requirements, the year's routine, that we never stop to ask, "Where is it all leading? If I 'arrived' where would I be?"

Where are your priorities? Who or what do you serve? Are you only hoping to live? Someday when you 'make it' then will you be happy?

One day Jesus told a group of people that real life isn't made up by an abundance of possessions. He's saying, "Don't let that job, or that title, or getting that degree, or buying that house, or achieving that end swallow up the meaning of your life. You're worth more than that. You're important. You count. You're loved.

Name of
Christian Church
(Disciples of Christ)
Address

SAMPLE

tive than the same ad repeated each month for an entire year. Churches may, for instance, wish to do a series of ads in September, another series between Thanksgiving and Christmas, then another series during the pre-Easter season.

An effective media combination is to saturate six weeks with three forms of advertising: Each week, use a fifteen- or thirty-second radio spot on Friday and Saturday mornings. During that same six-week time slot, run a quarter-page newspaper ad on Wednesdays (somewhere other than the church page). Sometime during that same six weeks, mass mail a letter (personalized with the name in the salutation, if possible) to at least 10 percent of the community population, directed toward those neighborhoods within fifteen minutes driving distance of the church.

Warning: Whatever form of media you use, remember that advertising makes a great "step one." But don't forget its limitations. Advertising gets people's attention; but don't stop there. One church mixed radio spots, newspaper ads, and mass mail in a well-tested commercial formula. Afterward, they wrote a manual describing their methods. While the manual was most informative, a check of that church's membership figures during those years reveals a declining chart. Why? They apparently did good advertising but little else. No amount of super-commercialism compensates for a congregation that doesn't *care* about visitors and doesn't provide need-meeting worship and programmatic experiences for people who show up at the building.

Parish Paper Power

Question: Should our church place evangelism prospects on the newsletter mailing list?

Answer: Absolutely! All growing churches do this. Leave them on your mailing list until they join another church or make it clear that they aren't interested in yours. Better to err by overmailing than underexposing. Many people remain on a prospect list for months. Failing to include them in regular church mailings signals nonacceptance and noncaring. If you want people to feel like family, treat them that way.

A few church leaders measure every decision by its cost rather than by its ministry potential. But even if viewed from a purely monetary perspective, mailing newsletters to evangelism prospects is a good buy. If only one family per year is influenced to join the church by receiving the newsletter, their financial support far exceeds the cost of mailing to *all* evangelism prospects that year. We can't get a nickle cup of coffee any more, but we still have a five-cent evangelism tool. At the price of third-class, nonprofit mail and a sheet of paper, where can you get a cheaper evangelism method?

Do not, of course, try to substitute the newsletter for personal contact. The newsletter can never *substitute* for those personal touches. Nothing does.

Every Which Way You Can

The variety of methods by which a church can raise its public visibility is limited only by the circumference of imagination. When a little girl saw her first rainbow, she turned to her mother and said, "Is that an ad for heaven?" Churches can't rent a rainbow from Hertz or hire skywriters, but a little concentrated creativity may drum up something even better.

Three times a year, First Christian Church (Disciples of Christ) of Noblesville, Indiana, reaches out in a unique way to a large group of people in their community, many of whom are unchurched. By setting aside three Sundays to honor all high school athletes, their parents and coaches, the church recognizes the significant contribution these young people make to their school and community. This practice also establishes positive contacts that have resulted in solid evangelistic growth. One Sunday in the fall, winter, and spring, each of the athletes participating in a sport for that season is invited to a special worship service. Invitations are extended to both boys' and girls' teams, as well as to cheerleaders. The fall "Sports Sunday" usually includes football, cross-country, tennis, golf, volleyball, and swimming teams. The winter Sunday honors athletes involved in basketball, wrestling, swimming, and gymnastics. Spring sports include baseball, track, golf and tennis. The athletic director of the high school or schools is contacted and informed of the events, and a list of athletes and their mailing addresses is requested. Each athlete and parent is written a personal letter of invitation to the special worship.

Athletes and coaches are asked to gather about thirty minutes before the worship begins and are then seated in a special section by teams. At the beginning of the worship, the entire group (athletes, coaches, and teams) is introduced and asked to stand. The sermon subject and the music on these Sundays fit the theme of the day. On this Sunday, athletes read the scripture and serve at the communion table. At the close of worship, each team is presented a Certificate of Appreciation for their contribution to the community. Each coach is given a minute or two to share anything he or she wishes to say. After worship, the fellowship time is held on the church lawn or in the fellowship hall, according to the time of year and the weather. These celebrations have been well attended by athletes and their families and have added a new dimension of service to the church.

The Noblesville congregation's growth has been meteoric during the past seven years (worship attendance has doubled and more than 700 persons have united with the church). "Recognition of Athletes Sunday" is certainly not the only thing they do to stimulate public visibility, but it is one of the most helpful.

133

Serving a Mass Society

In hearing this axiom about public visibility, we must take care not to overlearn. Christianity began with one. Then it spread to twelve. After Easter, 120 were praying together. On Pentecost, fifty days later, 3,000 more came into the church. By A.D. 325, the Roman Empire had 3.5 million Christians. By the Council of Nicea in A.D. 1,000, they numbered 50 million. By the Protestant Reformation in the early 1500s, 100 million. By 1900, 500 million. Now, one billion, 350 million. How did this happen? Predominantly by word of mouth and personal influence. That principle is not changed. Nothing substitutes for individuals communicating with individuals.

But in a society bombarded every second by mass communication, media methods have become as potent as the Gutenberg printing press in Luther's generation. "'Children, have you any fish?' They answered him, 'No.' He said to them, 'Cast the net on the right side of the boat, and you will find some.' So they cast it, and now they were not able to haul it in, for the quantity of fish'" (John 21:5-6). Media science is not a new messiah—all powerful. But it can help us fish in new places we couldn't get our nets into before.

Group Discussion Questions

1. List all the methods you can think of which our church presently uses to increase its public visibility.
2. In the light of the ideas presented in this chapter, comment on our church signs, their present condition and the need for additional ones.
3. Do you know of churches that have successfully used radio spots? What is your opinion about our congregation's trying them?
4. Do we have an aggressive system for getting frequent stories into the newspaper about what is happening in our congregation? If not, do you have any suggestions for how we might remedy that?
5. Has our church tried any paid newspaper publicity? If so, how did it work? In some congregations, individuals are often willing to pay for newspaper ads on a rotating basis, just as others are happy to furnish the sanctuary flowers once a year on Sunday morning. Do you think this might work in our church?
6. Do you have comments on how our church newsletter might be improved—especially at the point of increasing its appeal to visitors and evangelism prospects?
7. Do we presently sponsor any special Sundays similar to the "Recognition of Athletes Sunday" described in this chapter? Can you think of other special Sundays which might be evangelistically advantageous?

Love enables us to put up wholeheartedly with the imperfect people we otherwise couldn't stand.

13

Organizing a Sea Anemone Church

Everything living dies. Right? Wrong! Scientists now believe that the longest living multicelled animal—the sea anemone—has found a way to avoid death. This creature's tentacles have a fixed lifespan. But it has devised a way to replace these with new ones. So the organism perpetually renews itself. Congregations also live forever if they replace the parts that die and continually regenerate old cells. This occurs when new persons join the church with fresh ideas, great enthusiasm and new hope—providing they are fully assimilated into the organism.

China's enormous feat of feeding and clothing 900 million people went far beyond mere application of managerial principles. Mao succeeded in convincing hundreds of millions of manual workers that the entire destiny of the country hung on what each of them did every day. In so doing, he laid hold of a New Testament teaching: "As each has received a gift, employ it for one another, as good stewards of God's varied grace..." (1 Peter 4:10). Growing churches don't just take in members. They involve new persons at a high level of commitment and motivate them to achieve the best within them.

They, better than status quo churches, find ways to incorporate all comers into the vital purposes for which God has called his people out of nothingness. *Axiom #13: Growing churches quickly involve new attenders and new members in small groups, church activities, and leadership roles.*

Inclusion, Impact, Intimacy

When Karl Barth visited this country in 1963, he was asked to comment on the differences between the churches in America and Europe. He replied: "Unlike Europeans, Americans do not just attend church for divine service. Americans go to church to be with one another." That situation has not changed. A study among Catholic parishes by Dean R. Hoge confirms what everyone already knows about both Protestants and Catholics. Laypersons are looking for warmer, more personal parishes. Many complaints were heard about the difficulty in relating to impersonal churches, especially in the larger parishes. People often asked for more fellowship and wider opportunities for personal involvement. This was especially true in the larger parishes, but the size of the parish was not criticized nearly as much as its *climate*.[1]

The organizational systems in growing churches do an above average job of meeting three big needs: (1) inclusion—you as an individual are an important part of the church; (2) impact—your opinion is worth listening to and you can exert some influence in the church; and (3) intimacy—a feeling of liking and being liked by other people in the church. Different people have varying amounts of need for each of these. Intimacy, for example: some people fear close-range love. That's why they attend a large church—to keep their distance from people. That's why they refuse to participate in small groups. But generally speaking, overabundant amounts at any of these three points is positive for a church. People will take or leave according to their own needs. Better to err in the direction of excess than niggardliness. You can't take what isn't offered.

The Japanese and Chinese, with their super-strong family ties, are expert in developing esprit de corps. That's why they accomplish so much in their neighborhoods, factories, and armies. Growing churches become pros at the same thing. Their singing together, eating meals together, group inclusion processes, and idle chit-chat opportunities are tools for meeting deep yearnings. In these interactions, lonely people who feel that no one *cares* about them find meaning that transcends their empty oneness. Growing churches help members feel a strong sense of "we." People seek more frantically for this communal, first-person-pronoun feeling today than ever before. Society is just not as well organized to provide it as in the rural culture of four decades ago. This search for a positive self-

---

[1]Dean R. Hoge, *Converts Dropouts Returnees* The Pilgrim Press, 1981, page 171.

identity derived from inclusion in a solid social grouping is especially prevalent among youth and young adults.

The sign on a church marquee said, "New Friends Await You Here." Do most people hunt a church in the effort to find new friends? Perhaps a few singles do, and a few recently moved migrants who knew that churches are a good way to get acquainted. But most people don't go looking for new friends. They look for *old* friends who *accept* them and with whom they can feel at ease. Growing churches are adroit at helping friends remain *new* friends for the shortest possible time.

Flavil Yeakley interviewed fifty active lay members who had been in the church for at least six months. He found that people who stayed active had developed an average of seven or more friends in the church. Interviews with persons who had dropped out identified an average of less than two new friendship patterns.[2] Growing churches instinctively know that truth: facilitating friendship development counts big in evangelism statistics. And they organize to accomplish it.

Some congregations deceive themselves at this point. They encourage members to be friendly after church. They may even have a system for seeing that everyone gets his or her hand shaken upon arrival at the building. But some of these same churches have no real system for assimilating people into the church's fellowship and leadership circles. Form without function is like receiving the gift of an expensive-looking but inoperable television set. At first, you feel very appreciative. Later, when you learn the set has no picture tube, you feel differently. Any time an organization has form without functional follow-through, new persons catch on quickly. Phony friendship is repulsive. People may join due to the pull of warm, surface acceptance. But many will unjoin out the back door when they find this friendship is only handshake deep.

The Army and the Officer Corps

All fast-growing churches hit a crisis point at which the old guard resists the influx of new members. Rapid change in any social system breeds frustration. The same leaders who rejoice when God adds to the church weekly begin to grunch and groan when rapid growth stimulates a reshaping of the organization. Most of the time, church leaders can't see past their own feeling to the root of their upsetness. In some cases, however, seasoned leaders will flatly state, "With all these new people, it just doesn't seem like the same church anymore."

Another cause of this natural resistance to growth comes from "key leadership displacement." The church officers said with great feeling, "Our church needs to grow." But then it did. And they didn't. What they really meant was, "Our church needs to grow, but don't

---

[2]Flavil R. Yeakley, *Why Churches Grow*. Christian Communications, 1979, p. 54.

make any changes in leadership. I've grown accustomed to these faces. Make the army bigger, but don't change the officer corps."

Combating this natural resistance to change is particularly hard for the pastor. He or she would prefer that older members appreciate "what I have done to help the church grow." But the pastor always learns that numerical growth is a surprisingly two-pronged task—helping the saints to multiply and then helping them to be happy that they did. The pastor of a congregation that doubled in size was amazed to hear many of the older members saying, "The church doesn't seem to care about me any more. It just cares about all those new people." The same thing happened to Moses on his way to the promised land. As soon as he got the slaves out of Egypt, they "murmured" against him (Exodus 15:24). That is why growing churches must accelerate their effort to take good pastoral care of long-time members. Otherwise, growth becomes a hollow victory that soon tastes like a mouthful of ashes.

Closing the Back Door

Two things must happen to all new members if they stay active in the church and grow in spiritual maturity: (1) within a month or so after joining, they must relate to some small group in the church. This could be the choir, a Sunday school class, the women's group, a men's softball team, or any of a dozen other kinds of face-to-face groups. Only then will they feel themselves a real part of the church. (2) Within three to six months, they must get involved in some kind of job or responsibility in the church.

The pastor of one growing church says, "We put our new members to work very quickly after they join. Many people share with me that they were in churches for years before they were asked to serve. We use a lot of them in our worship services, communion, ushering, offering. We get them involved in study and prayer groups. We ask them to teach. We involve people even before they have placed their membership. We let them become part of the Body of Christ even before they become a part of the local church."

The pastor of another growing church says, "Some people move to our town from a church where they were depended on for everything. In moving to a suburb of the metro, they are looking for anonymity. . . .But allowing them to come to church and not do anything else is a disservice to them. If they do that, in thirty to sixty days most of them will either become an invalid or a corpse. . . .I can only count on keeping five percent of those who refuse to get into anything except morning worship."

A sure way to make this happen is by putting someone in charge of it. Saying that *everyone* is responsible for assimilation is another way of saying that nobody is. Appointing a new member development superintendent provides system and accountability. It ensures that as few as possible of those who walk through the front door end up flowing out the back door into inactivity. This person should be extremely detail-conscious and able diplomatically to motivate other church leaders. One of the new member development superintendent's most important tools is a "Talent and Interest Inventory" (see pp. 140-141). *How this card is used* is far more important than the format on which it is printed. But keep it simple. You don't need to know their social security number or how many years they were in the army. Personalize the card to meet the needs of your particular congregation, *but do not mail it to the home or leave it with the new members.* Immediately after persons place membership, a church leader should call in their home. The overarching purpose of this visit is delivery of a "New Member Packet." This folder may include such things as baptism certificate, roster of members' names/addresses, listing of teachers, pledge card, etc. As the visitor explains the packet's contents, he or she should verbally review the "Talent and Interest Inventory." This quickly determines what responsibilities new members might be comfortable with in their new church.

A good way to begin the conversation: "We try to avoid working anyone to death in our church, but we do know that you will want to use your talents in Christ's work. Let me ask you a few questions about the kinds of things in which you have had experience or in which you might be interested." At this point, remove the card from the New Member Packet and raise casual questions as you visually review the card. You may ask, for example, "Have you ever served as a church officer?" In the section that covers Sunday church school, if the person says that he or she has taught a class, ask what grade level. After the person responds, ask whether she or he enjoyed teaching that age group. Some will answer with an enthusiastic yes. Others will say, "I much prefer the younger children." Either way, you have obtained invaluable information that you might not otherwise have learned for years. This replaces the Russian-roulette method of asking people to take jobs, then finding that they neither enjoyed them nor did them well. By concentrating on what they have enjoyed doing in the past, you will gather information that you would never learn by any other method.

Work serves a double purpose in our society. It gets necessary chores done and provides the worker with a feeling of significance. The church needs many people to carry out its commission. But this cannot happen without concrete systems to match people with jobs.

Some kind of "follow-through-chart" can help the new member development superintendent motivate other church leaders to assist in the assimilation of new members (see pp 142-143). Modify this chart to fit the plan used by your particular church. Post it in the room where committees and church board usually meet. This will occasion its frequent review by persons in a position to carry out methods that lie beyond the control of any one individual. Reviewing the follow-through chart each month puts that principle into motion among key church leaders.

TALENT AND INTEREST INVENTORY
TIME AND TALENT SHARING CARD

"THE MASTER'S CHARGE" — "TIME AND TALENT SHARING"

MY PERSONAL COMMITMENT TO JESUS CHRIST as witnessed through "THE MIDDLETOWN CHRISTIAN CHURCH"

REALIZING that my personal CHRISTIAN growth is most meaningful when I give myself in CHRISTIAN SERVICE, I am willing to share my time and/or talent in the following ways during the coming fiscal year, (beginning July 1). (I understand that these commitments can be altered at any time by notifying the Church Office, should circumstances necessitate.)

Name _____ Today's Date _____

Address _____

(Mail, if diff.)

Bus. Phone _____

Home Phone _____

Occupation & Location _____ ;

If a student, grade and school _____ ;

NAME, AGE, & GRADE OF CHILDREN THAT ARE NOT CHURCH MEMBERS:

_____ ; _____ ;

INSTRUCTIONS:
1. **Children/youth**, please use Sections XI, A-R & XII; 2. **Adults**, use other Sections, but read Sections XI & XII;

I. DEPT. OF CHRISTIAN EDU.
A__Church School Teacher,
   Age level preferred _____
   Grd. level preferred _____
B__Youth Group Worker,
   Grd. level preferred _____
C__Nursery Worker
D__Art Work
E__Library Worker
F__Summer Youth Work
G__Vacation Bible School

II. DEPT. OF CHURCH MEMBERSHIP:
A__Church Photographer
B__Church Dinners/Kitchen Work
C__Sitter
D__Secretarial Work
E__Poster Artist
F__Telephoning

III. DEPT. OF COMMUNITY INVOLVEMENT:
A__Teach Ceramics
B__Gym Monitor: Community
   Youth Center
C__Clothes Closet Worker
D__Help persons/families
   in need
E__Provide Transportation
F__Help with Sr. Citizens

(over)

TIME AND TALENT SHARING CARD
Back Side
(Actual Size - 6 x 9 Inches)

IV. DEPT. OF CHURCH WOMEN:
A__ Special Events Worker
B__ Study/program Worker
C__ Projects Worker
D__ CWF Circles
E__ Mothers-Day-Out Volunteer
F__ Prayer Breakfast

V. DEPT. OF OUTREACH:
A__ Newsletter Worker
B__ Bulletin Board Worker
C__ Art Work

VI. WORSHIP:
A__ Usher
B__ Greeter
C__ Help prepare Communion
D__ Pick-up cups & straighten Sanctuary after Worship
E__ Wash cups after Worship
F__ Sing in Choir
G__ Play in Handbell Choir
H__ Play Piano
I__ Play other musical Instrument (what_____)
J__ Drama
K__ Help with Youth Choir Admin.
L__ Help with Youth Choirs

VII. EVANGELISM:
A__ Call on prospective members
B__ Publicity/promotion/ public relations
C__ Sign painting

VIII. PROPERTY:
A__ Carpentry
B__ Plumbing
C__ Electrical
D__ Yard Mowing
E__ Painting
F__ Care for Flower Beds
G__ Common Labor
H__ Church Bus Driver

IX. DEPT. OF MEN'S WORK:
A__ Help with Fish Fry
B__ Help with other Projects
C__ Prayer Breakfast

X. OTHER WAYS I AM WILLING TO HELP:
_____
_____
_____
_____

XI. CHILDREN/YOUTH INVOLVEMENT:
A__ Church School-all ages
B__ CHI RHO (grds/6-7-8)
C__ CYF (grds/9-12)
D__ Serve on a Committee, (Grds/6-12)
E__ Jr. Deacon, any church member thru Grd. 12
F__ Art work
G__ Crafts
H__ Nursery Helper, Grds. 6-12
I__ Choir, Primary, Grds/1-3
J__ Choir, Junior, Grds/4-5
K__ Choir, CHI RHO, Grds/6-8
L__ Handbell Choir
M__ Symbolic Choir, High School, 9-12
N__ Drama Group, Grds/6-12
O__ Pick-up & wash cups after Worship
P__ Straighten Sanctuary after Worship
Q__ Yard Mowing
R__ Candle Lighter

XII. OTHER WAYS I AM WILLING TO HELP:
_____
_____
_____

Follow-Through Chart

NEW MEMBER'S NAME	PACKET DELIVERED	RECEPTION	NOTIFY CHURCH OF TRANSFER	CHURCH JOB	CHURCH GROUP	MINISTER CALL

HOME	LETTER OF WELCOME	PLEDGE CARD RECEIVED	NEWSLETTER ARTICLE	IN A C.W.F. GROUP	LAYPERSON'S HOME	CHRISTIAN COURIER	MAILING LIST	NOTES

When unemployment rises to high levels in a capitalistic system, it threatens the structures of society. People lose that sense of belonging and merit which gives them personal psychological health. Church societies operate in a similar way. Congregations that put people to work (*everybody*, no matter what her or his talent) provide a feeling of worth that strengthens both individual and institution. Church things go better with work.

And So Forth

Methods to accomplish assimilation take countless forms. Don't be limited by the following list. Use it as an airstrip to get your imagination off the ground.

(1) Shepherding programs have failed miserably in many churches. But properly instituted and organized, they can be terrific assimilators. The pastor of one growing church says, "Once a family joins, they are assigned to a shepherding group. Each cluster is led by an elder with the assistance of two deacons. We underscore the importance of this shepherding work by counting on our deacons to chair the various functional departments. This frees our elders for the sole responsibility of leading the respective shepherding groups. To this end, we give them constant training and supervision throughout the course of the year. Our elders have a fall and spring retreat for this purpose. They meet once a month just prior to the board meeting and discuss the various activities of their individual shepherding groups. Each elder is expected to bring together his or her group a minimum of four times a year for fellowship and sharing. . . .

"In addition, each shepherding group composed of twelve to fifteen families is asked to provide the leadership for Sunday morning worship service during one month of the year. The Protestant Reformation's watchcry was "the priesthood of all believers." We place a corresponding emphasis on the participation of individuals in worship. Prior to the month in which a particular shepherding group has worship responsibility, the group meets and assigns individual duties commensurate with individual gifts and interests. Some will volunteer to serve as worship leader or say prayers at the communion table. Others will prefer to pass offering plates and communion trays or serve as ushers and greeters. But each member of our congregation through this involvement of the shepherding group in worship is given the opportunity to serve as priest to the other persons in the congregation.

"While our shepherding group activities are basically for adults, most of the groups stage at least one event each year that includes all members of participating families. (Our main means of building fellowship within our young people, however, is through our Sunday evening youth groups. We operate junior, junior high, and senior high programs.) Every other month, our fellowship committee hosts an all-church fellowship dinner and our new members are recognized at that time. We ask our elders not only to make the introduction, but to sit with new members who are part of their group. Our membership committee provides name tags for everyone in our church above the age of eight. These name tags are worn on Sunday mornings and also during the fellowship dinners in order to facilitate the placing of names with faces. Finally, at least once a year, activity sign-ups are held after Sunday morning worship."

(2) Another assimilation option: Organize a Sunday school teacher corps in which you have four, five, or more substitute teachers for each class. That gives new members a feeling of doing something worthwhile for the church but does not overload them. It also helps the Sunday school program, since all "master teachers" have several substitutes to call in an emergency; they never have to phone the Sunday school superintendent to find a replacement when they are sick or out of town. Under this system, the master teacher teaches during the nine months of the school year while the teacher corps members handle the three summer months.

(3) Another assimilation option: Have the church cabinet or other key leaders list every job in every section of church life that each current member is presently doing. This gives a job analysis of the present program, points up overloaded workers, and may suggest ways in which responsibilities could be spread among new members when the opportunity arises. This procedure is especially helpful in smaller churches where certain individuals may be accidentally (or because of personal inclination) overextended in church work.

LIFE with Capital Letters

Jim Fleming, pastor of a growing suburban church, tells this story: "Once upon a time, a couple of newcomers to town visited a certain church. It wasn't a large church, rather middle-sized, about like ours. Almost everyone knew everyone else. And they were all very eager to see and greet each other. A new couple entered the church and put their wraps on the coatrack. The foyer was abuzz with ricocheting conversation. Most of the faces were dressed with nice smiles. It looked like a good place to visit, maybe even to place membership. The couple entered the sanctuary. At worship's dismissal, they didn't just rush out but went with the flow of the crowd.

"The next Sunday they returned. Once again, a good number of people were present. These natives regarded them the same as they had the first week. And so they came, and then they went. On the third Sunday, the couple said to each other, 'Well, let's go back to the same church today. It is close. It is our denomination.' So they returned for the third Sunday. The chatter was still very charming. They went to hang up their coats, and other people were hanging up their coats. They went into the worship service. They went with the flow of the crowd as they left. When they got to their car, they said to each other, 'What goes here? We've attended this church three Sundays in a row, and on no occasion did one soul speak to us.' That can happen to any church. Let it not be said that newcomers can get into our worship but can't get into our church."

Jesus did not say he came so we could have *religion*. He didn't even say he came so we could have *churches*. "I came that they may have life, and have it abundantly" (John 10:10). Growing churches seek the same objective. They don't just try to get people to attend worship or join the church. They help people find a relationship with God and each other which provides LIFE with capital letters.

Lloyd Ogilvie says that loneliness is the greatest single problem in Los Angeles.[3] That analysis is accurate for every metropolitan area across America. Many people move there to be happy. Most of them just become lonely. Nobody knows anybody, and everyone seems disconnected. Churches that help reduce this loneliness factor find growth. When the love of God becomes concrete through personal contact, inclusion, impact, and intimacy, life becomes LIFE.

John Thompson, a pastor in Florida, tells a story about the night he and his family camped beside a beautiful lake in New Mexico. Even before he had the tent pitched, the children were making new friends. The family camped nearby had two children, also. For a while, the youngsters played well together—everyone was included. But then he noticed the smallest boy standing apart from the others. In his left-out feeling, the little boy cried, "I am here. I am here. Can't anybody see I'm here?" How many times a day do we hear this cry repeated in adults? But it is usually so silent or masked by other emotions that we don't hear it. Or our own needs so preoccupy us that we don't listen. Growing churches do a better than average job of listening for this cry.

[3]Lloyd Ogilvie, speech at the National Evangelism Workshop in Amarillo, Texas, May 1980.

Group Discussion Questions

1. In your opinion, how well does our church do in the task of involving members in leadership roles soon after they join?
2. Does our church have a systematic plan for being sure that new people find a group relationship and a responsibility in church work? How is this done?
3. Do you or do you not think most of our members feel their opinions are taken seriously and that they have "impact" on the direction of church life? If you don't think they do, suggest some ways we might improve this situation.
4. Do you feel there is resistance in our church to growth and the resulting change that comes with it? Illustrate.
5. Does our church use some form of Talent and Interest Inventory? Who is responsible for seeing that these are filled in by new members?
6. Has our church ever tried a "shepherding program"? Did it work? If it didn't work, what do you think went wrong?
7. How would you describe the climate toward Sunday morning visitors in our church? What suggestions do you have for improving our friendliness?

But in front of excellence the immortal gods have put sweat, and long and steep is the way to it, and rough at first. But when you come to the top, then it is easy, even though it is hard.

—Hesiod, ca. 700 B.C.

14

Contact Glue

One of history's great disasters took place in 1271. In that year, Marco Polo visited Kublai Khan. The great Khan at that time ruled all China, India, and the East. Attracted by the story of Christianity told him by the explorers, he said, "Go to your high priests and tell them to send me one hundred men skilled in your religion. I shall be baptized and all my barons and great men. Their subjects will be baptized, too. We will then have more Christians *here* than in your part of the world."

Somebody dropped the ball. Nothing was done for thirty years. Finally, two or three missionaries were sent. Too few and too late. What kind of difference might it have meant to the world if in the thirteenth century China, India, and the whole Orient had moved toward Christ? The same difference it makes when Christians personally contact unchurched persons in our own society. Nothing substitutes for that. No amount of prayer or "I wish they would visit our church" replaces contact cement.

A man sorting his mail glanced at an advertising circular from a local merchant. His eyes were attracted by the statement in bold, blue print: "Dear Preferred Customer." But as he looked below that appellation, he saw the mailing label that said, "Resident, 2616 75th." He had trouble imagining a business that didn't know his name saw him as a preferred customer. Even God couldn't make impersonal procedures work. When he wanted to get our attention, he did not erect a neon sign in the night sky. He sent a Son who moved about the landscape talking with people face to face. "And the Word became flesh and dwelt among us . . ." (John 1:14). Note that John does not say the Word was made into a book. God had already tried that with the Old Testament Jews. If he needed to get personal in order to communicate with us, how can we expect to succeed with less?

Axiom #14: Growing churches make a high volume of contact with non-members for the purpose of influencing them toward Christ and his church. Ask the members of your church board the following questions: (1) Do we have a systematic method for obtaining large numbers of names and addresses of non-church members, especially relatives, friends, and acquaintances of present members? (2) Do members of our church make a large number of face-to-face contacts each week with non-members they are trying to influence toward the church? (3) Does our pastor make a large number of face-to-face contacts each week with non-members for the purpose of influencing them toward Christ and the church? Growing congregations across the country answer these questions in the affirmative. They have not lost touch with biblical methods. They remember that the first apostles were attracted to Christ while fishing. Matthew was contacted while sitting in his IRS office. A lawyer was contacted on the highway. A wayward woman was contacted at the public water supply. Another was contacted during a meal at Simon's house. Zacchaeus was contacted in a tree. A thief was contacted while dying on a cross. Christ did not do his evangelism in church. He reached out to Jews, Greeks, Romans, rulers, Publicans, Pharisees, Sadducees, Herodians, lepers, beggars, wise men, soldiers, bandits, prostitutes, and little children—but he didn't do it in Sunday school or on the telephone. He let his feet do the walking.

Many churches are blocked from growth because their leaders work from three grossly fallacious assumptions: (1) They think people are tired of being asked to attend church. Not so! The average unchurched person is not offended by worship invitations, provided these are given in a positive, friendly manner. By far the largest percentage of Americans have not received a personal invitation to attend church in years. (2) They think people will come to church without being contacted personally. They seldom do. Letters don't get it. Personal contact does. (3) They think that average church members are not capable of making effective contacts. They are. The exact wording they use doesn't matter as much as using some kind of words. The concerned, caring voice of a nonabrasive church member has more impact than ten billboards or a telegram.

149

Jesus ends his parable about the lost sheep by saying that God doesn't want any of these little ones to perish (Matthew 18:12-14). Sheep don't go looking for shepherds; shepherds look for sheep.

God's Diplomatic Corps

Fact One: approximately one-half the young adult generation changes denominational affiliation when they move to a new community. Fact two: a majority of new adult members (70 to 90 percent) join churches as a result of person-to-person contact along existing friendship, kinship, or employment network lines. Conclusion: individuals talking with individuals is the strongest evangelism tool available. Paul's words were never truer: "So we are ambassadors for Christ, God making his appeal through us" (2 Corinthians 5:20).

The pastor of a growing church says, "When Jesus called Phillip, he went and found Nathaniel. Jesus didn't find Nathaniel; Phillip found Nathaniel and brought his friend with him. The Hastys in our community knew the Cavanaughs at the lake and brought them into the church. And the Cavanaughs at the lake have friends down the road. They brought the Chalmers, a family of five. Our evangelism department sometimes assigns one family to another family. That's fairly effective, but it may not work all that well. People with similar interests are likely to attract people with similar interests."

Historically, different church traditions have expected the power of their evangelistic influence to come from three different places. Some have depended on the words of the Bible to do evangelism: Protestants often tend in this direction. Catholics are more inclined to think evangelism is done through organized church structures and priests. A few groups have expected evangelism to happen through the influence of individuals. The Quakers, for example. But depending on any one of these alone for evangelism power tends to result in slim or short-term church growth. Not many persons are converted to Christ through the raw printed word packaged in Gideon covers and stored in motel rooms. A few are, but not many. An evangelism which utilizes only the church can end up as a superficial membership drive that gets a few people in the congregation, but not much of God into the people. An individual running about trying to convert people to his particular brand of spiritual enthusiasm can attract a few persons whose desperate psychological needs make them easy targets for manipulation. But many of these converts are planted shallow, bloom early, and wither soon.

While some results can come from each of these three methods, New Testament results come from a blend. Church, Bible, and personal contact are the holy trinity of effective evangelism in the modern world—just as they were in the ancient one. Growing churches try to bring unchurched persons into contact with the biblical message. They also use the work, teachings, fellowship, and programs of the church as evangelism tools. But they never depend on these alone. They understand that little evangelism happens if

Christian persons don't make personal contact with those outside the walls.

The following true story revolves around an anonymous young man called Joe Smith. Act One: Joe is twelve years old and on his way to church. In this earlier era, blue jeans were not the "in apparel." Poor people wore them to town if they didn't have any better. Joe was wearing his to church since he only had two pairs of trousers to his name—both blue jeans. The denims were clean but frayed from much use. Joe was greeted on the front steps of the church by an elderly gentleman who engaged him in conversation. In so doing, the man imparted the gracious information that "when you come to God's house, you should wear dress clothes in his honor." Joe said nothing, but his humiliation propelled him on through the building. He went out the back door, strode rapidly toward his grandmother's house (who raised him in absence of his parents) and never returned to any church for more than twenty years.

Act Two: Joe is seated in a pastor's office. Joe has been assigned to this minister for parole counseling. Just released for the Santa Fe, New Mexico, penitentiary, he had been sent up for completing twenty-seven successful burglaries and a twenty-eighth unsuccessful one in which he was apprehended. Joe was a pleasant fellow, easy to work with. The pastor enjoyed him. During the many hours he spent with Joe over a period of several months, he never once invited him to church. He was afraid Joe would think him "pushy" and somewhat unprofessional. After all, he had accepted this counseling assignment as a public service to the community.

Act Three—Several Years Later: The pastor unexpectedly meets Joe on the television screen. He stares at Joe's face in amazement, not believing his vision. Joe is doing a commercial for an automobile dealership. Several weeks later, the pastor has occasion to travel through the town where the broadcast originated, so he stops in to visit with Joe. As Joe fills in the blank years, the pastor reflects on the contrast between this sharply attired frame and the young man he had known before. After listening to Joe's success story, the pastor raises the inevitable question: "How did this all come about? You have really come a long way since I knew you last."

"Well," Joe said, "A friend of mine asked me to attend the church where he and his family go. I decided it was about time I made some changes in my life. So, I did."

Which of these three—the elder on the church steps, the pastor, or the man who invited him to church—was the real neighbor to Joe Smith?

Highly touted evangelism models of the late forties and early fifties were derived from salesmanship ideas. Church members were told they should sell the church like a salesman sells a product in the business world. This brought many positive results, but also some negative ones. Some of the people who bought the product returned it in a week after purchase. They had shallow or invisible conversion experiences.

The 1960s model of evangelism depended much on the "Rogerian" counseling approach. Ministers and laypeople alike developed the delusion that evangelism could not occur until someone approached them with a high desire to join the church. Even then, they must carefully respond in a nondirective way (which actually means a nonproclamation way—the very opposite of the New Testament model). That era produced what any era like it always produces—numerical decline. Can you imagine Paul saying to Barnabas, "What we need to do is wait until people come to us here in Antioch wanting to be Christians. Then we will very cautiously use responsive listening techniques. This will result in substantial growth and the planting of many new churches all across Asia Minor."

Growing churches in the seventies and eighties use a far more biblical model. Jesus said, ". . .I have called you friends. . ." (John 15:15). That is authentic evangelism—not salemanship or counselorship but friendship. How does a friend act? A friend forms a warm, positive relationship, trying to be helpful in whatever way possible. We do not agree altogether with everything our friend does or says. But we know that our friend is on a journey and is probably doing the best possible with the perceptions through which reality is currently viewed. Therefore, a friend is not judgmental, critical, or demanding. A working definition of friendship is found in First Corinthians, chapter thirteen. But neither does a real friend withhold honest opinion about what could make life better for another person. Imagine Jesus saying, "I have called you salesman" or "I have called you counselor." Doesn't quite fit, does it? But a friend? We can be a friend. Every Christian can be a friend to someone. And that is what Christian witnessing is all about.

Examine the four Gospels to see what Jesus' followers did. They studied what he taught. They lived with him. They watched his actions. They learned from him. But after Jesus' death and resurrection, we see a new behavior. They begin to look much less like disciples (learners) than they do witnesses (those who go out and tell good news). Christians today can easily imagine that being a *disciple* is all that counts. But if the first disciples had stopped at that point, the world would never have learned about the Galilean carpenter. Today, as then, all disciples arrive at a time when they need to stop being learners and start being teachers—stop being listeners and start being proclaimers—stop being observers and start being witnesses.

Organized Friendship

Psychiatric help is nothing more than specialized, organized friendship. Emotionally ill people go to offices and pay money for this. Ordinary and less ill people get it from their friends over coffee. All growing churches have some organized system for visiting people in their homes. The average church member thinks such calling, like psychiatry, requires years of training in specialized techniques. Not so. Some churches give these callers an hour or so of instruction to help them feel more at ease. Evangelism visitors simply lend their social skills to a structured system. Reaching out to people with the mechanism of their own friendship, they extend the friendship of Jesus Christ. Ministers with years of graduate training can certainly do this, too. But acting like a friend doesn't require extensive training.

Growing churches concentrate their visits in places where it does the most good. ". . .the fields are already white for harvest" (John 4:35). But the fields are not all *equally* white. So, expend your calling energy on the most responsive people first—those who visit your church services.

All vistors want to attend a church where people care about them personally. You can't adequately express this interest with friendly smiles and handshakes on Sunday morning. You must go beyond that to *active* caring. These visitors have already said by their presence, "We like your church. We don't know how much yet, but we like it some." Church members must therefore reciprocate. A call says quickly and clearly, "We like you, too." Go during the evening hours when family members are home. Send a different couple or individual back the second week and still a different caller the third week.

What is said in the call doesn't have nearly as much impact as the caller's physical presence. The pastor of a growing, small-town church was asked, "How do you do your calling?" He said, "We go in groups."

The interviewer had never heard of this approach, so he said, "What do you mean, groups?"

The pastor replied, "Well, three or four of us go. We sit down in their living room. Sometimes we can't all find a chair, so we sit on the floor. Each of us will take a minute or so to say something about why we like our church or why we joined our church."

The interviewer replied, "Tell me, why do you do it that way?"

The pastor said with some embarrassment, "When our people first started calling, they were scared to death to do it. So, I said, 'Let's just go together.' We've been going together ever since."

While this approach is rarely used in growing churches (and certainly not recommended), it illustrates the truth that presence is more important than what is said or who says it.

The variety of ways to organize church members for calling is infinite. The following outline is one sample from many alternatives. Whatever system you use, do not ask the entire congregation to come to the church and make visits on designated calling nights. This never works for more than one or two months. What would happen if you asked for volunteers to come each week and teach your Sunday school classes? The same principle applies to evangelism calls. You must enlist specific people to do calling on specific nights. Otherwise, the program malfunctions and self-destructs.

Try to enlist 10 percent of the congregation as callers. Thus, in the small church of fifty members, three couples might be sufficient. In the congregation of one hundred members, you will probably need five couples. If the church size is three hundred, shoot for fifteen couples.

Do not ask persons to *volunteer* for calling duty. The evangelism task force should look over the entire church membership list and select persons it feels would make effective callers. (In extremely large churches, a meeting of teachers or key leaders of all adult Sunday school classes is helpful in locating good callers.) Then, visit these potential callers in their homes and secure their commitment on a caller's commitment card. Tell them they will be calling on a specific night for one year and will attend a training session that outlines how to make such calls. Tell them that if after attending the training session they would prefer not to make calls, they can withdraw at that time. This promise of training always increases their willingness to sign up as callers.

Callers should be grouped into teams of six couples (or twelve individuals) per team. Place a team captain in charge of each team. *Do not create teams of more than twelve persons.* Nor should you make small teams of three to six persons. When teams are too large, members get lost in the crowd and may stop attending the calling nights (they think plenty of other people will show up). When teams are too small, members get discouraged and feel lonely if other members don't show up on a particular calling night due to illness or being out of town. A large church can divide forty to fifty people into four teams (which meet on four different nights of the month, or every week of a month every fourth month.) This creates team spirit and a much higher level of responsibility in each caller.

For the extremely small church of thirty-five attending on Sunday morning, discard the system described above. You will probably have no more than three or four couples available for calling. Ask these persons to meet for five minutes each Sunday morning between church school and worship, or right after services. They should meet *every* Sunday for the entire year. At these meetings, the team members report to each other on calls made during the past week and receive new assignments. Under this smaller church system, the pastor makes the first visit during the first week after people attend worship the first time. Then, three different calling team couples make three different calls during the following weeks. Make the three consecutive calls even when the prospects don't attend church the second and third Sundays after they visit the first time.

Someone always asks, "Shouldn't we telephone ahead before we make the visit?" The answer to that question is different for different communities and sometimes depends on the type of person on whom you are calling. By far the largest percentage of churches find it best *not* to call ahead. You can easily find the answer to this question for your church and community. Make five calls without phoning ahead. On five other calls, phone ahead for an appointment. By the time you have completed all ten of these visits, you will know exactly what procedure you need to follow in your community.

Whatever system you use, keep the visits brief. Some experts say that fifteen minutes is plenty.

After first-time worship visitors, the second most receptive persons on whom to call are new community residents who are already members of your denomination. In small towns, you can find these persons by systematically making front-door calls on all new residents. In larger towns, the water department, Welcome Wagon Service, or other such sources may provide you with these names.

The third most responsive persons are friends of present church members, especially your *newest* church members. These people are acquainted with a large pool of unchurched persons not known by your long-term members. When leaders make the New Member Packet calls during the weeks after people join your church, be sure they ask the new members to be thinking about the names of acquaintances and relatives who might enjoy the church, too. Telephone the new members two weeks later and ask for these names and addresses. New members are often God's best evangelists. But you must give them the opportunity.

The fourth most effective group on whom to call includes any new resident of your community. The ecumenical age has flowered in unexpected form. Most people now place more importance on the nature and quality of a particular congregation than on the sign in front of the building.

The fifth and least responsive group is found by block calling. This procedure is seldom cost-effective relative to time expended. The three exceptions to this rule are: (1) when starting a new church in a community; (2) when trying to penetrate a new housing development; and (3) the "target evangelism" method in which a specific concentration of houses around the church is blocked for repeated contacts over a period of weeks. Door-to-door calling effectiveness is limited in mainline denominations—except for the purpose of census-taking in order to find unchurched people.

Whatever group is called on, apply the principle of repetition. Don't stop with one call on people who seem only vaguely interested in your church. Many will respond to repeated contact who would let one call slip by unnoticed.

In Jesus' parable of the sower, 75 percent of the seed was wasted. It didn't reproduce. But the seed that did succeed multiplied prodigiously. That did not happen by accident. When the sower went out to sow, he *intended* to sow the seed (Mark 4:3-9). Churches that wait for "accidental evangelism" to occur seldom see much of a harvest. Churches that grow new members usually intend to. They have seed planting on their minds. They know that God ultimately gives the growth. But they know that seed must be put in the ground before God can do his part.

"God has visited his people!" (Luke 7:16). And he calls his people to visit others that *they* may become *his people.* "Go out to the highways and hedges, and compel people to come in, that my house may be filled" (Luke 14:23). God hasn't called many of us to be lawyers, but he has subpoenaed all of us as witnesses. Thankfully, this personal friendship contract is increasing in our society. A Gallup survey reports that the percentage of adults who say they have tried to encourage someone to believe in Jesus Christ or to accept him as Savior increased from 44 percent in 1980 to 53 percent in December 1981.[1]

A cartoon greeting card pictured five frogs sitting on a log. The caption on the card's first page asks, "If there were five frogs on a log and one decided to jump, how many would be left on the log?" A fold in the cartoon forms a pocket that invites the reader to take out a tiny card containing the answer to the riddle. It says, "Five would be left. Deciding to jump is not the same as jumping." Deciding to become an evangelistic church is not enough. You have to jump.

[1]*Emerging Trends*, February 1982, Princeton Religion Research Center, 53 Bank Street, Princeton, N.J. 08540.

Group Discussion Questions

1. What methods does our church use for making certain that Sunday morning worship visitors are called on in their home the following week?
2. In what ways do we obtain the names and addresses of persons outside our church whom we feel might be interested in relating to Christ through our congregation?
3. In what ways does our church try to motivate members to make personal contacts with their friends and acquaintances in order to extend them invitations to attend church?
4. Count the hands of those in the class who at one time in their lives were members of another denomination. What does this tell us about the kinds of people to whom we need to extend church invitations?
5. Brainstorm a list of all the reasons you think hold people back from making evangelistic contact with unchurched persons.
6. Have you known anyone who seemed to take the "salesman" approach to evangelism? The counseling approach? The friendship approach? Illustrate the reasons for your opinions concerning the effectiveness of these three approaches.
7. If any persons in the class have had experience in making home visits, ask them to explain why they prefer or do not prefer to telephone ahead for an appointment.
8. List any other ideas you think our church should use in making contact with not-yet-members.

> **Observe due measure, for right timing is in all things the most important factor.**
>
> *—Hesiod, ca. 700 B.C.*

15

Nobody Asked Me

George Lyon of Scotland was sixty-eight when he finally popped the question to Catherine MacDonald, age sixty. They had been dating forty-four years. When reporters asked Catherine why George waited so long, she said, "He is a bit shy, you know."

Mainline church leaders often practice similar tactics with potential new members. They hope people will join their church, but have trouble asking them in a straightforward way. Someone has estimated that the average church member has listened to 6,000 sermons and 8,000 prayers, sung 20,000 congregational hymns and asked zero people to accept Christ.

John Wesley seemed to depend on three things in his highly successful evangelism efforts: contact, impact, and decision. He made a large volume of contact with the unchurched. He impacted their minds with a definite message which called for re-examination of life priorities. And he asked them for a decision in specific terms. While today's growing churches work among people whose mindset is altogether different from the one Wesley encountered, they still depend on all three of the procedures he used: contact, impact, and decision. They don't stop with the first two, hoping the decision will take care of itself. *Axiom #15: Growing churches use systematic methods for encouraging prospective members to make positive decisions about Christ and church affiliation.*

During the past two decades, mainline churches have stood tensely between the two horns of a dilemma regarding the subject of asking people for a decision. One horn is the problem experienced in the 1950s. During that rapid membership expansion period, churches got large numbers of joiners by asking them to sign up on little cards. Some of the persons who came into churches through this salesman-like system became its best leaders. But the method also had disturbing flaws. Many people who signed these cards came and joined but never returned. They signed the order form but never picked up the merchandise. They decided for church membership without deciding for Christ. Many leaders therefore became disenchanted with the idea of asking people for a decision and discarded it altogether.

Adding to the fear of this horn of the dilemma was an increasing timidity. A survey among mainline clergy and laypersons across the continent gave people a list of forty-one possible causes of church decline and asked them to check the ones they personally felt most determinative. The second most frequently checked item was "Fear of appearing pushy with our evangelism." Mainline churches take pride in not being obnoxious about religion. But they have not found a middle ground between the two extremes of "irritating pushiness" and "influence anemia." Some 66 percent of the clergy and 64 percent of the laypersons checked this as an important cause of church decline.

The other horn of the decision dilemma mainline churches run away from involves their observation of methods used by parachurch groups like Campus Crusade. These evangelism workers may bring complete strangers to a decision about Jesus Christ at some particular moment in time, like on an airplane. But many of these new recruits never make the transition into church membership. They join the Head of the Body, but never the Body. The spiritual high is not followed by spiritual growth.

Mainline leaders find themselves stuck between the sharp tips of these two horns. On the one hand, they fear shallow membership recruitment. On the other hand, they fear manipulative spiritual surgical techniques that may cure the illness and kill the patient. For two decades, mainline churches have dealt with this dilemma by not dealing with it at all. Without consciously intending to, they became "closet Calvinists." They withdrew from logical thinking about the subject by resting back into the easy-chair assumption that God "predestines" people to enter the kingdom. In other words, God takes care of the task of asking the right people to join the church.

159

Statistics in most mainline denominations since 1960 indicate, however, that if God takes care of membership decisions by "predestination," he doesn't do nearly as well by himself as he did during the decades when his assistants thought they were supposed to help him. "Closet Calvinism" may be a comforting theology, but it shows poor bottom-line results. Nor do we find much evidence for this kind of theology in the New Testament. Jesus *asked* people to join his group. He *verbally* asked them.

Jesus didn't have 100 percent success with these decision calls. Some people did not follow. The rich young ruler came to Jesus, wanting to be a disciple. But when Jesus asked him for a decision, he got a negative answer. The young man decided the cost of discipleship was too steep. In another instance, Jesus said, "Follow me," and the man replied, "Lord, let me first go and bury my father" (Luke 9:59). In what sounds like a very harsh sentence, Jesus said, "Leave the dead to bury their own dead; but as for you, go and proclaim the kingdom of God" (Luke 9:60).

Just because he didn't succeed each time he asked someone to follow, Jesus didn't stop asking. People in growing churches across the country don't either. They deal with the decision dilemma.

A Matter of Timing

Eddie Hart and Reynaud Robinson, two of America's top sprinters, had incredible misfortune during the Munich Olympic Games. Because they misunderstood the scheduling, they failed to appear at the appointed time for a quarter-final heat and missed their chance to bring home a medal. In those brief minutes of confusion, years of preparation, time, and energy dropped through the drain. They were well prepared but missed being in the right place at the right time.

Failure to seize opportunities when they are ripest happens in tragic ways to everyone. People invest significant pieces of their lives in getting ready for something big. They get an education. They pray. They toil. But the big moment comes and they miss it— perhaps never to meet it again. Nowhere is this more true than in evangelism. Timing is not everything, but without timing nothing else matters. Most people can be influenced toward Christ and the church at certain periods in their lives but not others.

Regardless of whether the human mind is pondering the decision to buy a new car or give commitment to Christ, it goes through five stages. Between the time an idea is initially introduced into consciousness and the time the person affirms that idea and begins living her/his life in the light of it, the following five mental states are experienced: awareness, relevance, interest, trial, and adoption. Sometimes people travel very rapidly through these stages. More often, however, the trip takes weeks or months. Growing churches have their priorities straight and their timing on target. They ask for a decision, not too soon and not too late.

A few growing churches set up a "Membership Sunday" once each month, prior to which they ask several people for a decision. But most do not. Rather than targeting dates on a calendar, they concentrate on the readiness of particular individuals for a decision. They continually ask themselves the question, "Whom will I ask to join the church this Sunday?"

An Open-Ended Direct Approach

Methods for asking people to decide vary endlessly. Here, as in the contact process discussed in the previous chapter, actually asking is far more important than how you ask. But most pastors and lay leaders want some clues regarding do's and don'ts for such conversations.

The pastor of one of America's fastest growing Christian Churches (Disciples of Christ), Glenn Wilkerson, uses what might be termed the "open-ended direct approach" in asking people for a decision. The following comments give a general picture of how this conversation proceeds.

"I like to make advance appointments for this call. If people keep putting me off and don't want to talk with me, I'm really not interested in making that call. I don't want to cram the church down anybody's throat. I always make this first-decision call myself. After that, if the person continues to attend but doesn't place membership, we have two or three laypersons who are also comfortable making that kind of call. Since we have an average of twenty-five visiting families each week, our lay callers are kept busy just making the initial contact visit.

"I like to talk with all the adults in the family and as many of the children as possible. The call takes a varying length of time. It could last fifteen minutes or run as much as an hour. The average call probably lasts forty-five minutes. There is no hard and fast rule. Just whatever time is needed to tell the church's story. I don't believe there is a right or wrong way to make a decision call. I don't see any Moses on the contemporary evangelism scene who has the Ten Commandments for Decision Calls chiseled in stone. Nobody can lead us to the promised land in regard to exactly what to say in order to elicit a faith response.

"I'm not comfortable with a hard sell. Nor do the residents in my community seem receptive to such an approach. I simply get to know my hosts and share with them the vision and the mission of Cypress Creek Church. Whenever it's appropriate to do so, I also jump at the opportunity to share my faith perspective with them concerning the Good News of Jesus Christ. My typical decision call is broken down into six basic components: I always begin by inquiring into their background. Simple questions like, 'Where are you from? How long have you lived here? Where do you work?' My intent is to let them know I am genuinely interested in getting to know them as persons.

I'm willing to let them talk about their background until it becomes apparent that they have exhausted that subject. Second, I ask, 'What is your religious background?' If it turns out that they come from a different religious tradition than ours, then I will give them a brief overview of our denomination's history and traditions. Third, I share with them the uniqueness of our local congregation. This is an opportunity to share not only the programs but also the theological emphasis of our church. Fourth, I then ask them if they have any questions about our church that I might be helpful in answering. Also, if some of the family have disclosed the fact that they are non-Christians, I seize the opportunity at this point to share my faith. And then finally, I always close my presentation by saying, 'If you believe that Cypress Creek Christian Church can be a spiritual home for you and your family, we'd love for you to become a part of our fellowship.' I always offer that invitation, share a few pleasantries, and then leave.

The Key Question Conversational Approach

Other growing church leaders hang up a decision conversation on the hooks of specific key questions. The following outline comes from a sheet used to train laypersons in this method. The three sentences cast in italics indicate key turning points in the conversation. Unless these key questions are used, the process falls apart, producing an unsuccessful call.

    I. Forget everything you learned about contact calling. This is a different kind of call.

    II. What keeps people from making a final decision:
        1. Nobody asked them
        2. Procrastination
        3. Crowd fear
        4. Misunderstanding about membership transfer process
        5. Fear of baptism
        6. Misunderstanding about baptism requirements

    III. When to make the call:
        1. Only after people visit the church several times and seem interested.
        2. Generally speaking, four to six weeks after their first visit to the church would be the earliest time for making a decision call.
        3. With some individuals, there are special reasons for waiting several months before making a decision call. The pastor and other leaders usually sense when the time is right for a decision call.

IV. How to make the call:
1. Read your master prospect card carefully and prayerfully. Pray for the individual on whom you are about to call.
2. Go to the home and make your entrance in the usual manner, as with other calls. Before entering, decide on a lead person. The lead person should be seated close to the prospect or head of the house. Do not make a decision call on the wife alone, or if the family has company present.
3. Visit with the people for about three minutes, then come to the point in something like the following manner.
   A. *Key Question—"Have you folks given any thought to placing your membership with our church?"* Alternate approach—"Did you folks get the letter from our minister telling you about our membership day next Sunday?" Another alternate approach—"Several people will be placing their membership with our church this Sunday. I knew you folks would probably be thinking of joining sometime soon. Since many folks like to do this with other people rather than alone, I wanted to stop by and let you know. I thought it might be a good opportunity for you to come in with a group."
   B. Then ask some questions that bring an affirmative response (some callers like to ask these questions first, before they bring up joining the church), questions such as: "You do enjoy our church? You have liked our worship services? You and your children have appreciated the Sunday school program?"
4. Then say something like the following, depending on which applies:
   A. "I'm sure you know how the membership process works in our church. On the singing of the invitation hymn, you come forward and stand facing the minister."
   B. "Our church does not require you to be rebaptized if you have already been baptized in another church. We already accept you as a Christian."
   C. For adults who need to be baptized (applicable with initial converts and in denominations that practice immersion), say something like, "Our church follows the biblical method of baptism—immersion. The Greek word *baptizo* means to dip under. This is why we immerse. We like to baptize people with the whole congregation present because it is inspirational and educational for them, but it can be done privately."

5. *Key Question—Would there be any reason why you folks couldn't be there to place your membership this Sunday?*
6. If you use a decision and transfer type card or folder, this is the point at which you should remove it from your pocket and say something like: "What we do is fill in these cards in the home so that we can get the information to transfer your membership for you. This also enables us to introduce you on Sunday morning." Then begin filling in the blanks on the card, asking the person the appropriate questions to complete the blanks on either the membership/transfer section or the decision/baptism section. After completing the blanks (except for the signature), say: "Now, would you just *write* your name here as you want it to appear on the church roll." (Do not ask about children who are old enough to join until *after* you have asked the parents.)
7. *Key Sentence—If excuses are offered, meet each one directly.* Do not accept excuses without challenging them. Don't take no for an answer or be put off.
   A. If absolutely necessary, make an appointment to come back later in the week. In such cases, leave the cards in the home and ask them to think it over. But concentrate on getting a decision on this first call. Ninety-five percent of the time, an experienced caller will not need to return a second time.
   B. Don't argue, and they won't. Just be direct in your responses. This allows them to stop kidding themselves about their reasons for not making a decision. You always move them closer to a decision by not agreeing with their excuses.
   C. The excuses most people offer are ways of asking you for a good reason why they should decide positively. By meeting these excuses directly, you always leave them closer to the church because you have indicated that you care enough about them to want them in the church.
   D. Remember that almost all persons who say yes on this kind of call give *one* excuse before they do so. The fact that they offer this excuse before saying yes will have no bearing on the quality of their commitment or church participation after they join.
8. After the card is signed or the decision is made verbally to be there on Sunday, a brief word of prayer should be offered (perhaps thanking God for this decision and for these fine people).
9. If they cannot be there next Sunday, press for the next date possible.
10. In rare cases, as with invalids, a "membership in absentia" might be explained.

The Miniature Flip-Chart Approach

A layman in Oregon had poor success at decision calling. He continually got no for an answer and couldn't understand why. Finally, he talked with his pastor about this problem. The minister soon learned that this dedicated evangelist began his conversations like this: "I don't suppose you're interested in joining our church, are you?"

Many laymen (and pastors, too) don't know what to say and how to say it. Yet they don't feel comfortable with a memorized conversation. Some of these leaders say they like to use a small card or folder outline in decision calling. This approach has several advantages. They don't have to memorize anything and suffer anxiety about forgetting it. The gospel message is presented in a systematic, clear way. The persons on whom they call tend to focus on the printed material and their decision rather than on the caller. This method is like a miniature flip-chart. Most leaders know how useful these are in helping people make decisions during stewardship campaigns. They can perform the same function in evangelism calling.

In most decision-calling systems that use this approach, the caller sits down near the prospect. After brief initial chit-chat, he or she asks permission to review some of the basic ideas that anyone considering becoming a church member or a Christian would want to think about. People always agree to this. (A pastor who has made more than 10,000 such calls says he has yet to have someone refuse.) Then the caller reads through the booklet, perhaps stopping to comment or illustrate. Or, the caller can just read the material as printed on the folder.

The remainder of this type of call is very much like the "Key Question Conversational Approach" illustrated above. The caller asks for a decision. If the prospect offers an excuse (most people do offer one, sometimes two), the caller meets this directly and then asks for the decision again. The card (pp. 166-7) is a good example of this type of material. Theologically, it communicates effectively in mainline churches as well as more conservative groups.

Answering the Excuses

In what has traditionally been called the "cultivation call," visitors should give little attention to the excuses for not affiliating with a church that those called upon always offer. Acknowledge the fact that you heard the excuse, perhaps with a pause—just enough pause to let them hear in the silence the emptiness of their own hollow noise—then move the conversation on to other things. These excuses are seldom the real reason for people staying out of church anyway, so it is probably better to avoid reinforcing and strengthening them by giving them conversational attention.

A

BIBLICAL

OUTLINE

OF

GOOD NEWS

FOR YOU

I believe that Jesus is the Christ and accept him as my Lord and Savior.

I intend with his help to lead a Christian life.

I desire to unite with Christ's Church.

_____
Signature

Address _____

_____

_____

Zip code _____

I expect to unite _____ Date

by confession of faith and baptism ☐
by transfer of membership ☐

from (Church) _____

(Town) _____

Additional copies available from:
National Evangelistic Association
5001 Avenue N
Lubbock, Texas 79401

GOD SENT JESUS TO BRING YOU A RICH, FULL LIFE.

"I am come that they may have life, and have it abundantly." (John 10:10)

"These things I have spoken to you, that my joy may be in you, and that your joy may be full." (John 15:11)

"Therefore, if any one is in Christ, he is a new creation; the old has passed away, behold, the new has come." (II Cor. 5:17)

HERE IS HOW YOU FIND THE NEW LIFE JESUS WANTS TO GIVE YOU:

1. You realize that new life doesn't come from following religious rules or doing good works.

"Therefore, since we are justified by faith, we have peace with God through our Lord Jesus Christ. (Romans 5:1)

"For by grace you have been saved through faith; and this is not your own doing, it is the gift of God - not because of works, lest any man should boast." (Ephesians 2:8-9)

2. You have a change of heart by repenting of self-centeredness.

"And Peter said to them, 'Repent, and be baptized every one of you in the name of Jesus Christ for the forgiveness of your sins...'" (Acts 2:38)

"The times of ignorance God overlooked, but now he commands all men everywhere to repent...." (Acts 17:30)

3. You publically state your belief in Christ.

"...because, if you confess with your lips that Jesus is Lord and believe in your heart that God raised him from the dead, you will be saved." (Romans 10:9)

"So everyone who acknowledges me before men, I also will acknowledge before my Father who is in heaven...." (Matthew 10:32)

4. You seal your decision to follow Christ by being baptized.

"Then Philip opened his mouth, and beginning with this scripture he told him the good news of Jesus. And as they went along the road they came to some water, and the eunuch said, 'See, here is water! What is to prevent my being baptized?' And he commanded the chariot to stop, and they both went down into the water, Philip and the eunuch, and he baptized him." (Acts 8:35-38)

"We were buried therefore with him by baptism into death, so that as Christ was raised from the dead by the glory of the Father, we too might walk in newness of life." (Romans 6:4)

"...for in Christ Jesus you are all sons of God, through faith. For as many of you as were baptized into Christ have put on Christ." (Gal. 3:26-27)

5. You begin to help with Christ's work in the Church and the world as your life is enriched by the Holy Spirit.

"You are my friends if you do what I command you." (John 15:14)

"So we are ambassadors for Christ, God making His appeal through us." (II Cor. 5:20)

"...you shall be my witnesses in Jerusalem and in all Judea and Samaria and to the end of the earth." (Acts 1:8)

"So those who received his word were baptized, and there were added that day about three thousand souls. And they devoted themselves to the Apostles' teaching and fellowship, to the breaking of bread and the prayers." (Acts 2:41-42)

"Let us hold fast the confession of our hope without wavering...not neglecting to meet together, as is the habit of some...." (Hebrews 10:23-25)

But in the "decision call," where a concrete commitment for Christ and the church is being sought—probably for next Sunday morning—it is usually necessary to deal with these excuses in some way. If you don't, they may block the conversation from moving forward to a positive conclusion. But even here, don't deal with the excuse at length. Let the callee say it, make your reply to it and then move quickly on to other things. The real problem is almost always something other than the excuse presented, so hit it a brief, glancing blow—enough to get it out of the conversational pathway—and move on.

Regardless of what excuse a person offers as a block to decision, keep several universal principles in mind if you intend to make an effective response: First, there is a big difference between arguing and "meeting an excuse directly." Never engage in argument. Few people are argued into the kingdom of God. But do people the courtesy of meeting their excuses directly and honestly. This nudge helps them to stop kidding themselves about their reasons for not making a decision.

The logic of your response to an excuse is never as important as the simple unwillingness to accept an excuse as a valid reason for a negative decision. As soon as the person realizes that you recognize the weakness of the excuse, he or she usually admits that weakness and makes no further comment.

When a blocking excuse is offered, many experienced callers like to reply with a smile, a light-hearted chuckle, and preface their response with, "I can understand why you would feel that way, but. . . ." The caller then adds to this beginning whatever remarks seem appropriate to meeting that particular excuse (see samples below).

The following excuses are samples from a list of thirty commonly given by people just prior to making a positive decision. The suggested responses printed under each excuse provide insight regarding the manner in which callers should reply. Few people use more than one excuse, or two at most. So, the decision caller who meets that first excuse in a direct manner is usually finished with that part of the conversation in thirty seconds. The callee has exhausted her or his ammunition and moves on toward a decision.

Excuse: "I am waiting until my husband (or wife) is ready."

Possible response: "How long have you been waiting for your husband? Waiting hasn't been a very successful method, has it? One member of the family waiting on the outside of the church usually keeps the other member waiting on the outside." Alternate response: "Doesn't each of us have to work out our relationship with God individually, apart from other people, even our wives and husbands? You are not really responsible for your husband's actions, but you are responsible for your own."

Excuse: "I want to think it over some more."

Possible response: "You do think the church will help you to live more meaningfully, don't you? Do you really need to think over whether you want to live a better life?" Alternate response: "Is coming into the church a right thing to do? Of course it is. If this is the right thing to do, why wouldn't *now* be the right time to do it?"

Excuse: "I can be as good a Christian outside the church as I can in it."

Possible response: "Could you be as good a soldier outside the army as in it? You might, but aren't you likely to be a better soldier inside the army?" Alternate response: "Could you be as good a student outside a school as inside? Perhaps you could, but aren't you likely to be a better student by attending school?"

Whatever approach you make to answering excuses, remember that decision calls are not a place to let your "responsive listening skills" dominate the interaction. Set those skills aside and do something completely different. In the typical "contact call," you should build relationshps and respond to the conversational pattern of other people. The decision call is built more on the New Testament model of "proclamation." In a contact call, you put the other person in charge of the conversation. In a decision call, you go with the attitude that *you* will take charge of the conversation.

Two nuns were sent to a certain part of Africa by their religious order with the assignment of Christianizing the "heathen" in that part of the world. Five years went by, and no reports were received concerning conversions. A superior was dispatched to investigate. When she interviewed the two nuns, she asked them why nobody had been converted. They replied, "Oh, we are still trying to understand these people. We haven't attempted any conversions yet. We thought that should wait until later." Can you imagine the apostle Paul writing home to Jerusalem from Thessalonica, saying that he was trying to create a "Christian presence" in their culture but hadn't attempted any conversions yet?"

Training and Presence

A young pastor in Harrodsburg, Kentucky, went out to call on a middle-aged man who had attended the church several times during the past few years. The young minister dropped by because the church was holding a revival, but he expected nothing to happen. This man just didn't seem like the church type. Using one of the methods outlined above, the young pastor asked the man for a decision. Surprisingly, the man said, "Yes, I want to do that." He came forward the next Sunday, was baptized, and is now an active church member. One day sometime later, the clergyman asked him why he had waited so long before joining the church. "Nobody asked me," he replied.

Soren Kierkegaard told a story about a man walking down a street in Europe. Passing a store front, he read a sign in the window that said, "Pants Pressed Here." He immediately entered the front door of this business establishment. Once inside, he went behind the counter, and began taking off his trousers. The shocked clerk asked, "Sir, what are you doing?" The man replied, "I want to have my trousers pressed." The clerk said, "We don't press trousers here." The man, pointing to the sign in the window, said, "But your sign says, 'Pants Pressed Here.'" The clerk, finally recognizing their communication problem, responded, "Oh, we don't press pants here. We just paint signs."

God has many nice buildings around the country, setting comfortably behind green lawns. Each has a sign in front whose letters communicate some assertions about what goes on inside that institution. How easily we fall into a stance of painting signs rather than making disciples. But Jesus did not ask us to become sign painters. He called us to be disciple makers.

Group Discussion Questions

1. What procedures does our church use in asking people to make a decision for Christ and church membership at an appropriate time?
2. Have members of the class share their good and bad experiences regarding times when they were approached for a decision about Christ or church membership.
3. Of the three methods John Wesley used—contact, impact, and decision—in which do you think our church does the best job? The poorest? Illustrate your opinion.
4. Have you ever felt extremely negative about some personal decision—like buying a new car or a home—then found yourself changing to a positive decision within a few moments or an hour's time? Does your own personal experience of deciding about Christ seem to validate that theory?
5. Do you recall ever having someone "meet your excuse directly" when you were trying to put off a decision for Christ or the church? How did that feel to you?
6. Some pastors feel that explaining the mechanics of "how people join our church" is extremely important, especially to persons who come from other denominations. If you have at some point in your life transferred to our church from another denomination, would you share with the group your opinion regarding the importance of such explanations?
7. Most pastors in growing churches, even large ones, find time to call in the homes of prospective members. Do you think these calls by the pastor are important? Why?

The superior man is distressed by his want of ability.
—Confucius, 551-479 B.C.

16

Staying Power

The first man who owned the greatest gold deposits in western Nevada didn't find them. He unearthed some of the yellow metal, but not much. One day when the boiling sun was high and his spirits low, he gave up and sold his claim. In a very short time, the new owner struck the Comstock Lode. Millions of dollars in gold emerged from those shafts during the next few years.

Growing church pastors stay with it. Many of them keep digging for five years before anything significant happens. Most of them have served their present congregations for at least seven years. *Axiom #16: Growing churches have long-term pastoral leadership.* "The kingdom of God is as if a man should scatter seed upon the ground, and should sleep and rise night and day, and the seed should sprout and grow, he knows not how," Jesus said (Mark 4:26). Seed *is* like the God relationship. Although containing mysterious power within itself, it can't be controlled. You can try to set up the conditions for growth, but you can't actually make it produce. Good pastors don't grow churches. Only God can do that. But the longer a pastor stays in one field, the better he seems to till the ground and scatter the seed; consequently, the greater God makes the harvest.

Love Power

During announcement time in the morning installation service for a new pastor, the lay leader urged worshipers to attend a fellowship dinner/talent show that evening. "You will see several people doing things they are not capable of doing," he said. The synod executive seated on the platform felt that statement applied equally well to himself and every pastor he knew. Being clergy is like performing at a perpetual talent night. It forever involves doing things of which nobody is capable. Churches are miracle systems: God takes small-talent people and accomplishes missions impossible. He sets imperfect leaders in the midst of imperfect people and gets something great going.

In the frustrating midst of all this organized imperfection, how can a pastor find the endurance to stay around until things start happening? That requires several personality qualities, ". . .but the greatest of these is love" (1 Corinthians 13:13). Bob Bates, president of a Bible College in Glennallen, Alaska, defines love as an unconditional commitment to an imperfect person. That describes a quality essential for growth church leadership. Pastors who see their task as "perfecting the saints" have their vocational role confused. Only God can perfect the saints. The pastor must accept the saints and patiently wait while they gain maturity. Trying to rush the saints toward perfection succeeds about as well as attaching a rocket launcher to a roller skater in order to increase his speed. Many of life's best things require much time, patience, and waiting on God to finish his work. Going the distance with the "calculated inefficiency" of local congregations is one of these.

"He who is a hireling and not a shepherd, whose own the sheep are not, sees the wolf coming and leaves the sheep and flees. . ." (John 10:12). What divides the shepherds from the hirelings? Love of the sheep. What divides the shepherd from loving the sheep? Bitterness: bitterness at members, bitterness at budgets, bitterness at salary, bitterness in general. If you let it sneak through your fences, it will surely kill your sheep. Only love—active, forgiving love—can make rancor hold its distance. It takes concern for one another, being there and being dependable. It takes patience, perseverance, and time.

Purpose Power

A young flag-bearer in the Civil War, far ahead of his advancing regiment, planted the colors near the enemy lines. The captain yelled after him, "Bring back the flag, you fool!" But the soldier called over his shoulder, "You bring up the regiment!" Moving through the heavy shell fire, his comrades found him dead. His hands still clutched the base of the flag, which stood proudly erect.

Most growing church leaders don't die for their cause, but they hold their purpose as firmly in mind. They are God-connected people.

Difficulties don't distract them because they remember what they came here to do. Ministry requires a healthy blend of four things: education, motivation, perspiration, and spiritualization. But the fourth packs more power than the other three together. A shot of spiritual purpose will induce motivation, perspiration, and education, but none of the other three produce dedicated purpose. Ministers can have three degrees but no spiritual temperature. Motivation or perspiration create high activity levels. By themselves they are like hooking a 300 horsepower motor to a boat with no rudder.

The sooty tern is a seabird with unique staying power. After leaving the nest, it remains in the air for more than three years before returning to earth. The sooty tern manages to stay up so long because it has developed the facility for "resting in the wind." It can rest and fly at the same time. In order to maintain the high endurance required, pastoral ministers must do something similar—rest in God. Without that spiritual quality, even the highest energy level leaders can't keep on keeping on through the steady wind of demands on their busy lives. ". . .they shall mount up with wings like eagles, they shall run and not be weary, they shall walk and not faint" (Isaiah 40:31). That comes true for ministers every day, just as it did in the Hebrew trek from Babylon to Jerusalum. That kind of strength emanates from the internal perception that God will help us do what he wants done in spite of our personal power failures.

As Jesus begins his ministry, he goes into a desert place without food and faces forty days of temptation. Every ministry moves through barren spots where nothing seems to grow: little hope for the future, little affirmation from other people, a feeling of distance from God. For Jesus, this low valley experience was set on a high mountain. Paradoxically, it came on the heels of a real mountaintop experience at the river Jordan—his baptism. God said, "This is my beloved Son, with whom I am well pleased" (Matthew 3:17). Then came the barren place.

West Texas farmers who grow cotton year after year on arid land feel the brunt of similar experiences. In one of the biggest cotton-crop years ever experienced, 1973, some farmers profited so much that expensive new homes sprung up everywhere—replacing poor wooden dwellings that had suffered four decades of weathering. But the next year was a barren place. How do farmers deal with these barren places? They are tempted to quit, turn back. They feel the urge to sell their land and make bread from those dusty stones. But most of them don't. They keep on keeping on, knowing that in the midst of even this barren spot, God is still around and will see them through to another mountaintop.

A small-town church suffered years of decline and stood on the brink of starvation. Through many lean years, members streamed away to the big cities. That church is now thriving and growing. Why? Because a few members and several pastors traversed those desert years in faith. Tempted to quit, they didn't. Like Jesus, they clung to their purpose. They felt that God wanted them there and would see them through. He did.

One young pastor hangs onto this principle through the words of an ancient, unknown poet:

> Live for something.
> Have a purpose, and that purpose
> Keep in view.
> Drifting like a helpless vessel,
> Who canst 'er to life be true?
> Half the wrecks that strew life's oceans.
> If some star had been their guide,
> Might have long been safely riding,
> But they've drifted with the tide.
> Let us then be up and doing
> With a heart for any fate,
> Still achieving, still pursuing.
> Learn to labor and wait.[1]

Hanging in There

John Creasy is one of the world's most prolific mystery novelists. His 560 books have sold more than sixty million copies and are translated into twenty-three languages. But Creasy collected 743 rejection slips before getting his first word into print. James J. Corbett, former world heavyweight champion, was asked to describe the most important thing necessary to becoming a champion. "Fight one more round," he said.

The pastor asked a visiting denominational executive, "Do you have any words of wisdom for me before you leave?"

The bishop replied with a smile and three words: "Hang in there!" He then went on to say that he gives this advice to every pastor in every church. "If you can't do that, you can't do anything else," he said. The apostle Paul put it this way: "And let us not grow weary in well-doing, for in due season we shall reap, if we do not lose heart" (Galatians 6:9).

A pastor in Louisiana says he would hate to look at his church's graph for the first five years he was there. "Sometimes it takes five or ten years to see the results," he said. "That's where the patience comes in." A pastor in Kentucky worked four years before seeing numerical results. A New Mexico pastor served five years before growth began. These leaders didn't just sit on their hands during this period, waiting for God to do something. They built relationships and constantly sought for better community reach-out methods. But waiting was part of the necessary commitment.

---

[1]Author unknown. Taken from "The Messenger," newsletter of First Christian Church, Paducah, Texas, July 1, 1981.

Part of this lengthy time requirement comes from the need for communication redundancy. People do not instantly act on the pearls of wisdom from even the wisest leader. A psychiatrist and a pastor doing group therapy were evaluating a session they had just finished. Seeing that the minister was frustrated because a certain group member was progressing so slowly, the psychiatrist said, "Sometimes you have to tell a patient something six times on six different occasions before he understands you and gets an insight." Then, too, few pastors know at the very beginning of their tenure exactly what that church needs to do in evangelism. Several early years of ministry are used up in getting on board, evaluating and experimenting.

Another pastor asks, "How long does one preach the same old thing to the same old people? How long does one put up with folks who reject the message of good news? How long is evangelism to be a priority for the church? But mystery breaks in and says, 'Do it as long as it takes till the job gets done . . . till hell freezes over . . . till the cows come home.'"[2]

Making It Through the Stages

"He is just going through a stage," his mother remarked. "He'll get over that later on." Childhood is a continual series of stages. But now we know that these stages never stop. Adults, too, move through stages all their lives. In addition to these normal transition phases, ministers are subject to "pastorate stages." From the beginning of service with a particular church on through to its end is a constantly unfolding set of new stages. Another reason growing church pastors hang in there is because they learn how to survive the hinges of these stages without getting mashed.

Stage One—The Honeymoon. This one-year, getting-acquainted period is a glorious time. Unless the new pastor does something awfully stupid or immoral, these are happy months. Since neither party in the marriage is very well acquainted with the other, each has little about which to complain.

Stage Two—The Hidden Iceberg Stage. This "getting to know all about you" period runs from one through two years in a small church, one through three years in a middle-sized church and one through five years in a larger church. Icebergs whose tips were only faintly seen at earlier stages begin to appear bulky and formidable. During this time, the real truth gets known about both parties—the good, the bad, the ugly. Some of that information is encouraging; most of it is not. This period is similar to the same stage in a marriage. Conflict is the word for this adjustment phase.

---

[2]From a speech by David Blondell at the National Evangelism Workshop, Amarillo, Texas, May 1980.

When Exodus says, "And the people murmured against Moses . . . " (Exodus 15:24), he had hit the iceberg stage. When he broke the tablets of ten commandments, he was at the iceberg stage. One wonders if he anticipated these problems that day at the burning bush when he got the big dream of freedom for his people?

Stage Three—Liking You Anyway. This pleasant phase is entered after a major crisis or series of small confrontations. It comes at approximately three to five years—sometimes seven years in a gigantic church where the pastor follows a long-term predecessor. A new bride always has a picture in her mind of the ideal husband; the groom likewise believes he has married the perfect wife. After a few years, both parties reach a crisis consisting of two choices. They decide to tear up the picture and throw it away. Or, they decide to tear up the person and throw him or her away. The latter procedure is called divorce. In churches, it is called "terminating the ministry," or "moving on to an opportunity for greater service."

Rather than having an installation service for the new minister, congregations should perhaps consider having a similar service about three years later. This would signal the fact that pastor and people have now worked through their differences sufficiently to go on doing ministry together. They now know each other, flaws and all. And they like each other, anyway.

Stage Four—The Specialization Stage. At this point, the pastor is getting bored, though she or he may not recognize or admit it. Seven times around the cycle of church seasons leaves you with few surprises. The warm glow from frequent praise in early years of ministry has faded. People still appreciate you, but they don't say so as much. In a conscious or unconscious response to boredom and affirmation needs, the pastor begins to specialize in something. He or she keeps on doing the church's work, but transfers more time to a specialized field. For some, this is counseling. For others, it is civic work. For many, it is denominational officerships and board services. Sometimes, it is Holy Land tours. Occasionally, it is a plethora of public speaking. For a few, it is writing. But whatever the specialization, it fills an important personal need. Everybody who stays long in a pastorate does it. Pastors of growing churches are no exception. The big difference between them and their colleagues: specialization does not distract them from their primary purpose. They still shepherd their flock with patience and love. They continue to evangelize the unflocked with determination and zeal. Their hobby does not displace their vocational calling.

Stage Five—The Rocking Chair Temptation. This comes at ten to twelve years beyond the starting gate. Things are easy now. The pastor knows all the parish personalities and foibles. He or she knows how to politic quickly, with a minimum of time expenditure. The three great temptations at every stage are to whine, shine, or recline. In this fifth stage, the "recline temptation" comes to the foreground. That's why some pastors feel they have lost all their creativity. By this time, everyone in the church has decided that things are going pretty well, so we ought to let the pastor do things the way she or he wants to. Growing church ministers fight their way through this temptation to homestead in a rocking chair on the church's front porch. They attend seminars. They read books. They research new ideas and programs. They don't grow stale; they grow wiser. And their churches continue to grow larger.

Stage Six—The Benevolent Grandfather Years. By this time (fifteen to twenty years into the pastorate), you are marrying the children whose mothers you visited in the hospital at delivery time—perhaps you even married mom and dad. If you make it this distance, you have developed immense pastoral skills. Your people love you. They no longer see your faults. You can do no wrong because you are family. This is the best and worst of ministerial stages. Best because it is the most fun; your professional self-confidence has never been higher. Worst because you are tempted to rest on your laurels instead of sprinting for the finish line. That is why a study of fifteen large mainline churches whose pastors served them more than twenty years shows a five-year numerical decline pattern immediately before they retire. This curve appears on the chart of most long pastorates. A few ministers pass through the twentieth year in high gear. But most don't.

None of the above means that all pastors should move on at a certain stage, or that they should never move. It means that all ministry is like a balancing act on a three-legged stool. The pastor must build a positive relationship with God, a positive relationship with people, and continue an aggressive search for programmatic ideas that help persons inside and outside the church relate positively to God.

Growing church pastors don't just stay, they stay balanced.

Group Discussion Questions

1. What can local church members do to encourage capable pastors to stay longer in each congregation? Make a list on the blackboard or flipchart.
2. In addition to those mentioned in this chapter, what other ministerial qualities do you think are important for people who serve long pastorates?
3. Do you know of churches that went through barren years of decline and then increased in vitality? Illustrate. Why did they experience new growth?
4. Do you feel that the six stages of ministry sketched in this chapter are accurate descriptions? Have different members of the class give illustrations of pastors they have known who went through these stages.

No man is wise enough by himself.
—*Titus Maccius Plautus, 254-184 B.C.*

17

Build a Quality Circle

A reporter once asked Frank Leahy, the great Notre Dame football coach, whether the nuns' prayers helped his team to win. Leahy thought for a moment and replied, "Their prayers work better when my players are big!" Faith and prayer are major factors, but growing churches also field big players. They ask for and get high personal commitment from the laity. *Axiom #17: Growing churches have strong lay leadership involvement in church life.*

Generals Need Lieutenants

Charles de Gaulle succeeded in leading France because he won and held the allegiance of several outstanding officers. Pastors who fail lack this sparkling capacity. Ezra didn't kid himself. He knew that a God connection is essential and said so. But he also knew he couldn't do alone what God wanted done. So, he appointed magistrates and judges. "I took courage, for the hand of the LORD my God was upon me, and I gathered leading men from Israel to go up with me" (Ezra 7:28). Good leaders are always thus. They never try to row the boat by themselves. They gather other leaders and teach them how to lead.

Approximately 35 percent of mainline congregation members are inactive, though they may attend occasionally. Another 35 percent participate actively, but they are more Indian types than chief material. Fifteen percent are youth and children who can seldom give leadership. The remaining 15 percent are workers, leaders, tithers, very occupied with helping the church reach high goals. Growing church pastors have great leadership skill. Their lieutenant circle is always intensely dedicated and often larger than this typical 15 percent. "Laypersons are crucial and vital to evangelism happening," says one of these pastors. "It can't be done by the minister alone." That congregation has a highly systematic shepherding structure which involves one elder working with four deacons, who in turn work with forty church members.

In this congregation, elders cannot be nominated unless they meet very high standards. They assume a pastoral role in caring for the members and are expected to be the twenty-four most committed members of the church. They attend frequent training sessions in order to improve their skills. Each elder participates in many activities that keep him or her extremely knowledgeable about the congregation's goals. The following list illustrates what these key leaders do.

An elder must:
1. have strong stewardship (time/talent/treasure).
2. attend church school regularly.
3. attend worship regularly.
4. provide spiritual/administrative leadership and counsel.
5. preside at the Lord's Table and assume the following worship duties on a rotated basis.
   a. serve convalescent communion.
   b. serve as greeter after worship at the rear exit doors.
6. attend elders' meeting monthly.
7. attend board meetings bi-monthly.
8. attend yearly elders' retreat.
9. spend at least one hour per week doing "elder work."
10. meet one new person or family per week.
11. support/assist/counsel/pray for ministers.
12. be knowledgeable of all church programs.

This church also expects elders to participate in the church's flock/shepherding in the following ways.

An elder must:
1. meet with deacons in July and plan at least the first flock function.
2. visit with and instruct deacons to call in homes of each flock family by September 1.

    a. encourage deacons and flock families to get involved in programs—church school/youth/etc.

    b. encourage strong stewardship.

    c. encourage all to meet one new person or family per week.

    d. explain bereaved family procedure.

3. have three or four flock functions each year.

    a. get to know each other.

    b. promote/inform about church programs.

4. function as a mini-minister.

    a. visit flock members in hospitals.

    b. check on absentee members.

    c. be a liaison to church board—listener/communicator as needed.

    d. help new members find their niche.

5. explain/promote prayer chain to deacons and families.

    a. tell them that ministers pray for each elder and family *by name* each day.

    b. tell them that elders pray for ministers and each deacon and family *by name* each day.

    c. ask each deacon to pray for each family and elder *by name* each day.

    d. encourage the families to reverse this process by praying for deacon/elder/ministers *by name* each day.

6. deliver New Member Packets as assigned.

7. check church mailbox weekly for messages.

8. in concert with deacons, help with Every Member Commitment Program as required.[1]

The systems used to develop strong lieutenant groups vary in different growth churches. But each has some kind of structured interaction plan. Japanese industrialists use similar principles. They understand that great creativity and productivity comes from small, tightly-knit circles of leadership.

A World Council of Churches spokesman several years ago said that "the laity are not helpers of the clergy so that the clergy can do their job. The clergy are helpers of the whole people of God, so that the laity can be the church." Pastors of growing churches don't just have great dreams for lay involvement; they organize air-traffic-control systems so these theological 747s can come to earth at their church.

Most denominations now agree that the clergy-laity dichotomy is unbiblical and therefore invalid. It grew up as an accident of church

---

[1]*Situational Evangelism,* edited by Herb Miller, "Finding and Assimilating New Members" by Jim Baughman. Net Press, 1982.

history and marked a drift away from scriptural faithfulness. At the same time, most Protestants have retained the Catholic one-bishop rule in form of one-minister rule. They don't recognize this carryover because they so strongly emphasize lay officers. They think these democratic elections are proof that they are carrying out "the priesthood of all believers." For most Protestants, however, this is a mirage. Just because a church elects officers and calls them lay leaders, that doesn't automatically produce a strong, shared leadership involving both clergy and laity.

Growing church pastors understand the dramatic disparity between an ostensible constitutional democracy and an actual, collegial, quality-circle leadership.

Only after Moses began to share his leadership did the quails come and the Hebrews have meat to eat. While these two items may not be cause and effect in the Exodus, they surely are in modern churches. Without shared leadership, churches perish in the wilderness. As an ancient Shinto saying puts it: "Decisions on important matters should not be made by one person alone."

Smart Lieutenants Don't Attack Alone

Theodore Roosevelt said, "The best executive is the one who has sense enough to pick good men to do what he wants done, and self-restraint enough to keep from meddling with them while they do it." The classic mistake of all great monarchs—from Alexander the Great to Napoleon to Hitler—was in overextending their power of influence without building an organizational linkage strong enough to support it. They lengthened their supply lines too far, allowed their internal systems to weaken and tried to govern too much. If they had been content with smaller spheres and more mutual alliances, they could have governed longer and better. Growing church leaders understand this principle. They know that when you try to control everything, you eventually end up controlling nothing.

Growing churches recognize the differences between people who like to *do* things and people who enjoy *deciding* things. They involve the lieutenants in the *deciding functions* because they enjoy that sort of thing and do it well. They involve the bulk of church members in meaningful *activity* because they enjoy that sort of thing and do it well. Of course, some of the church's "discussing functions" always involve some doing (as illustrated by the list of elder functions from the church mentioned earlier in this chapter). And some "doing functions" always involve a bit of deciding. But the differences are still major between these two types of activity and the two types of people who enjoy them. Because growing churches recognize that difference and don't confuse the two roles, much larger clusters of persons gather to participate in what each personally finds meaningful.

American cults, though potentially negative and destructive to personality, understand the tremendously different emphasis needed in working with their core leader group and the less involved, less verbally skilled, outer-membership circle. They confuse these two functions much less fequently than most Protestant groups.

Another part of the reason for increased member involvement in growing churches comes from their higher quality of esprit de corps. Their members work harder, but they also have more fun together. How does this happen? Mostly through the pastor, who has the knack for bringing it about, but also through the lay leaders, who work to accomplish it. Then, too, Christians are never really happy unless they know they are doing God's work. Evangelism is so obviously a right thing to do that it begets a high enjoyment level.

Ordinary People

When Wycliffe translated the Bible from Latin into a common tongue, he was criticized by the intellectuals of his age for scattering the evangelical pearls "to be trampled by the swine." These critics were making the same mistake that intellectuals in the church make in every age—that of looking down sophisticated noses and questioning the ability of the common man to rise to uncommon insights. The great reformers (and the great religious renewal movements) of every age built skyscrapers of change on precisely that bet.

Growing church pastors have immense and honest respect for common, ordinary people. These pastors are true intellectuals. *Real* intellectuals respect the people they work with and understand that each has a gift which, though different, is equally useful for doing the work of Christ.

We live in a professionally oriented society. We glorify professionalism in athletes, physicians, teachers, lawyers, preachers, and architects. As the director of the Toledo, Ohio, Symphony Orchestra said, "There is no room for the amateur among our musicians." But translating this attitude into church life gets us into big trouble. The dictionary defines an amateur as one who does something for pleasure, out of the sheer joy of doing—someone who loves what he or she does. This is why the most important people in the church are always amateurs. You can't *hire* that kind of commitment. You can hire pastoral, professional leadership. But you can't *hire* the amateur leaders who are so essential to a strong congregation, and this can only be precipitated through great respect by leaders for common people.

The key question growing church pastors ask of potential church workers is the same one Jesus asked Peter: "Do you love me?" (John 21:17). Jesus didn't ask, "Are you capable? Are you smart? Will you follow directions?" He asked, "Do you love me?"

If God gives you a job to do, he will teach you how to do it as you go along. He will provide the knowledge, strength, or ability to do it as the need arises. Do not ask to know whether people are smart enough, but whether they are willing. That is why Jesus called

Matthew from a tax office instead of a rabbi from the synagogue. That is why he called Simon Peter from a fishing boat instead of a college professor from Athens. And that is why growing churches lift up majestic objectives and ask ordinary people to respond to that vision. Jesus said, "But seek first his kingdom and his righteousness, and all these things shall be yours as well" (Matthew 6:33). When people set themselves toward high aims with enthusiasm, the talent to accomplish them soon appears.

Many growing churches involve women at the same leadership levels as men. One pastor says, "Our congregation seeks a fifty-fifty ratio between men and women while selecting elders and deacons. Quite frankly, our women probably do a better job as elders because by nature they are better nurturers, better mothers." Another pastor says, "Our elders and deacons are male or female based on commitment, not age or sex. We have no stipulations that half or a third be female. It might turn out some year that 75 percent of them should be women; if twenty out of the twenty-four most committed persons we have are women, then we ought to have twenty women elders. If twenty of the most committed persons are men, then we ought to have twenty men. Our church did a theological study on the role of women. We concluded that Paul, from whom most of the ideas regarding women not speaking in the church and women submitting to the authority of men are taken, was a product of the first century. As such, he reflected the cultural expectations of his age, but Paul also taught that in Christ there is neither male nor female. In saying that, he was clearly reflecting the thinking of Jesus himself. So, we took all these scriptures into consideration and came to the conclusion that we ought to give women equal leadership responsibilities and opportunities."

Motivation Is the Golden Key

How do you motivate ordinary people? Try this formula: (1) Give them the facts of reality. (2) Give them responsibility. (3) Give them encouragement and recognition. (4) Show them how. (5) Show personal enthusiasm. (6) Intensify the quality of your interpersonal relationships. (7) Dissolve emotional blocks by unconditional acceptance of people.

With people, you usually get what you ask for. If you ask for little, you get it. If you ask for much, you get it. Be careful what you ask for. You shall surely get it.

Group Discussion Questions

1. Is the key leadership group of our church more than 15 percent of the total membership? Less? If it is less, how can we increase that percentage?
2. Which does our church emphasize most—asking people to participate in committees, or the actual doing of Christian activities?
3. Comment on the observation that only about 30 percent of people feel comfortable in church roles that require high ability in verbal skills?
4. Examine the list of elder's duties and check the ones in which key leaders of our own congregation engage. Discuss your findings.
5. In what ways do key leaders of our church show respect for ordinary members of the congregation?
6. This chapter mentions the importance of esprit de corps (having fun together in working at common goals). How would you characterize our church in that regard?
7. Do we tend to appoint people to church tasks because they are talented or because they are committed? Comment on your past experiences in this regard.
8. Do you think we appoint some people to church offices just so we can get them to become more active in the church? What is your opinion about this procedure?

> Well begun is half done.
>
> — *Aristotle, 384-322 B.C.*

18

Your Place or Mine?

First Christian Church of Santa Fe, New Mexico, has shown rapid growth in spite of a terrible location. Though not on a deadend street, it stands near a "dead corner" at the tip of a steep hill which drivers seek to avoid. Secluded in a quiet, residential area, passing traffic is limited to lost tourists and neighborhood residents. But this congregation is an exception among growth churches. A high visibility location where many persons drive past every day is another crucial factor in evangelism success. *Axiom #18: Growing churches are located at an appropriate place in the community.*

"But what if you have a seventy-five-year-old building situated in the wrong place?" asks a pastor. "What can you do about that?" You have three options: relocate, compensate, or slowly die. In some cases, you should sell the building and move to a more desirable spot. Your place and God's place may be in different places until you relocate. A church in the small town of Brownfield, Texas, began rapid growth after moving from a dreary location to a busy highway on the growing edge of town near a shopping center. Same pastor for twenty-one years. Same congregational leadership. Same community population totals. A different place changed the growth pattern drastically.

If an immediate relocation seems impossible, try to overcome your poorly located base camp by experimenting with compensating devices. Occasionally, an institution finds vitality and strength in spite of a negative setting. One example is the Hebrews arriving at a promised land that flowed with rocks and dust more than milk and honey. The American colonists, accidentally landing at Plymouth Rock instead of Virginia, is another. One of the giant posters in a card shop said, "Bloom Where You Are Planted!" That sometimes happens. But only with highly motivated people and exceptional leadership.

The ways to attempt "location compensation" are endless. An automobile dealer is Dallas uses television spots that say, "The worst location in Dallas, but the best deals." That slogan might not fit a church, but one congregation with a hard-to-find location has compensated with a large map on their calling brochure. By pointing out the poor location, they get people's attention.

But most location compensations require far more aggressive efforts. First Christian Church, Lincoln, Nebraska, furnishes us with several successful examples. In 1976, this 416-member "old first church" located near the state capital building stood at the bottom of a fifteen-year membership decline—only thirteen additions by baptism and transfer for the past twelve months. By 1980, a growth pattern had reversed that trend. Forty-five persons joined the church in 1979; fifty-one came during 1978; and fifty during 1977.

One of the main reasons for this turnaround was the P.I.E. (Persons Involved in Evangelism) Group. Edward Kolbe, the pastor, says that P.I.E. seeks to raise the consciousness-awareness of the congregation to evangelistic opportunities. "We meet for an hour and a half about once a month, from September to June. And we serve pie. This helps people remember the name of the group. We review our list of prospects and discuss ways we can relate them to Christ and his church. (The total list is copied and distributed. It contains the name, address, phone, and previous denominational background of each individual or family.) We hear reports from persons in the group who have had contacts with these prospective members. We primarily use 'fellowship evangelism' and seek to relate people to our groups and church program. During the last thirty minutes, we have some kind of presentation concerning the nature of evangelism. We seek to give a biblical base for evangelism, to illustrate various evangelism methods and to share the evangelism goals of our denomination. We are positive but realistic about our past history as a congregation. Then we serve pie."

The Lincoln congregation uses several other excellent location compensation techniques. Among these are the following: (1) A group of single women, most of them ages 40 to 60, have formed a "lunch brunch" after church on Sunday. For single women, having someone to eat with on Sunday is most important. (2) A coffee every Sunday after the worship service gives members an opportunity to get acquainted with visitors and creates a friendly atmosphere. (3) Church youth serve lunch occasionally after the Sunday service. These lunches create fellowship, provide funds for youth projects and save time/travel cost for youth parents driving long distances. (4) Young people babysit in the church nursery during lunch on some Sundays. This gives young couples an occasional Sunday meal free from the responsibility of their small children. It also provides an opportunity for friendship circles to develop naturally between young adults and new members. (Some other congregations offer this babysitting service regularly with paid nursery personnel and sack lunches provided by parents.)[1]

The creative contemporary artist, Joan Miro, who was still producing in his eighties, completed the sketch work for a painting while eating lunch. A drop of strawberry jam fell on his drawing. He looked at the blob a moment, then enlarged it with his finger and incorporated it into his design. This is much easier to accomplish in a picture than in a mislocated building. But it's worth trying— for a year or three. If compensation efforts don't work and the building is clearly in the wrong part of town, sell it and move. Strawberry jam fits well in some paintings, but not all.

Group Discussion Questions

1. How would you evaluate the location of our church's building in the community? Excellent, good, fair or poor? Why?
2. If our location is poor or fair, make a list of every possible way you can think of that we might compensate. If the class has a consensus on any of the ideas, pass them on to the appropriate planning group in your church.
3. Do you feel that our congregation should strongly consider selling the building and relocating? Make a list of all the reasons why that would be hard to do. Make a list of all the reasons why it would be a good idea.
4. Ordinarily, the people from whom we can learn the most are those who have succeeded at something we are thinking about doing. Do we know of any churches in our part of the state or region that have successfully relocated from a poor site to a better one? Is it feasible to invite a representative of that congregation to come and speak to us?
5. Can we do anything to our building's exterior, such as signs, spires, bell tower, etc., which might heighten our visibility to passing traffic?

---

[1]Adapted from material in a column by the author entitled "New Ideas You Can Use" in *The Disciple,* April 20, 1980, St. Louis, Missouri.

There is nothing more difficult to take in hand, more
perilous to conduct, or more uncertain in its success,
than to take the lead in the introduction of a new order
of things.

Niccolò Machiavelli, 1469-1527

19

Swimming Upstream?

Anyone can succeed in evangelism," quipped Jim Blodget, "providing they serve a new congregation in a fast-growing suburb." That
frequently heard comment contains a thimbleful of *true* and a truck-
load of *false*. Yes, thirty-five of the forty fastest-growing Christian
Churches (Disciples of Christ) in North America are found in towns
or cities whose population expanded rapidly since 1970. Twenty-
seven of these forty churches are located in one of the twenty-six
population areas described by *U.S. News and World Report* as "strip
cities." Each of these twenty-six areas contains at least one million
people and usually embraces several metropolitan sprawls. And
since two out of three Americans now make their home in one of
these huge population blobs, we should not be surprised to find a
majority of growing churches there.

One of these congregations is near Peoria, Illinois, where the
Caterpiller Tractor Company's home office and other industries have
in past years boomed the population. Another is at Slidell, Louisiana,
a community thirty miles north of New Orleans which enlarged

with the advent of the aerospace program and the Saturn Five rocket boosters for the Apollo Program. A church in Houston is located in an area described by the *Wall Street Journal* as the fastest growing residential community in the United States. This suburb is populated by a middle-and upper-middle-class constituency to whom traditional mainline theology has great appeal. *Axiom #19: Growing churches are usually situated in a growing community.*

Two visitors were walking along a street in Washington, D.C., during the days before air pollution became a national issue. They happened to pass within sight of the Washington Monument at the time a janitor was putting trash out to burn. At the point where they were walking, the fire was so situated in their line of vision that it appeared to be at the base of this tall, slender monument. One of the visitors shook his head in mock despair and exclaimed, "They'll never get it off the ground!"

If your church is located in a declining community, you may think the odds for numerical lift-off are similar. In some situations, that is accurate. One is the inner-city church (or semi-inner-city—the ring of older neighborhoods just outside the central city). The departed population has been replaced by other races or no race at all. Another complex growth challenge lies at the other end of the sociological spectrum—the small town anywhere is North America that has less than 10,000 population and is already overchurched. If the population is shrinking and the median age-level rising, church growth is a tough, uphill task.

And yet the positive correlation between growth churches and growth communities contains a truth that often blocks out two other truths from our range of vision: *Some churches in declining population situations do grow. And many churches located in exploding metro-conglomerates do not grow.* By far the largest majority of Christian Church (Disciples of Christ) congregations in four of the fastest-growing United States population centers, for example, have declined sharply in membership between the 1970 and 1980 census reports: Houston and Dallas, Texas; Southern California; and Florida. *Rapid population growth is obviously not the only determining factor in evangelistic success.* Did you ever swim upstream against a strong current? It's possible, but difficult. Certainly harder than swimming downstream. But if you don't know how to swim, the current's direction won't matter; you may drown no matter which way the current flows. Doing evangelism successfully in static or shrinking population areas is like swimming upstream. But facilitating church growth in a rapidly growing city may prove equally difficult, if you don't know how to swim.

A biologist watched an ant carrying a piece of straw that seemed impossibly large for its small size. The ant came to a crack in the earth that was too wide to cross. It stood for a moment as though pondering the situation, then put the straw down across the crack and walked over on it. Picking it up again, the ant went on its way.

That ant had the two qualities necessary for church growth in a declining community: faith and ingenuity. Without faith, nothing is attempted. Without ingenuity, nothing is achieved.

Group Discussion Questions

1. Did our community population grow or decline between the last two census counts? How much?
2. Are other churches in our community growing or declining? Illustrate.
3. Some smaller towns are now experiencing a slight upward surge of population because younger adults are moving out of the cities. Is that true in our situation? What are we doing to capitalize on this?
4. Is our church located in either a static small town or an inner-city setting where evangelism is especially difficult? If so, what are we doing to compensate for these upstream community contexts?
5. Why do you think so many churches in mainline denominations are declining even though situated in growing urban sprawls? What can be done about that? Make a list of all the possibilities your group can dream up.

Appendix

Examples of Verses That Illustrate
Jesus' Twenty Teachings

Entering

1. God is here and you experience him by entering what Jesus called "the kingdom of God"—new level of consciousness that makes possible new ways of thinking and behavior. "Jesus answered him, 'Truly, truly, I say to you, unless one is born anew, he cannot see the kingdom of God'" (John 3:3). In John 3:4-8 Jesus adds that we don't know where the wind comes from or where it goes, and so it is with those born of the Spirit. In Luke 12:32-34 he says, "Fear not, little flock, for it is your Father's good pleasure to give you the kingdom." In Luke 11:20 he tells people that the kingdom of God has already come upon them. In Luke 17:20-21 he says that the kingdom of God is present now "in the midst of you." In Matthew 18:14 he makes it clear that great religious knowledge is not a requirement for those who wish to enter the kingdom of God because we must enter it with the naiveté of a child. In Matthew 13:1-9 his parable of the soils seems to indicate that this new state of consciousness comes to different people in differing degrees.

Aids

2. You are able to enter this new level of consciousness only by a changed attitude of the heart, not by following a list of religious rules. "You hypocrites! Well did Isaiah prophesy of you, when he said: 'This people honors me with their lips, but their heart is far from me; in vain do they worship me, teaching as doctrines the precepts of men'" (Matthew 15:8-9). Jesus recognizes the Jewish Law as an important means to an end—achieving God consciousness—but indicates that it must not be seen as an end in itself. In Luke 16:14-16 he says that the Jewish Law (found in the Old Testament) was preached until John the baptizer came, but now the kingdom of God is proclaimed. In Matthew 12:1-14 he permits his disciples to break the Old Testament rules against grain gathering and healing on the Sabbath, then defends himself against his critics by saying that rules are not as important as attitudes and motivations. In Matthew 15:10-20 he says that eating taboo foods does not make people as ritually unclean in God's sight as some of the words they spit out of their mouths, because the words reflect the state of their hearts. In Matthew 16:11-12 he speaks of the bad yeast of the Pharisees and Sadducees, who stress good rituals more than good hearts and lives. In Matthew 20:1-16 he uses a story of vineyard laborers hired at different times during the day to show that the kingdom is entered in a moment of mental decision, not worked into by following religious rules for long periods of time. In Matthew 23:13-28 he speaks of the hypocrisy of religious rules without the practice of mercy, honesty, and justice in our relationships with other people. In Luke 18:9-14 he contrasts the phony righteousness of the Pharisee who followed all the religious rules with the obvious virtue of the tax collector who had followed no rules but changed his heart.

3. *Concentrating your mind's attention on Christ strengthens your ability to enter this new consciousness and experience it in greater fullness.* "Again Jesus spoke to them, saying, 'I am the light of the world; he who follows me will not walk in darkness, but will have the light of life'" (John 8:12). Jesus says in John 15:4-5: "I am the vine; you are the branches." He says in John 15:15: ". . . I have called you friends, for all that I have heard from my Father I have made known to you."

4. *Prayer strengthens your ability to enter this new consciousness and experience it more fully.* "Ask, and it will be given you; seek, and you will find; knock, and it will be opened to you" (Matthew 7:7). In Matthew 7:7-11 Jesus elaborates on the idea that God will give us the good things we ask him for. In Matthew 6:10 he teaches his disciples to pray for the Kingdom to come. In Luke 18:1-8 he uses the story of a wicked judge to illustrate the need for urgent and continued prayer. In Mark 11:20-25 he tells a parable about a fig tree to illustrate the importance of praying with faith and confidence.

Blocks

5. *You are blocked from entering this new level of consciousness unless you turn away from (repent of) self-centeredness.* "From that time Jesus began to preach, saying, 'Repent, for the kingdom of heaven is at hand'" (Matthew 4:17). In Matthew 7:13-14 Jesus' metaphor about the narrow gate teaches that those who enter God's kingdom must make a clear choice between two alternatives. His statements of "Follow me, and leave the dead to bury their own dead" in Matthew 8:18-22 and ". . . if your eye causes you to sin, pluck it out. . ." in Mark 9:42-48 dramatize with literary hyperbole the principle that we must guard against falling under the control of any responsibility that deters us from seeking his kingdom *first* in our life. In Matthew 10:34-36 he indicates that for some persons

this decision to enter God's kingdom will even necessitate the setting aside of important relationships with friends and family. In Luke 14:15-24 his parable of the great feast indicates that we enter the kingdom only by a desire to turn away from other life preoccupations. In Matthew 22:1-14 he tells a parable about a wedding dinner that can only be eaten by those who are willing to come and accept it.

6. *Those who take pride in their religious achievements find it difficult to enter this new consciousness.* "Whoever humbles himself like this child, he is the greatest in the kingdom of heaven" (Matthew 18:4). In Matthew 18:1-4 Jesus elaborates on the need for erasing religious pride in order to enter the Kingdom. He says in Matthew 5:3 that the spiritually poor find God consciousness more easily because they aren't blocked by their religious pride. In Matthew 6:16-18 he warns against the religious pride that so easily arises from ostentatious fasting. In Matthew 6:1-14 he says we should avoid ostentation in prayers and charities. In Matthew 8:11-12 he says that the Jews shouldn't be so proud of their religious achievements, since people from all countries and races will enter God's kingdom with them. In Matthew 19:13-15 he says that children have qualities of humility which allow them to easily enter the kingdom. In Matthew 23:1-12 the perils of religious pride are contrasted to the virtue of religious humility. In John 10:16 he says that he has other sheep in other pens, inferring that the disciples should not get puffed up with pride because of their role as his closest followers, anymore than the Jews should get hung up on themselves because they are God's chosen people. In Mark 9:38-41 a person unknown to Jesus and his disciples is found driving out demons in Jesus' name, but Jesus indicates that he should be permitted to continue.

7. *The financially wealthy find it difficult to enter this new consciousness because their money brings a false sense of power that distracts them from seeking something better.* "It is easier for a camel to go through the eye of a needle than for a rich man to enter the kingdom of God" (Mark 10:25). In Matthew 6:19-34 Jesus urges us to seek *first* God's kingdom rather than riches, since putting something else at first priority can block us from our God relationship. In Matthew 19:16-26 Jesus tells a wealthy young man to sell all he has because it is blocking him from entering God's kingdom. In Luke 6:20 Jesus says that the poor are happy because they are not distracted by the false god of wealth. In Luke 16:1-13 the story of a rich man and his employee is used to paint a satire about the folly of relating to money instead of God.

Rewards

8. *Entering this new level of consciousness paradoxically gives you rich rewards.* "If any man would come after me, let him deny himself and take up his cross and follow me. For whoever would

save his life will lose it; and whoever loses his life for my sake and the gospel's will save it" (Mark 8:34-35). In Matthew 13:44-46 Jesus' parables about a treasure hidden in a field and a pearl of great price indicate that the kingdom *seems* like a sacrifice but really isn't. In Matthew 5:1-12 he lists among the beatitudes numerous rewards for those who enter the kingdom. In Luke 11:28 he says that those who keep God's word are blessed. In Luke 14:7-11 he says that those who sit humbly at the lowest places shall be exalted. In Mark 10:29-30 he notes that the last shall be first. In Matthew 5:10 he infers that persecuted disciples find much happiness and personal satisfaction in knowing that they are doing God's will. In Matthew 5:11-12 he mentions rewards for those who suffer persecution. In Matthew 10:32 he promises the disciples that he will reward them by personally commending them to God. In Mark 9:41 he promises rewards for those who serve well. In Matthew 11:29 he says that those who take up his yoke will find rest for their souls. In Matthew 19:27-30 he promises hundredfold rewards to those who have followed him at great personal sacrifice. In Matthew 6:19-20 he speaks of rewards laid up in heaven. In Luke 20:34-38 he says that those who attain the resurrection will become like angels. In Mark 10:21 he says that those who take up their cross of sacrifice will be rewarded in heaven.

9. Those who enter this new consciousness find a sense of security that comes from believing that their personal needs will be cared for. "But even the hairs of your head are all numbered. Fear not, therefore; you are of more value than many sparrows" (Matthew 10:30-31). In Matthew 6:25-33 Jesus says that we should not be anxious about our need for food and clothing; God will care for us. In Matthew 10:5-10 he says that special providence will be given to the twelve apostles as they are sent out; they therefore have no need to take money or food with them.

10. Those who experience this new consciousness find a new power released in their lives and thought processes that transcends the normal cause and effect patterns of their environment. "And whatever you ask in prayer, you will receive, if you have faith" (Matthew 21:22). In Luke 9:1-6 Jesus sends the twelve disciples out with the power to heal the sick. In Luke 10:9 he instructs the seventy to heal the sick and informs them that the kingdom has come near to them. In Luke 10:17-20 he says that the seventy will have power over snakes and evil spirits. In Matthew 10:19-20 he tells the disciples that the words they need to say will be given to them in their hour of need. In Mark 16:17-18 he predicts that the eleven remaining disciples will have power to help the sick recover and to cast out demons, and will not be hurt by poisonous snakes.

11. Those who experience this new consciousness live and worship joyfully, not in sadness with long faces. "These things I have spoken to you, that my joy may be in you, and that your joy may be full" (John 15:11). In John 10:10 Jesus says, ". . . I came that they may have life, and have it abundantly." In Matthew 6:16 he urges the disciples not to practice the Jewish ritual of fasting with dismal faces. In Matthew 9:14-17 he says that his disciples don't fast because they have the Christ with them. In John 16:22 he predicts that he will see the disciples again and that their hearts will rejoice.

12. Those who experience this new consciousness continue to live in that consciousness beyond the time of physical death. "My sheep hear my voice, and I know them, and they follow me; and I give them eternal life, and they shall never perish, and no one shall snatch them out of my hand" (John 10:27). Similar statements appear in Matthew 19:29, 25:46, Mark 10:30; Luke 18:30; John 3:15, 16, 36, 4:14, 5:24, 6:27, 40, 47, 54, 10:28, 12:25, and 17:2-3.

By-products

13. If you enter this new level of consciousness, you experience increased love and concern for other people. "And he said to him, 'You shall love the Lord your God with all your heart, and with all your soul, and with all your mind. This is the great and first commandment. And a second is like it, You shall love your neighbor as yourself'" (Matthew 22:37-38). In Luke 10:25-37 Jesus uses the parable of the good Samaritan to connect loving God with the qualities of neighborliness and mercy. He implies in Matthew 5:27-30 that a respect for other persons logically leads to a desire to avoid adultery. In Matthew 19:1-12 he infers that a concern for other people promotes the avoidance of divorce. In Mark 9:50 he speaks about the salt of friendship as a positive quality. In Luke 14:12-14 he urges us to invite the poor to our banquets.

14. Those who experience this new consciousness are not judgmental about other people. "Judge not, that you be not judged" (Matthew 7:1). In Matthew 13:24-30 Jesus illustrates the principle of leaving judgment to God instead of trying to do it ourselves.

15. Those who experience this new consciousness have a forgiving spirit. "Then Peter came up and said to him, 'Lord, how often shall my brother sin against me, and I forgive him? As many as seven times?' Jesus said to him, 'I do not say to you seven times, but seventy times seven'"(Matthew 18:21-22). In Matthew 18:23-35 Jesus illustrates with the parable about an unforgiving debtor the need for showing mercy on those who wrong us. In Matthew 5:21-26 he warns against anger. In Matthew 5:43-48 he speaks of the need to forgive and love enemies. In Luke 6:27-36 he speaks of the need to love enemies and to lend our cloak to those who have already taken our coat.

16. Those who experience this new consciousness work to help other people to enter it too. "Go therefore and make disciples of all nations, baptizing them in the name of the Father and of the Son and of the Holy Spirit, teaching them to observe all that I have

195

commanded you . . ." (Matthew 28:19-20). In Matthew 5:13 Jesus calls his disciples the salt and light of the world. In Matthew 18:10-14 he tells a parable about the urgency of finding lost sheep. In Matthew 9:35-38 he speaks of sending workers to ripe harvest fields. In Mark 16:15 he gives the clear imperative to preach the gospel all over the world. In Luke 15:3-32 he says we should as eagerly seek to communicate with people about God's kingdom as we would seek to find a lost coin, a lost sheep, or a lost son. "Feed my sheep," Jesus says to Peter during their last conversation on the seashore (John 21:15-19).

17. Those who experience this new consciousness live their lives in a spirit of self-giving. "If any man would come after me, let him deny himself and take up his cross and follow me" (Matthew 16:24). In Matthew 10:38 Jesus says that the person who does not take up his cross is not worthy to be his disciple. In Matthew 20:26-28 he says that the person who wants to be greatest among his followers must be the servant of all the other servants. In Mark 12:41-44 he uses a story of a widow's penny to illustrate the virtue of extreme sacrifice. In Matthew 10:16-24 he says that entering God's kingdom will bring some people into persecution and a need for making sacrifices. In Luke 17:7-10 he pictures the self-giving servant who does his duty as a model disciple. In Luke 22:24-30 he says that the greatest servant in his kingdom is the one who serves everyone else.

Continuing

18. You cannot continue to experience this new level of consciousness unless your thinking and actions remain consistent with this new state of mind. Returning to self-centeredness causes a loss of the new consciousness experience. "Not every one who says to me, 'Lord, Lord,' shall enter the kingdom of heaven, but he who does the will of my Father who is in heaven" (Matthew 7:21). In Matthew 7:15-27 Jesus illustrates the need for *continued* right attitudes and actions by saying that a tree is known by its fruits and by telling a story of two different kinds of house builders. In Matthew 21:28-45 he tells a parable about tenant farmers who reap the reward of unfaithfulness in their vineyard work. In Matthew 18:23-35 he says that when the unforgiving servant didn't practice his experience he lost his place in the kingdom. In Luke 13:6-9 he illustrates the fig tree's urgent need to bear fruit in order to avoid being destroyed. In Matthew 25:14-30 the parable of invested and uninvested money illustrates the need to act in faithful service, or lose the opportunity to participate in the kingdom experience. In Matthew 25:31-46 the parable of sheep and goats illustrates the need to act out the experience of the kingdom in order to avoid losing it. Jesus everywhere says that we must live the truth as well as hear it. Living the truth involves making the outside behavior match the interior feelings and attitudes. Unless that happens, the resulting split splits us from the kingdom we are trying to experience.

Not Entering

19. If you do not enter this new level of consciousness, you experience negative results from your failure to do so. "So it will be at the close of the age. The angels will come out and separate the evil from the righteous, and throw them into the furnace of fire; there men will weep and gnash their teeth" (Matthew 13:49-50). In Jesus' wheat and weeds parable of Matthew 13:24-30;36-43 the weeds are eventually burned up. In Matthew 23:29-36 he describes the punishment of the Pharisees who refuse to enter God's kingdom. In Matthew 24:45-51 he pictures the dire fate of an unfaithful servant. In Matthew 25:1-13 he tells a story which ends badly for the unthinking bridesmaids who run out of lamp oil. In Matthew 25:14-30 he gives a parable about three servants and the ill fate of those who don't use what God gives them. In Matthew 25:31-46 he describes a grim end for the goat characters in a sheep and goats parable. In Luke 14:34-35 he illustrates the fate of worthless salt. In Luke 16:19-31 he contrasts the extreme opposite fates of the rich man and Lazarus. In Luke 10:13-16 he paints a black day for the towns who didn't believe in him. In John 5:19-29 he plainly says that the unsaved are damned.

Future Hopes

20. Your new level of consciousness experience will at an unspecified future time become more fully and obviously manifested in the whole of creation. "Jesus said to him, 'You have said so. But I tell you, hereafter you will see the Son of man seated at the right hand of Power, and coming on the clouds of heaven'" (Matthew 26:64). In Matthew 24:3-44 Jesus deals extensively with an end time when the kingdom will become apparent and vividly real to all. In Matthew 25 he tells parables about ten girls and their lamps, a master and servants, and sheep and goats in order to say that there will be a final curtain on human history in which the kingdom will come visibly. In Luke 21:5-37 he speaks of the temple's destruction at the end of time, earthquakes, battles, and other physical signs of the last days. The reader can hardly avoid his clear point here: heaven and earth will pass away at some future time and will be replaced by a full-bloom kingdom of God.